08 Shadows (Black/white/ gray)
Arya Bahram Art Photos Collection

عکس های هنری سایه از آریا بهرام (مجید بهرام بیگی)

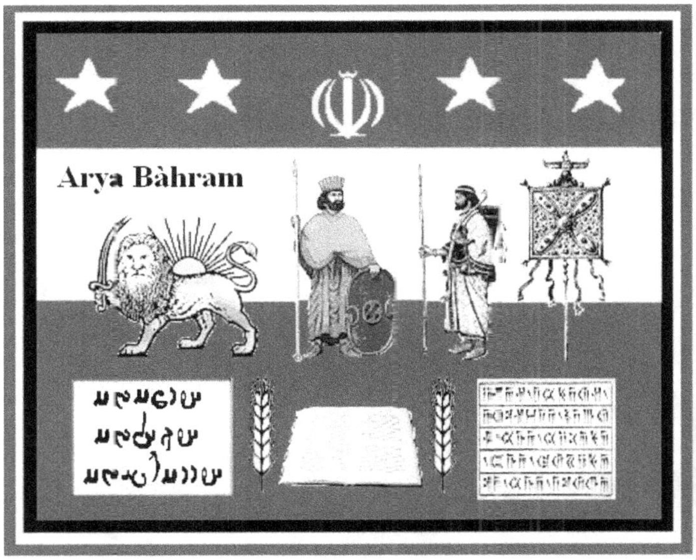

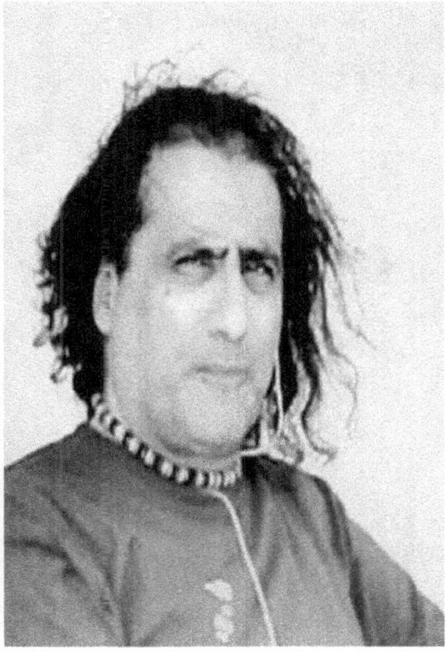

Musics for book - musiques pour livre - Musiken für Buch – آهنگها برای کتاب - Ahàng ha bàraye nibig ha

http://www.majidbahrambeiguy.at/my-foto-books---mes-livres-des-photos-.html

Arya Bàhram (Majid Bàhram beiguy) , Österreich

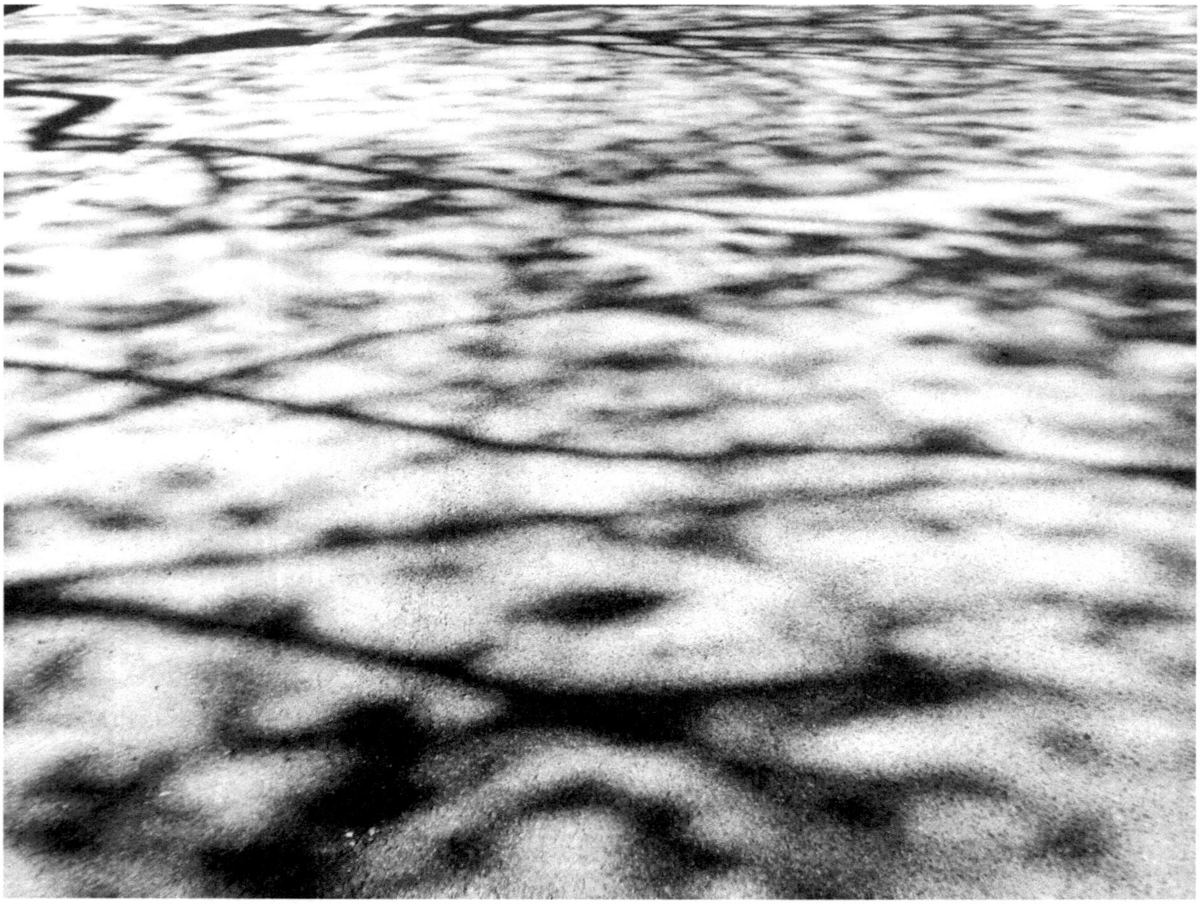

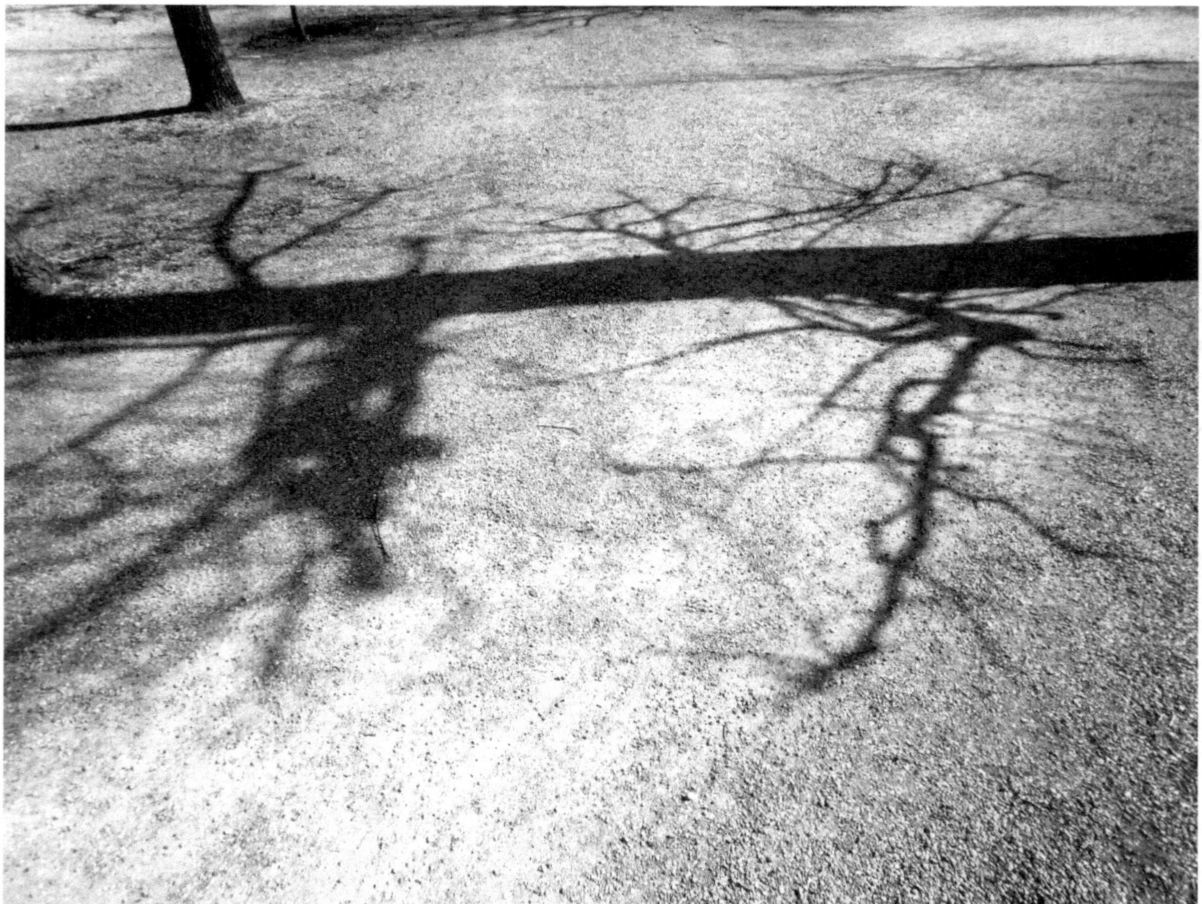

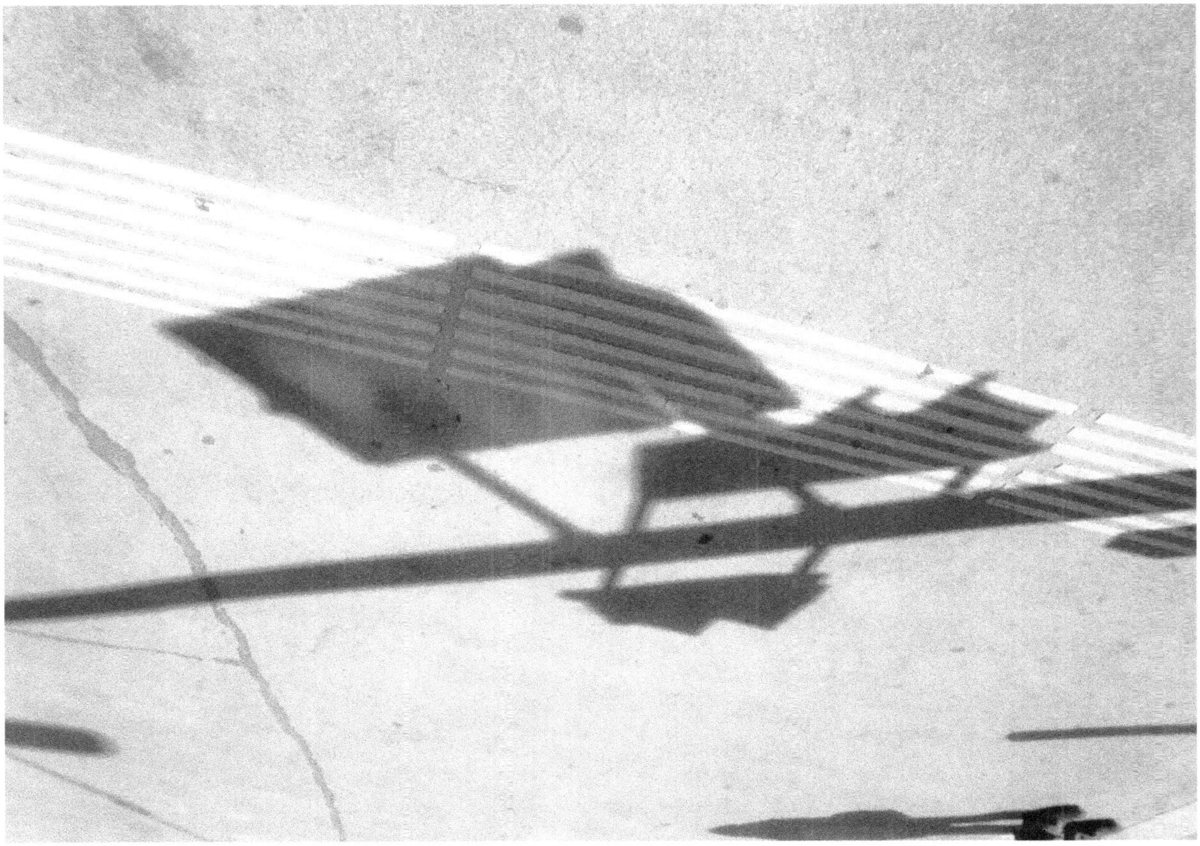

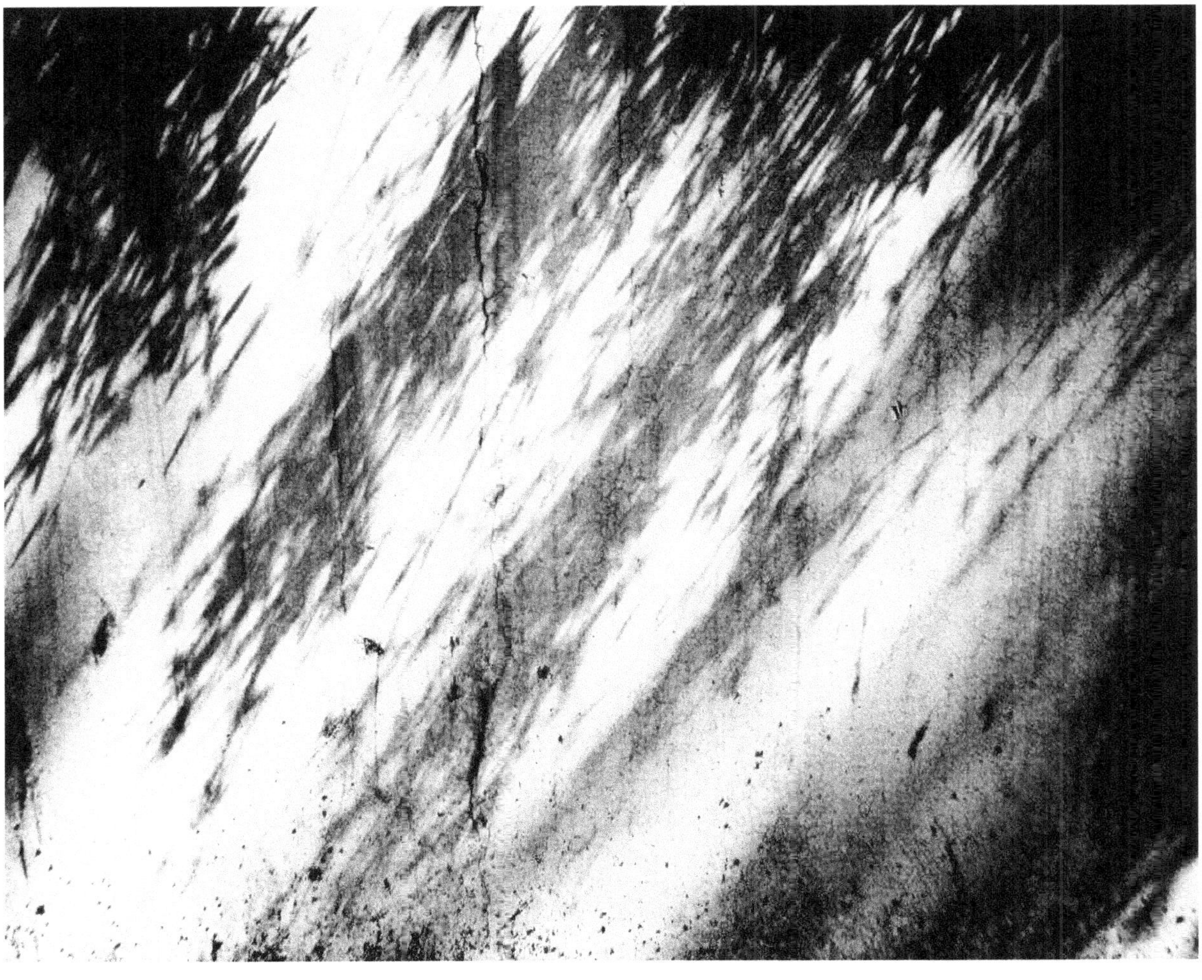

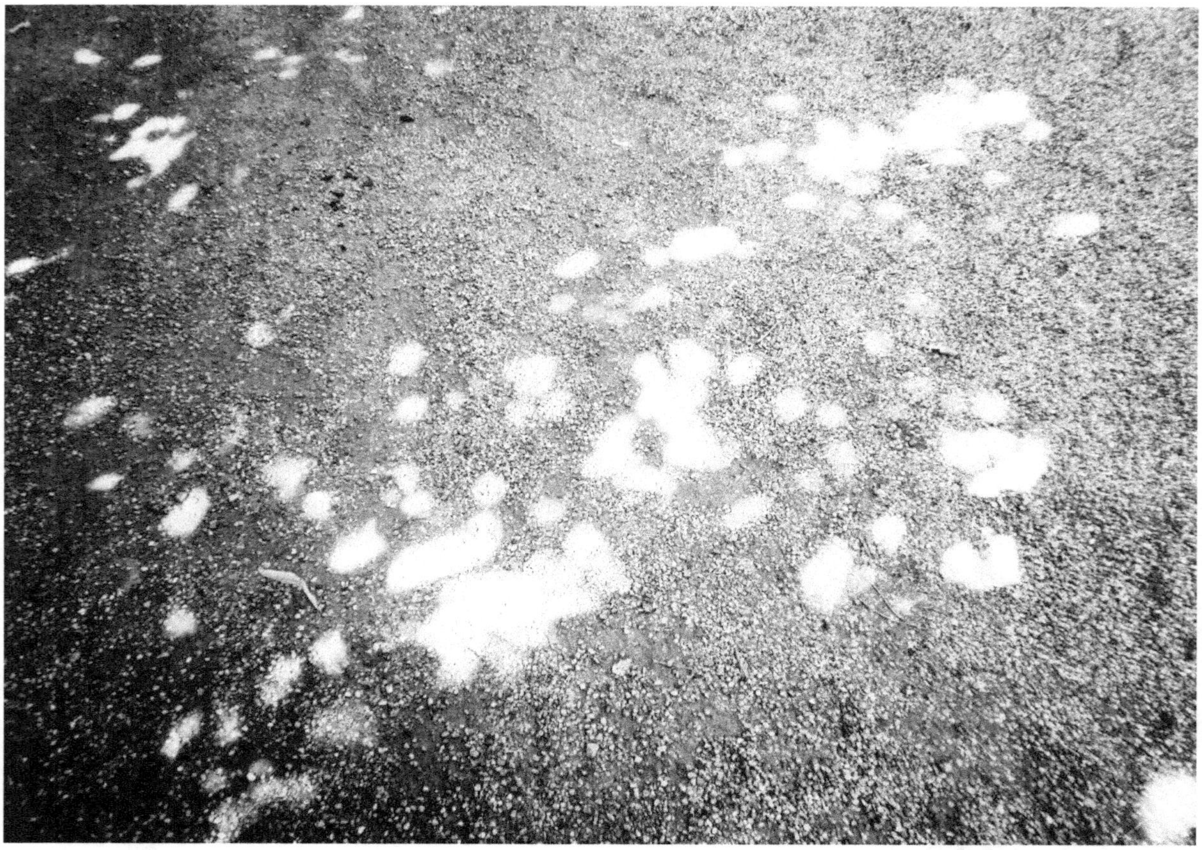

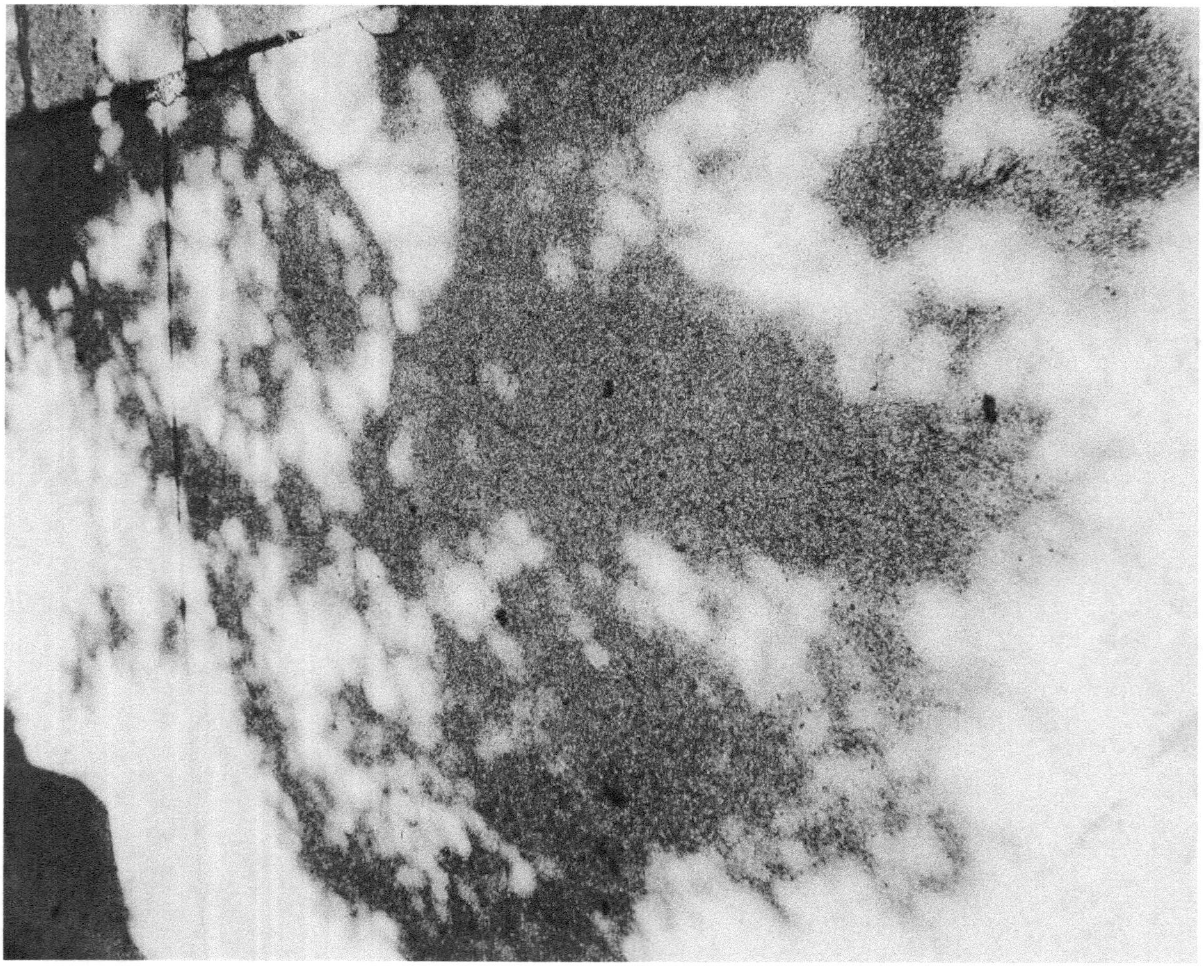

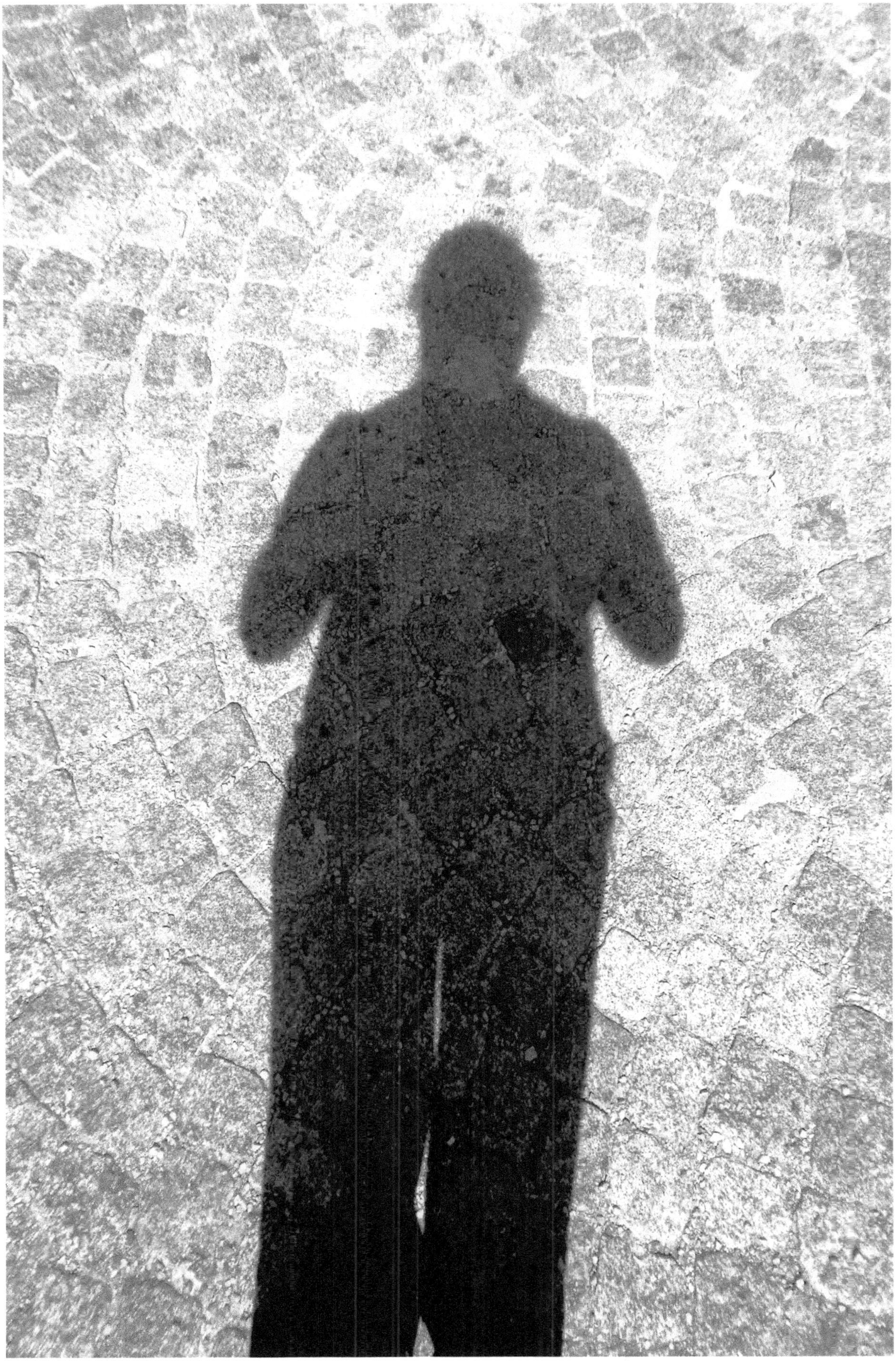

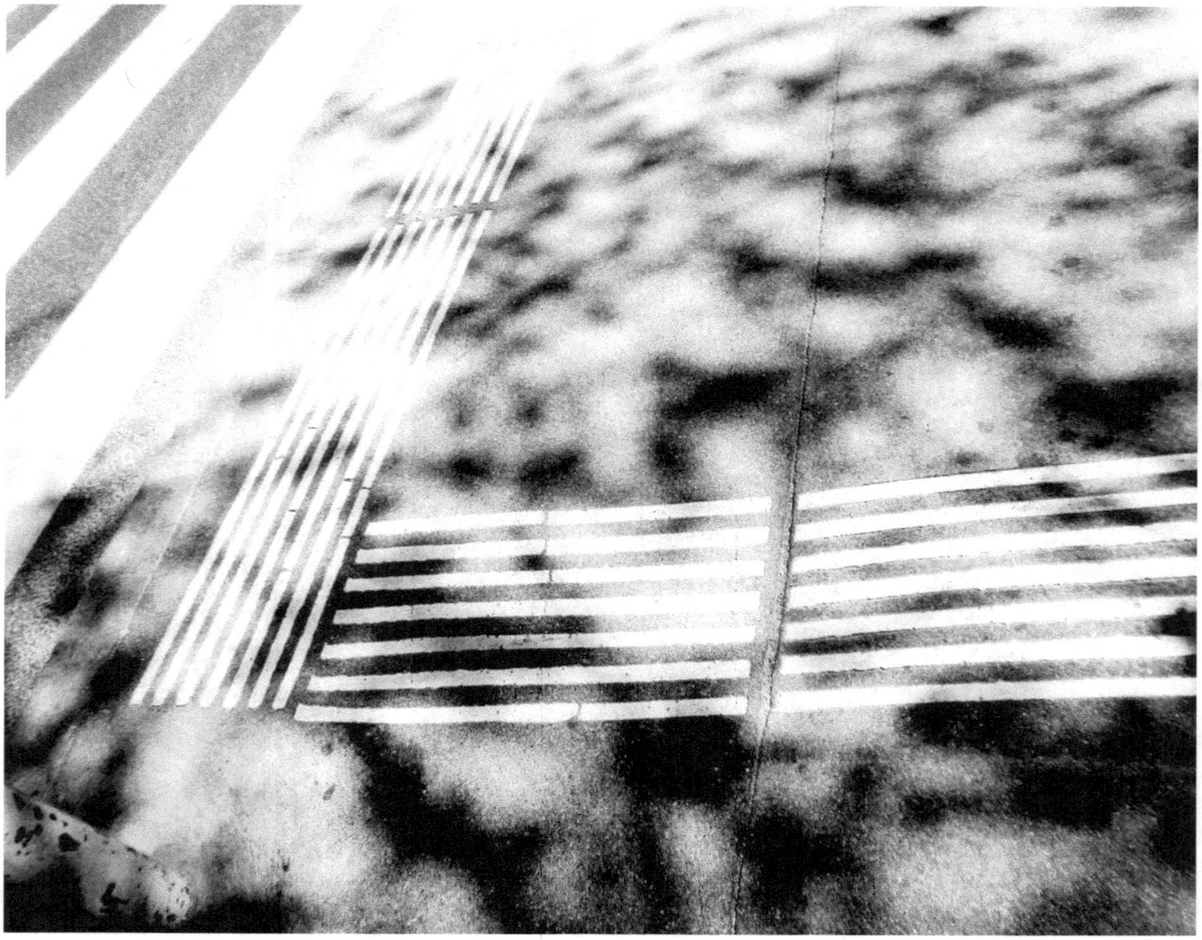

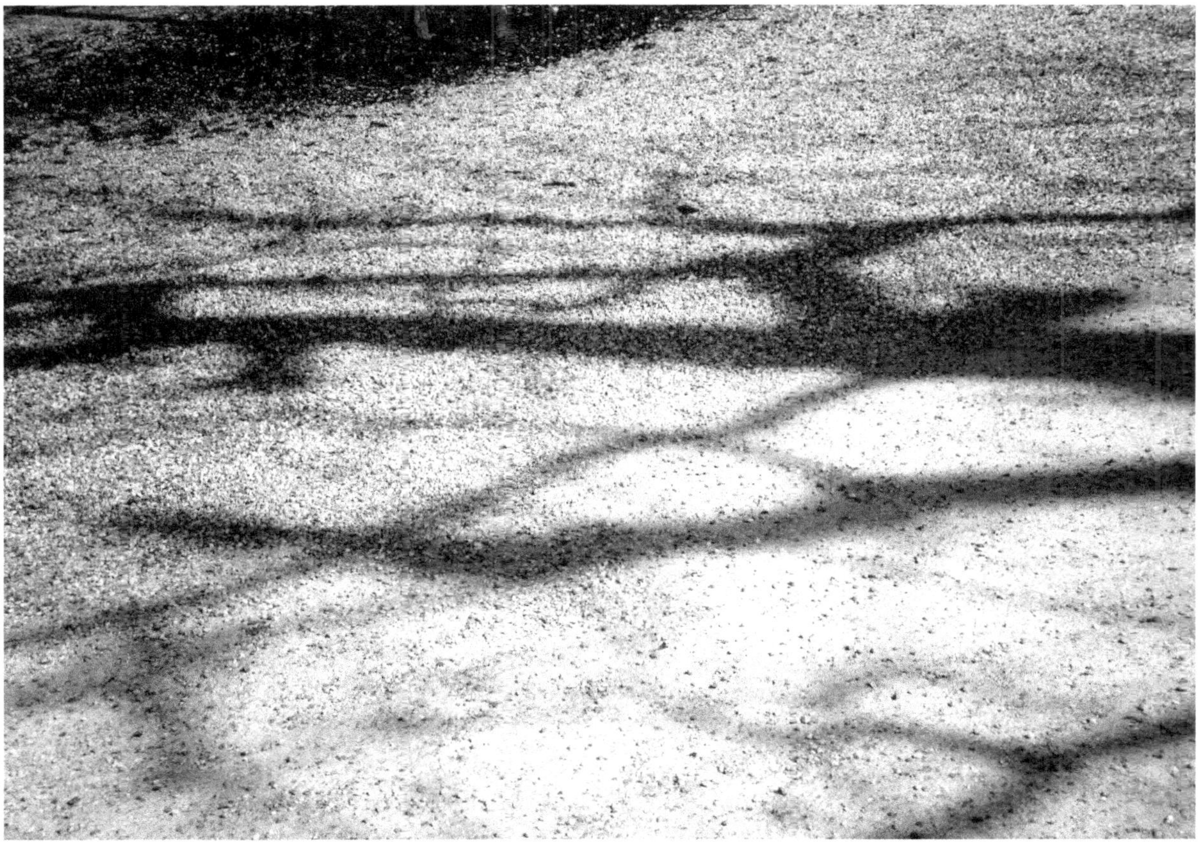

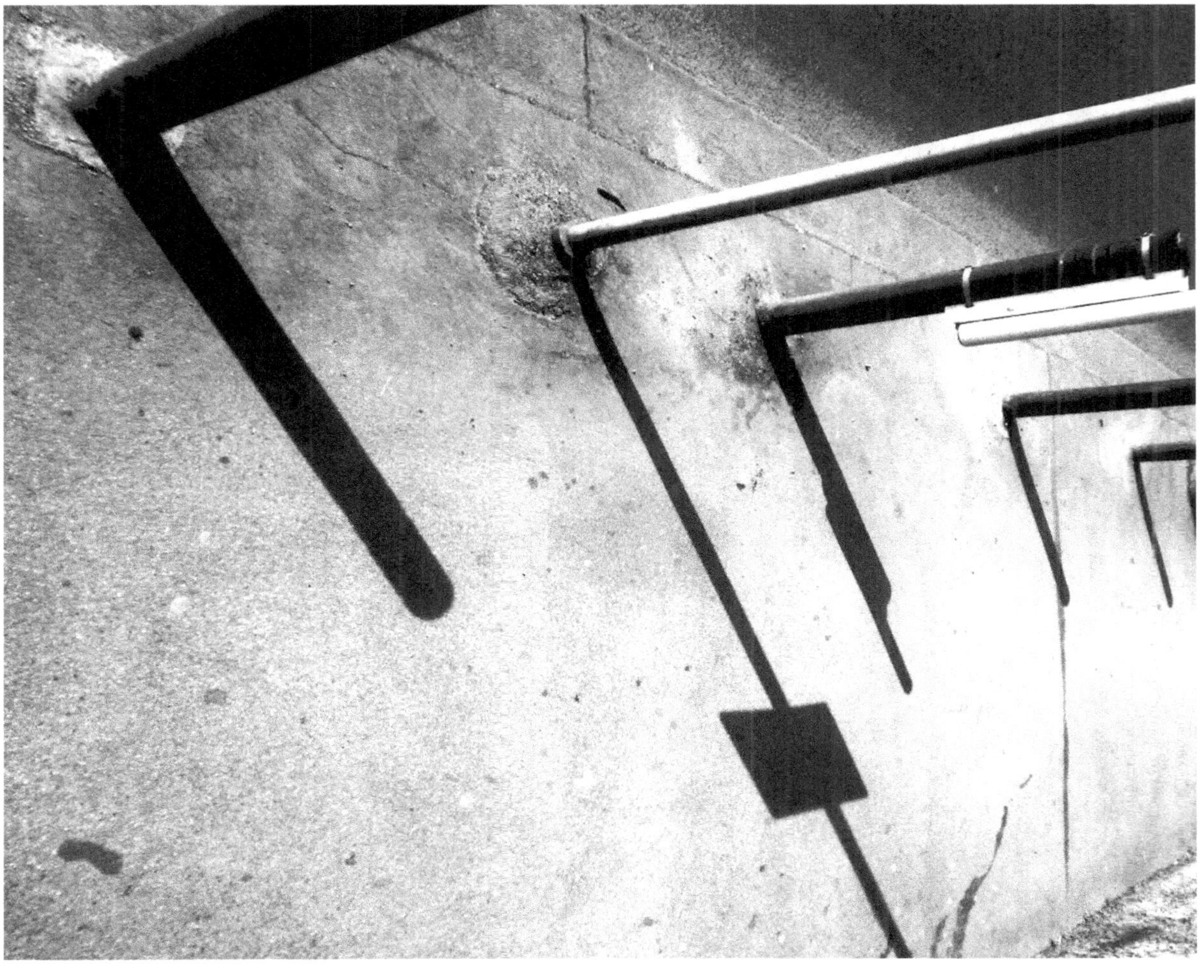

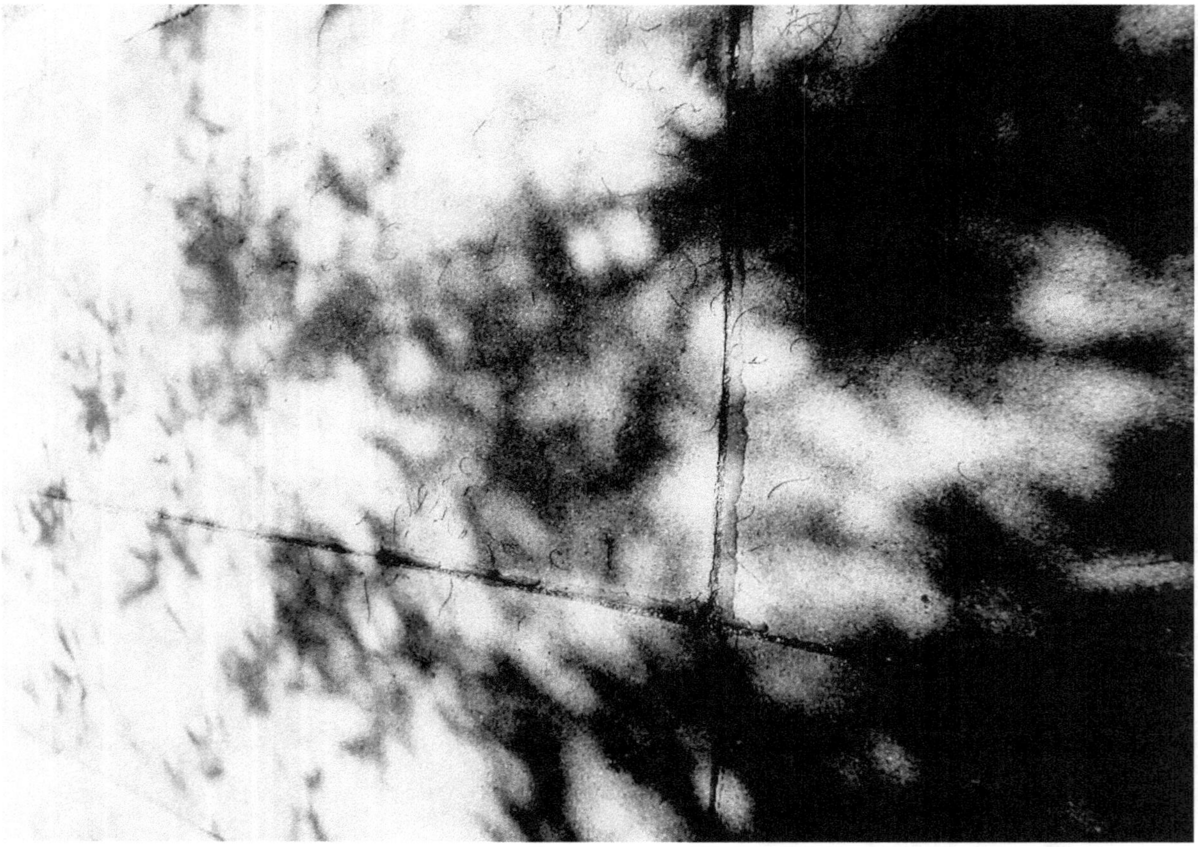

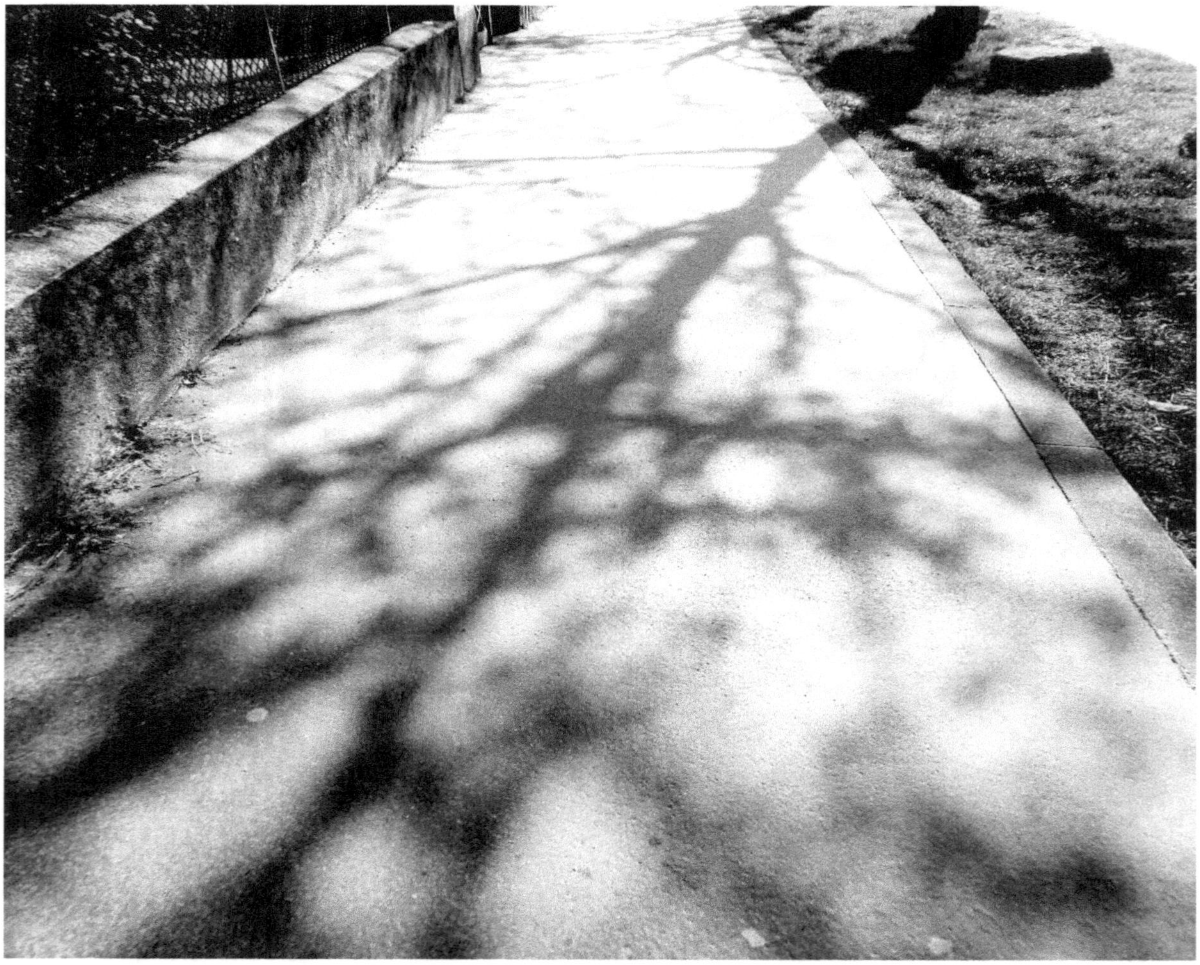

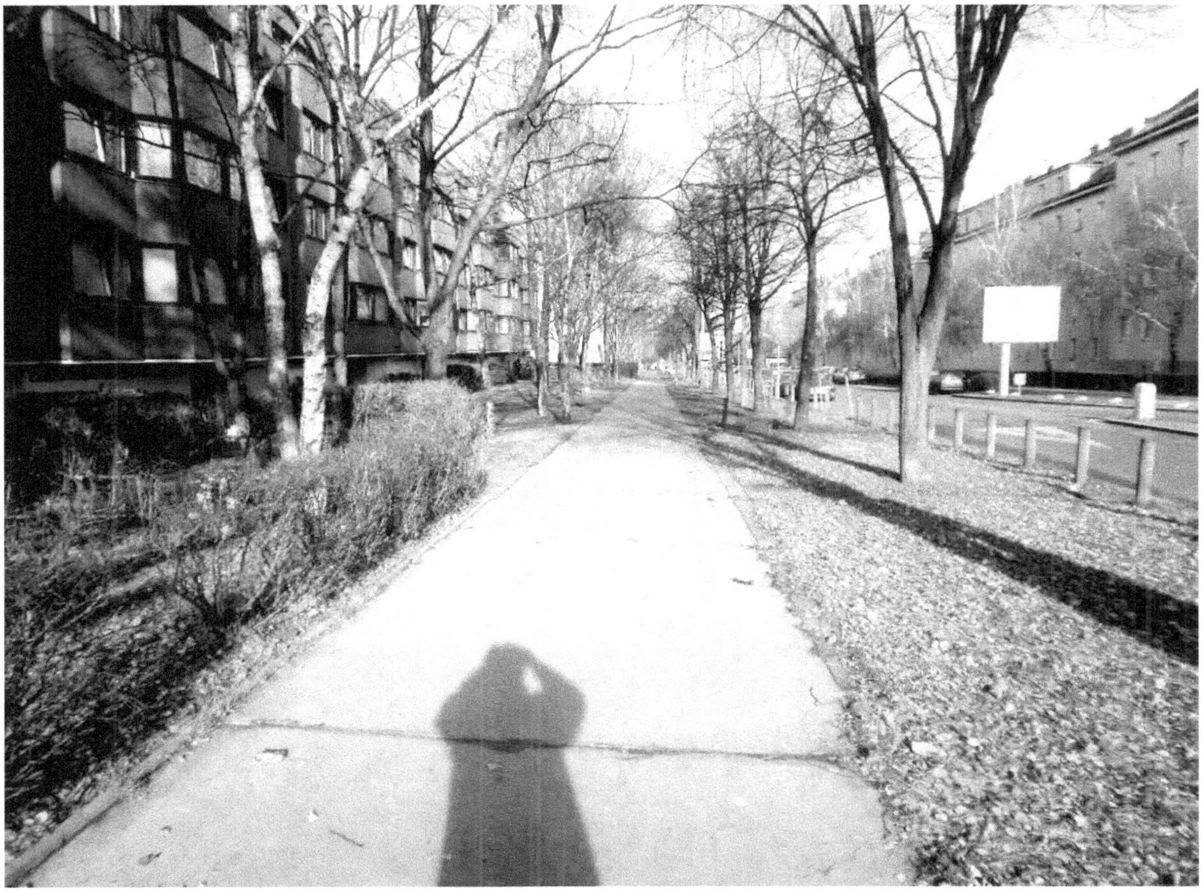

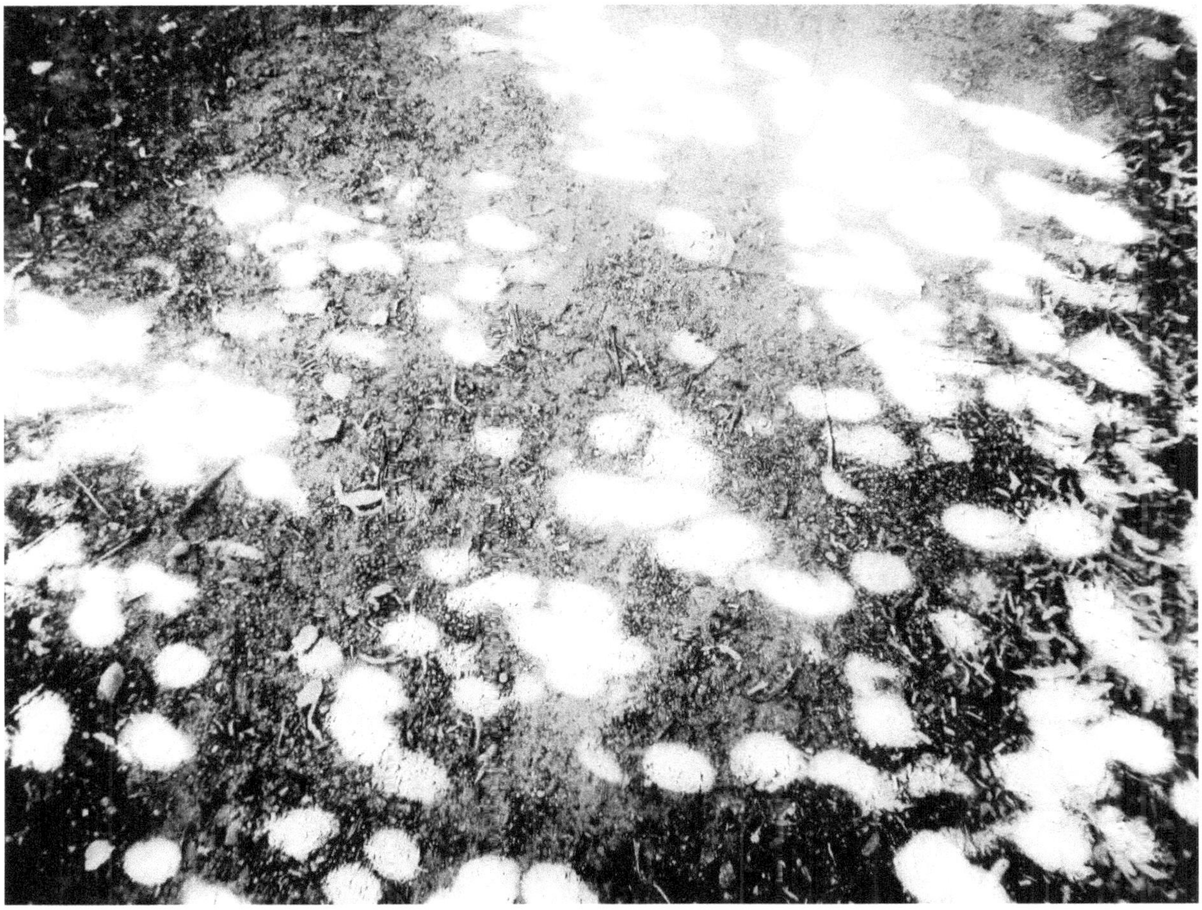

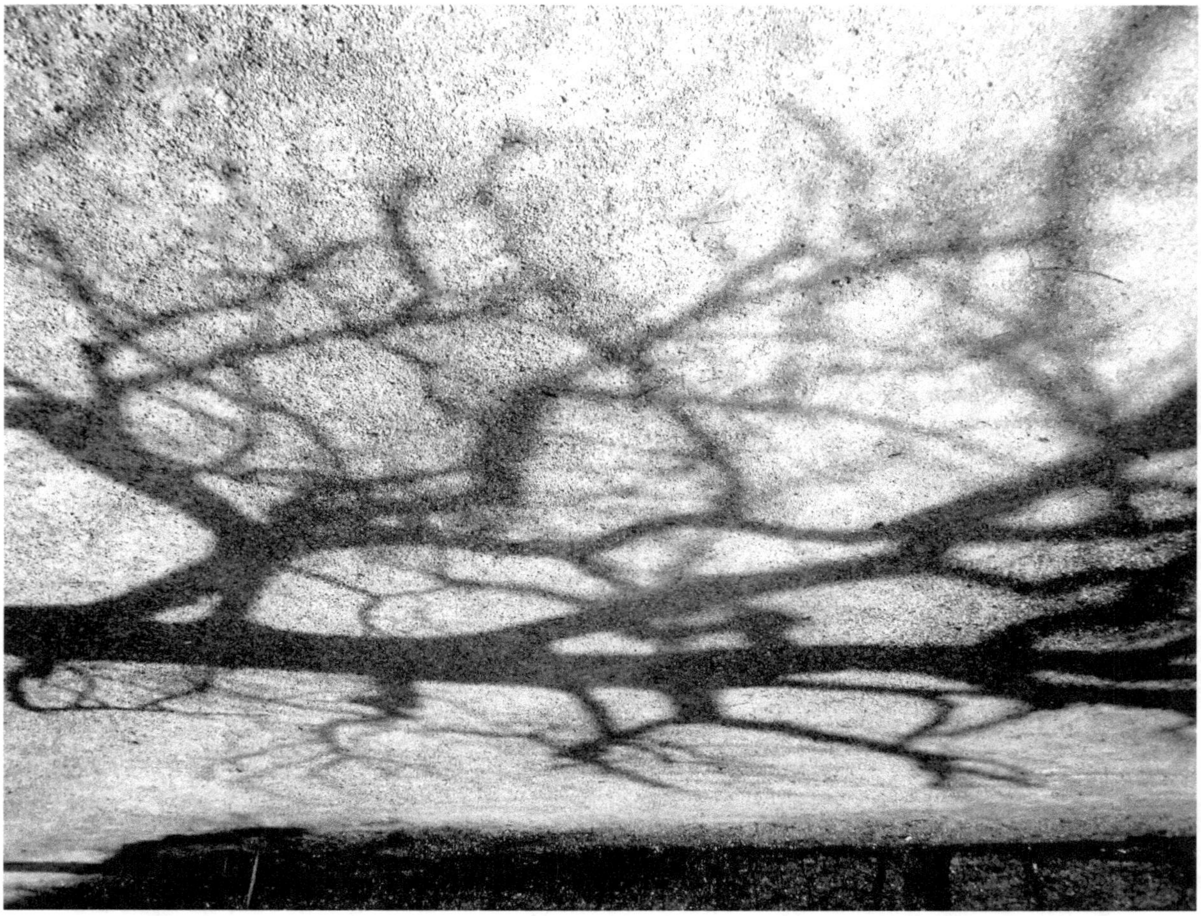

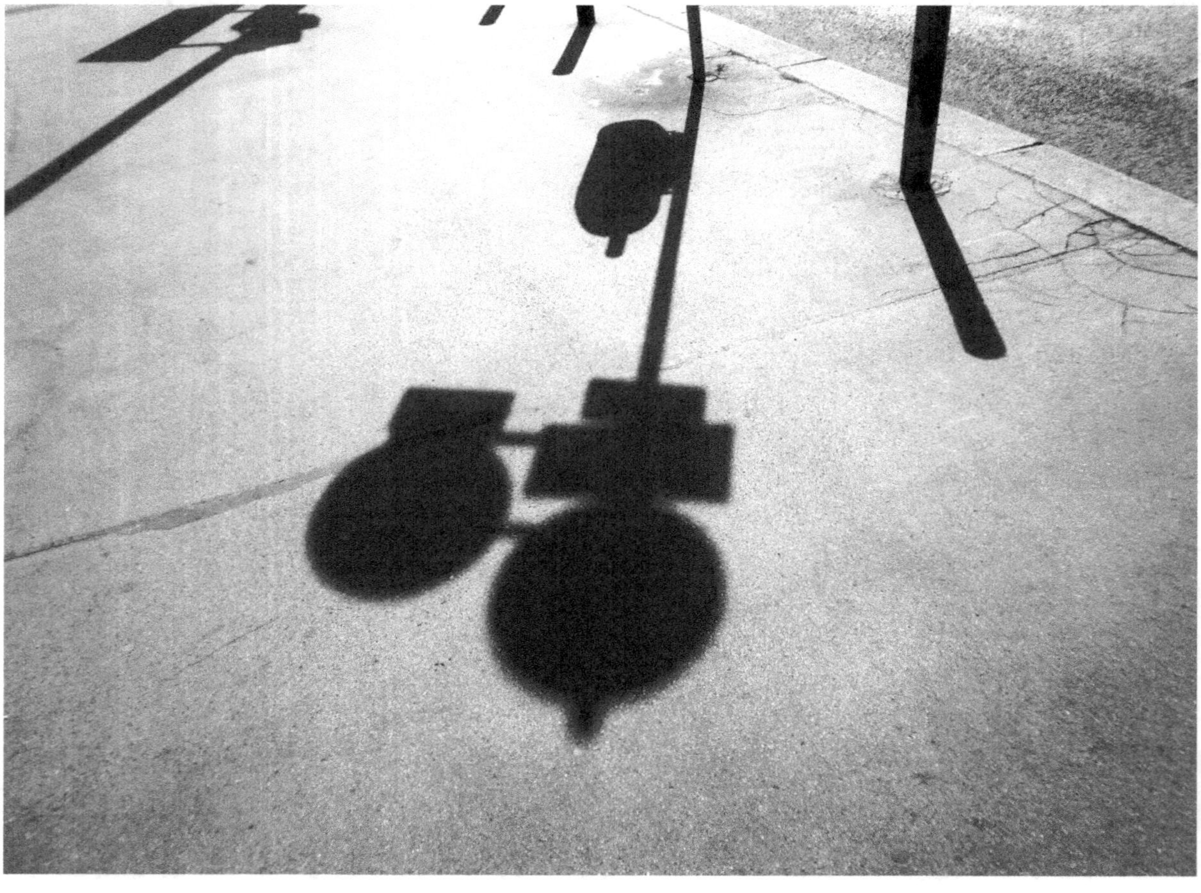

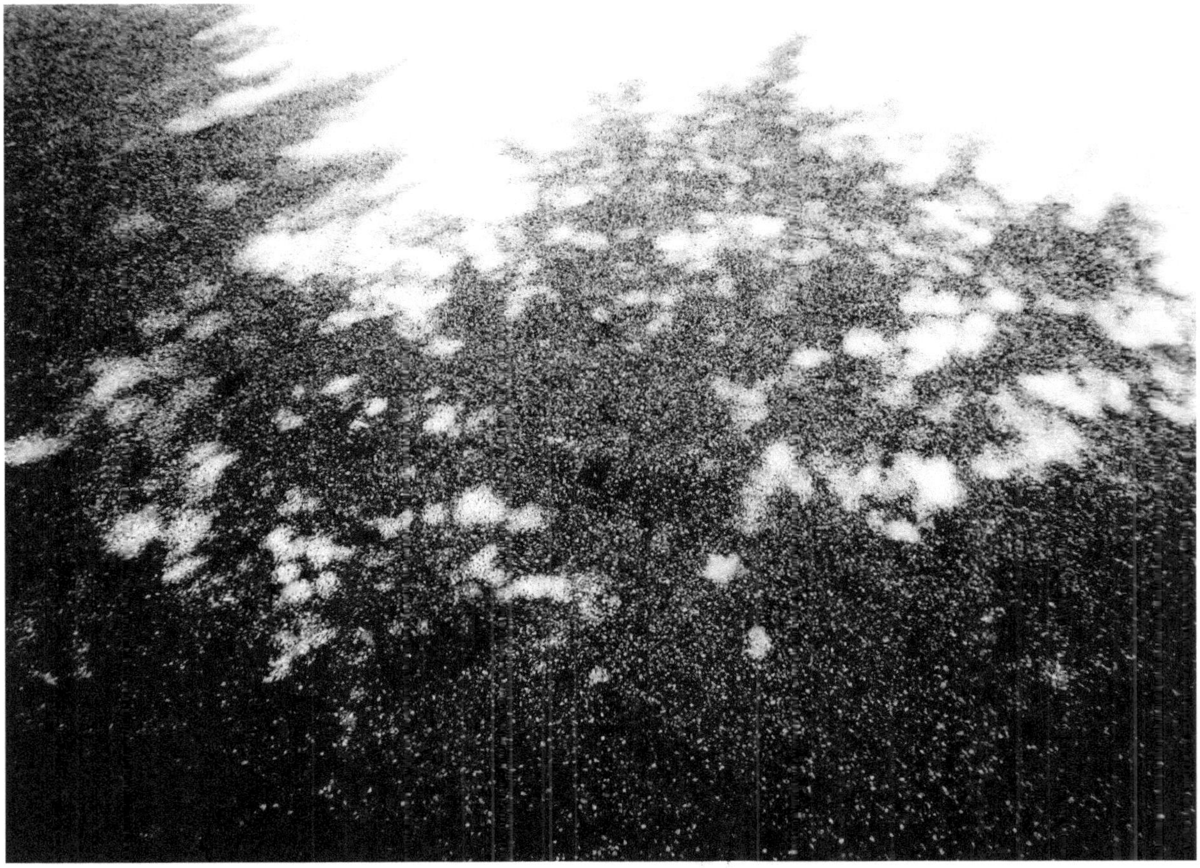

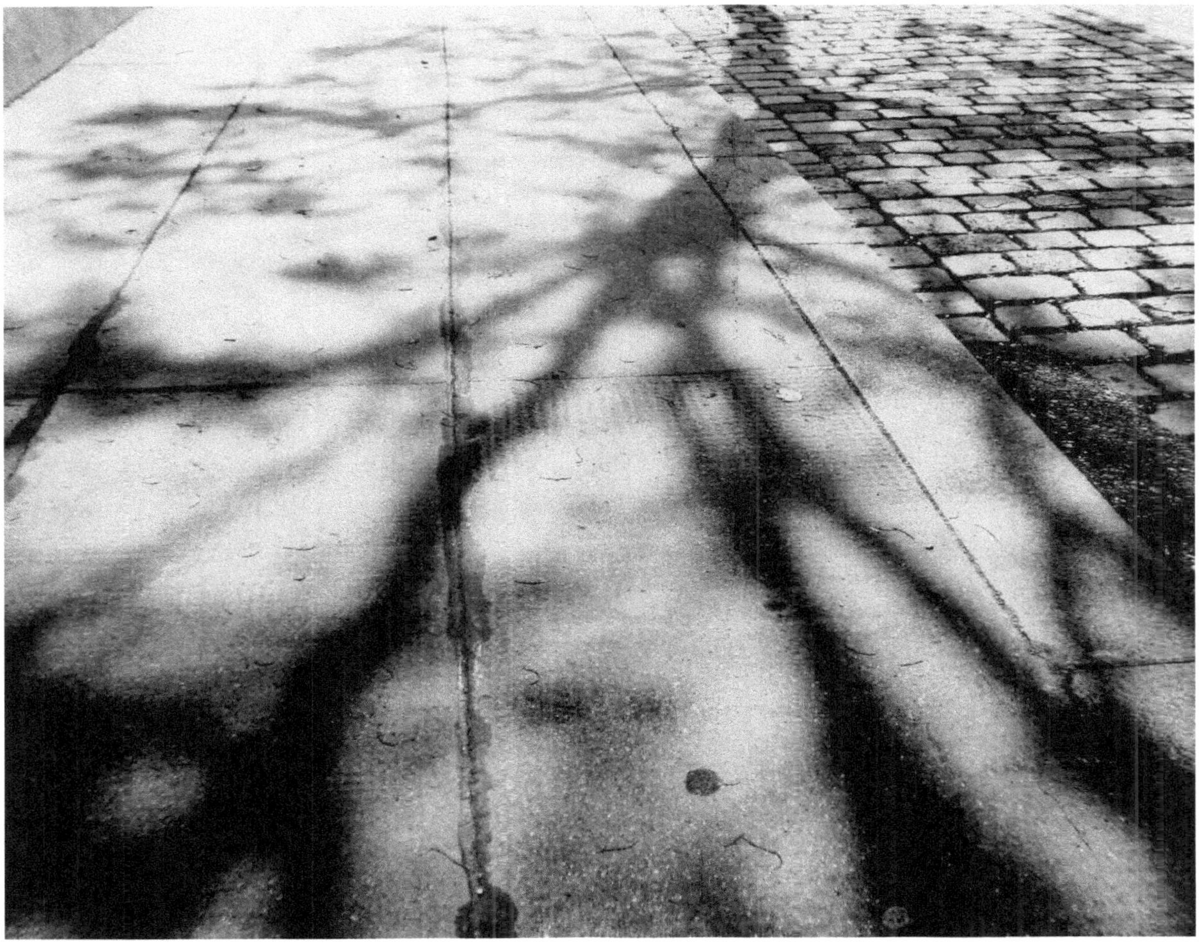

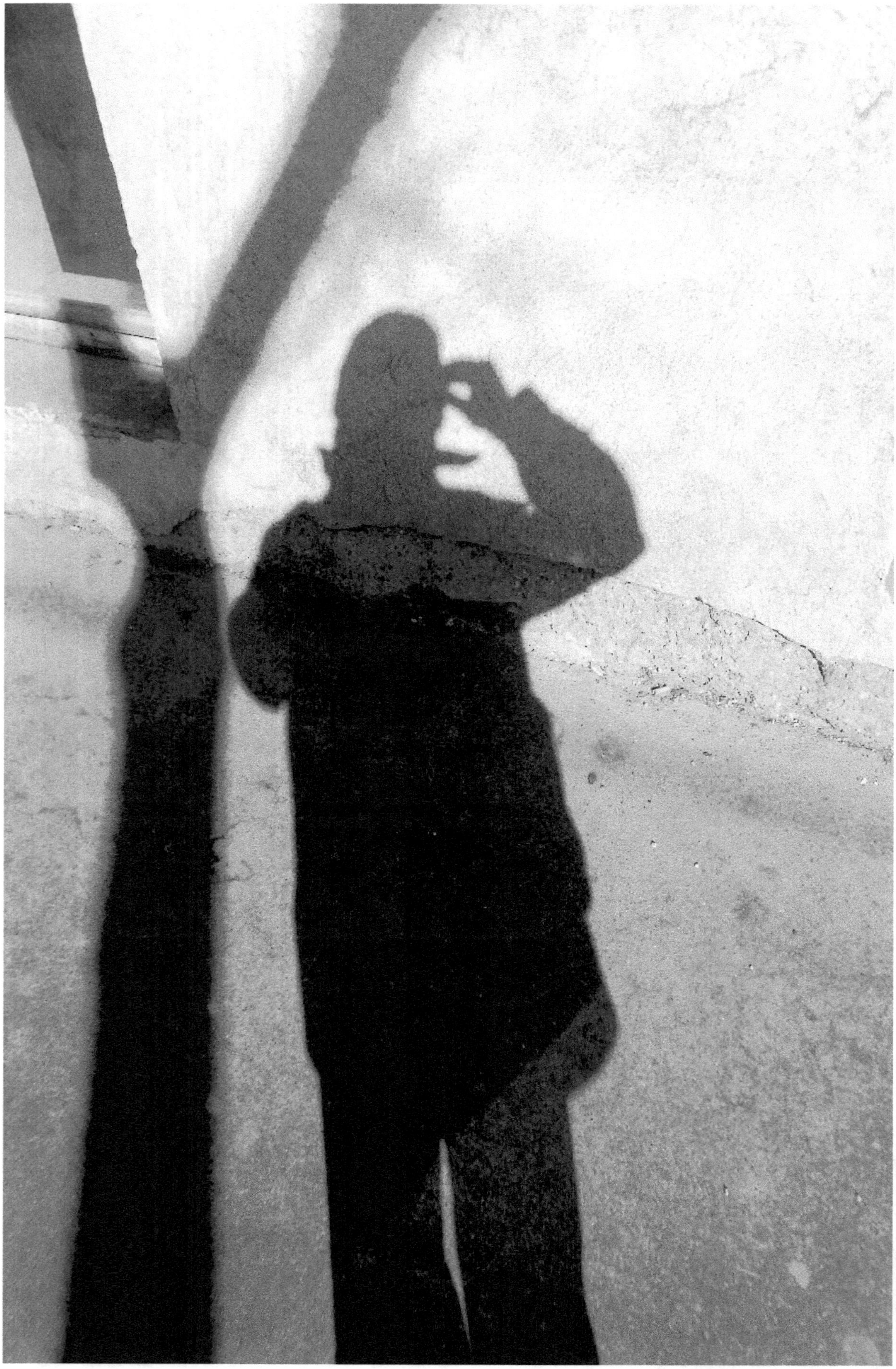

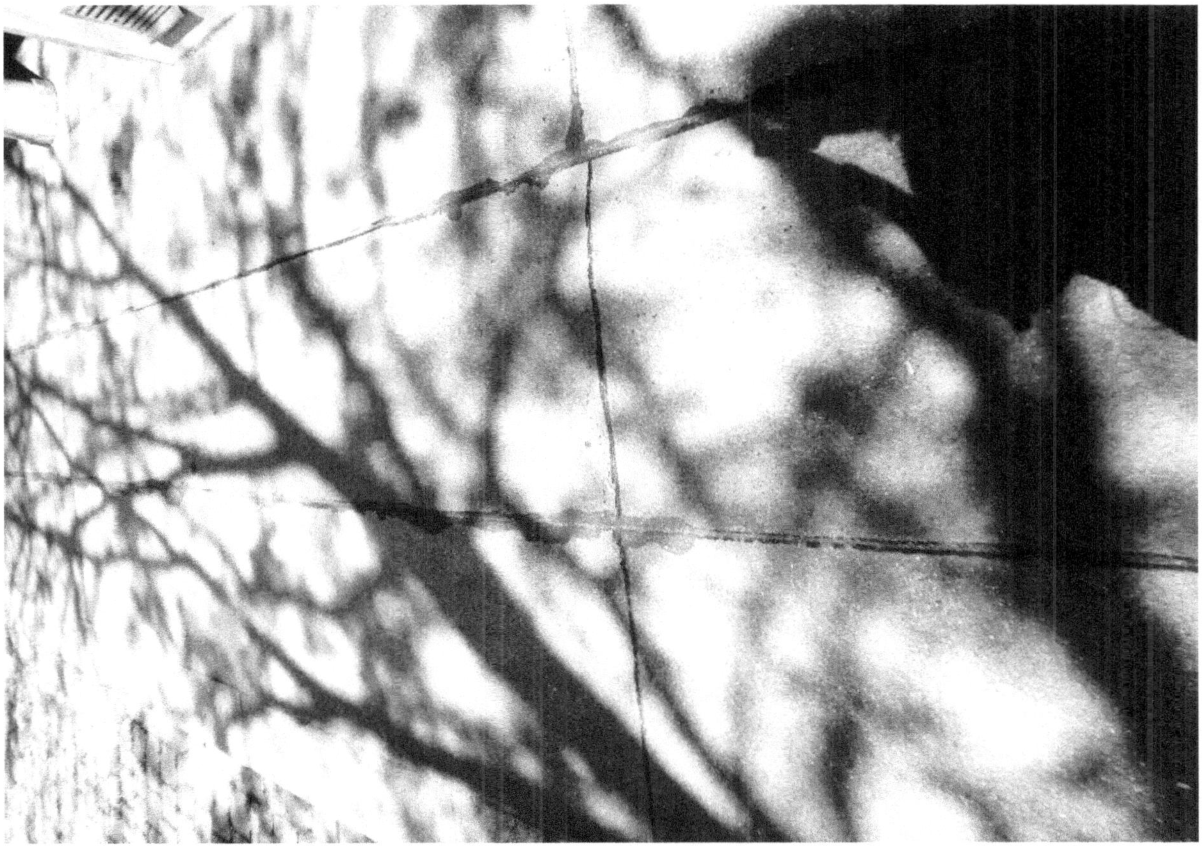

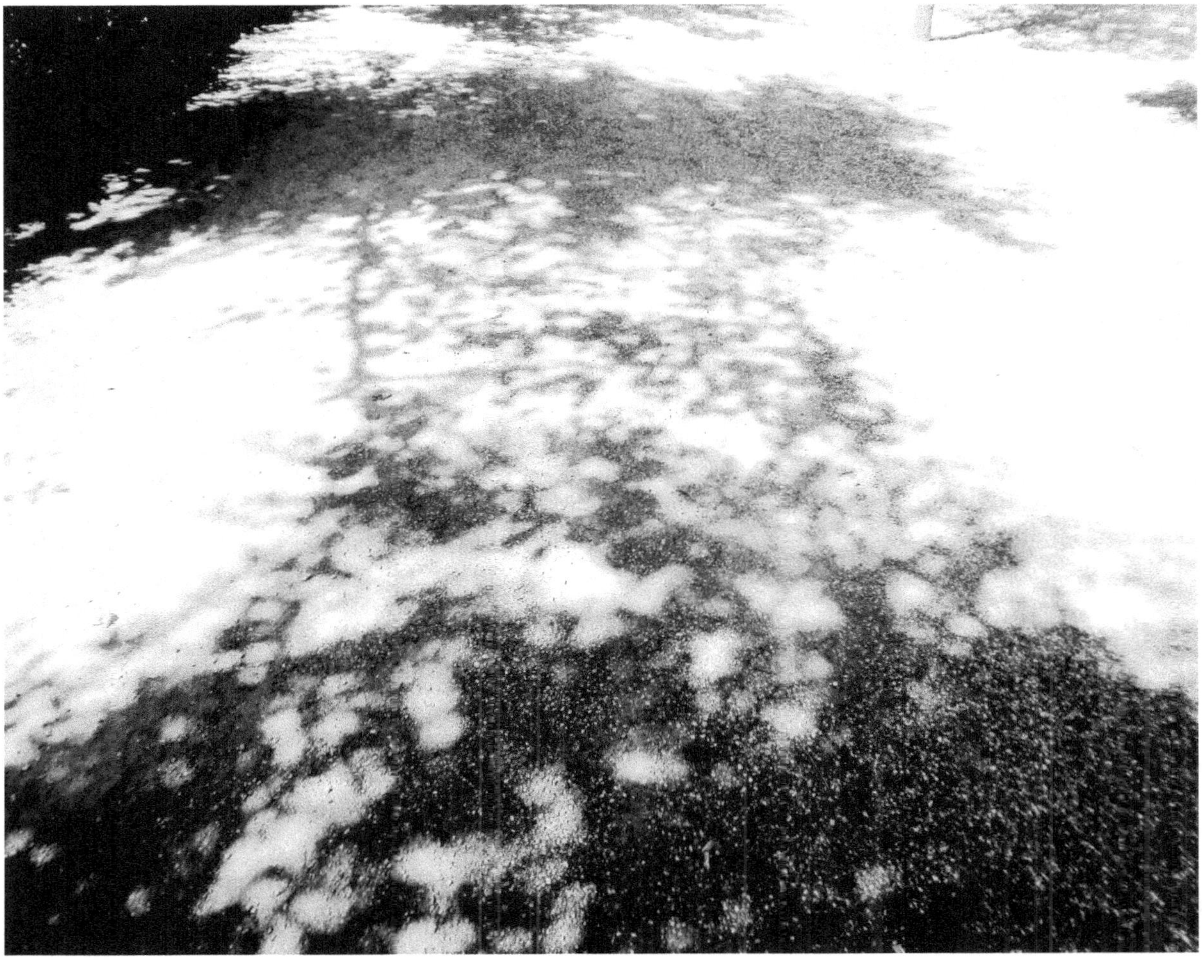

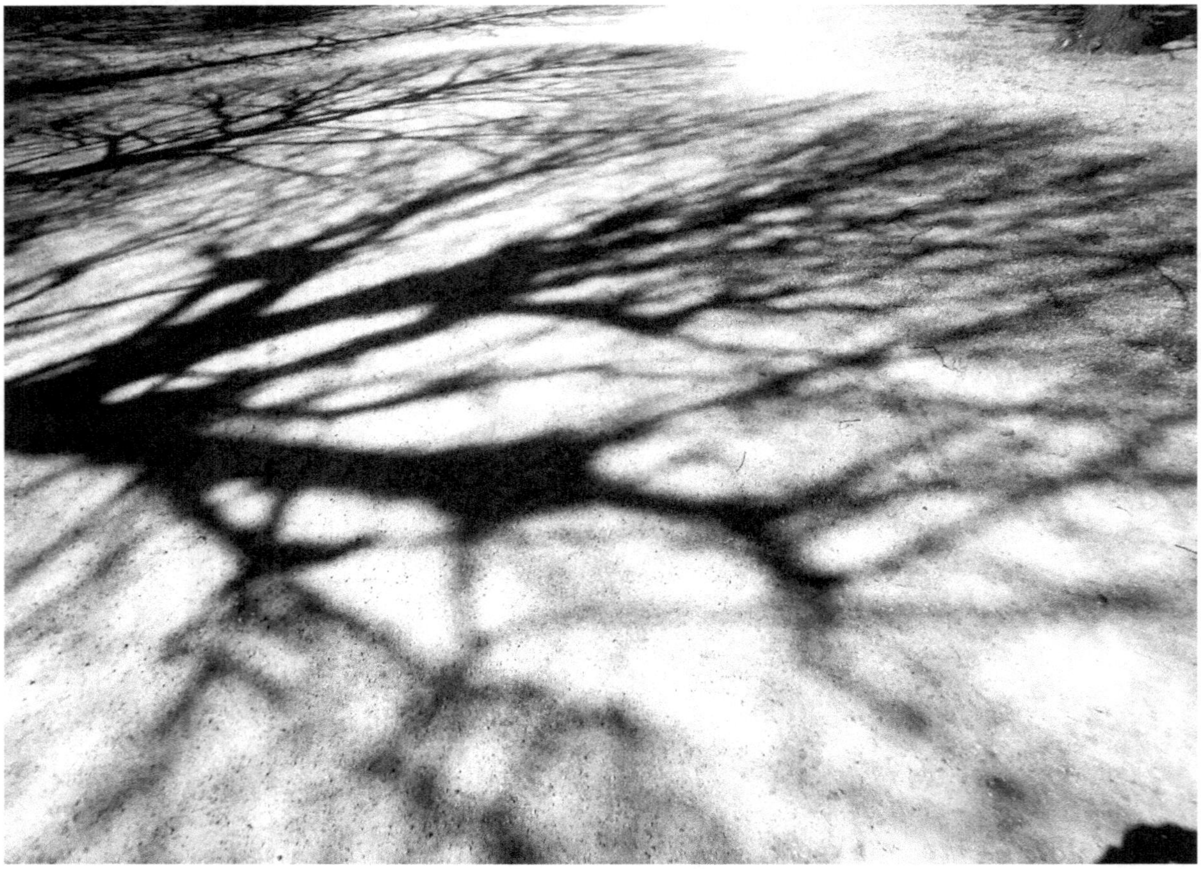

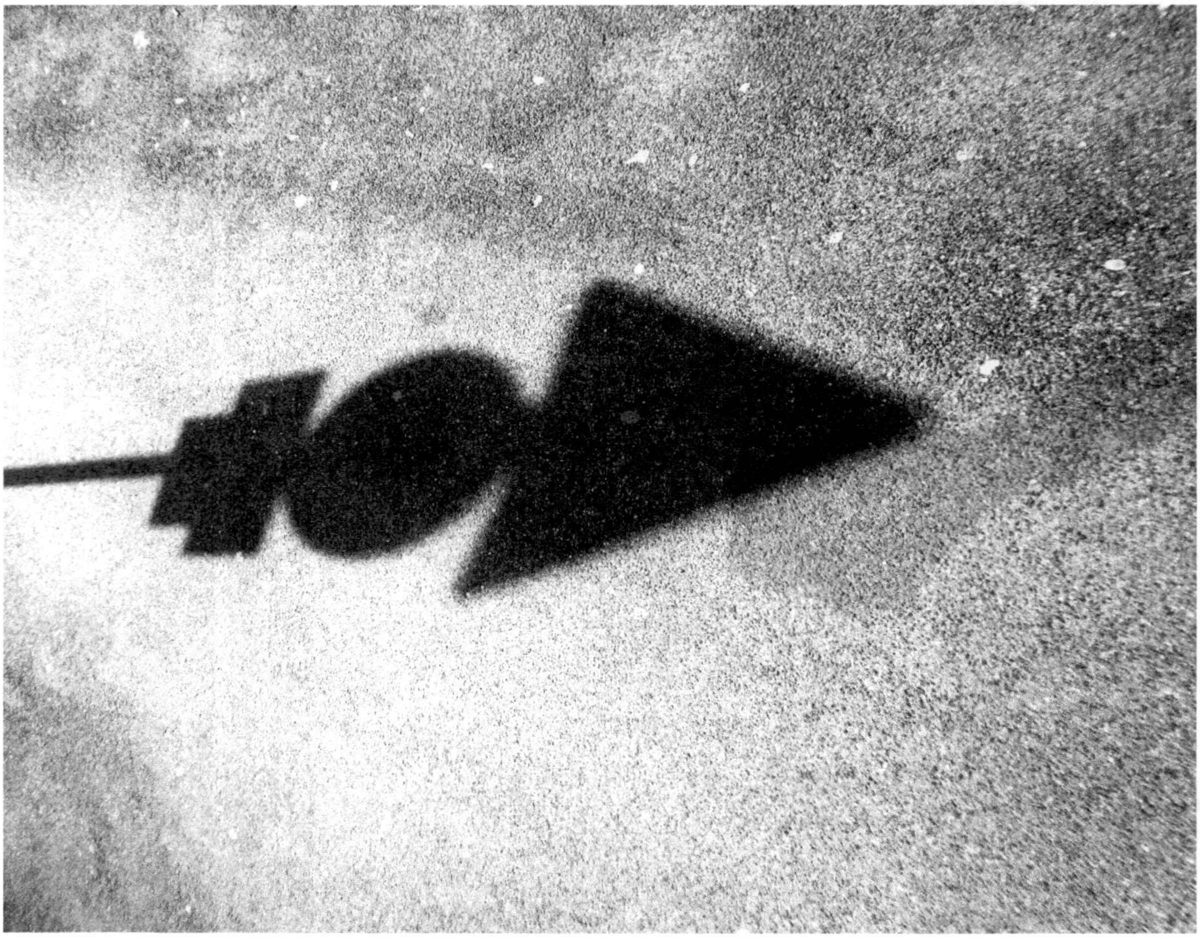

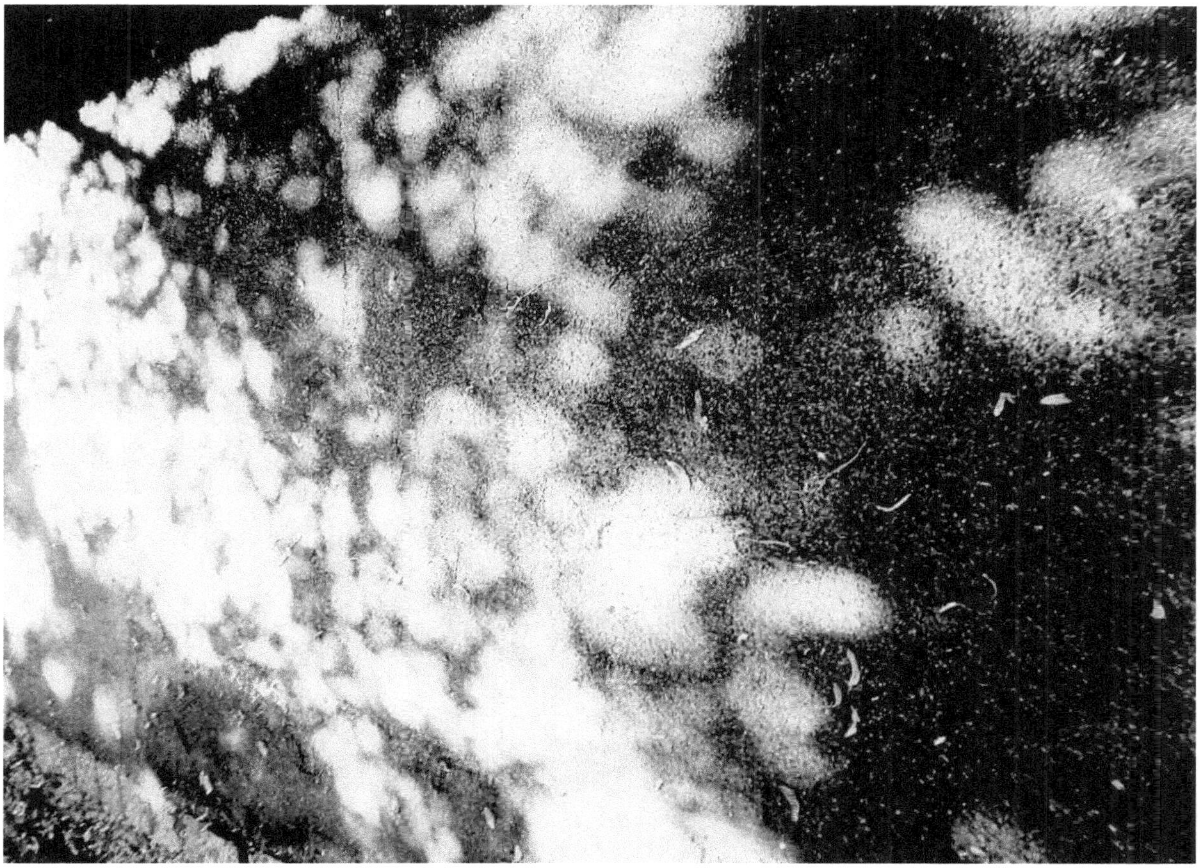

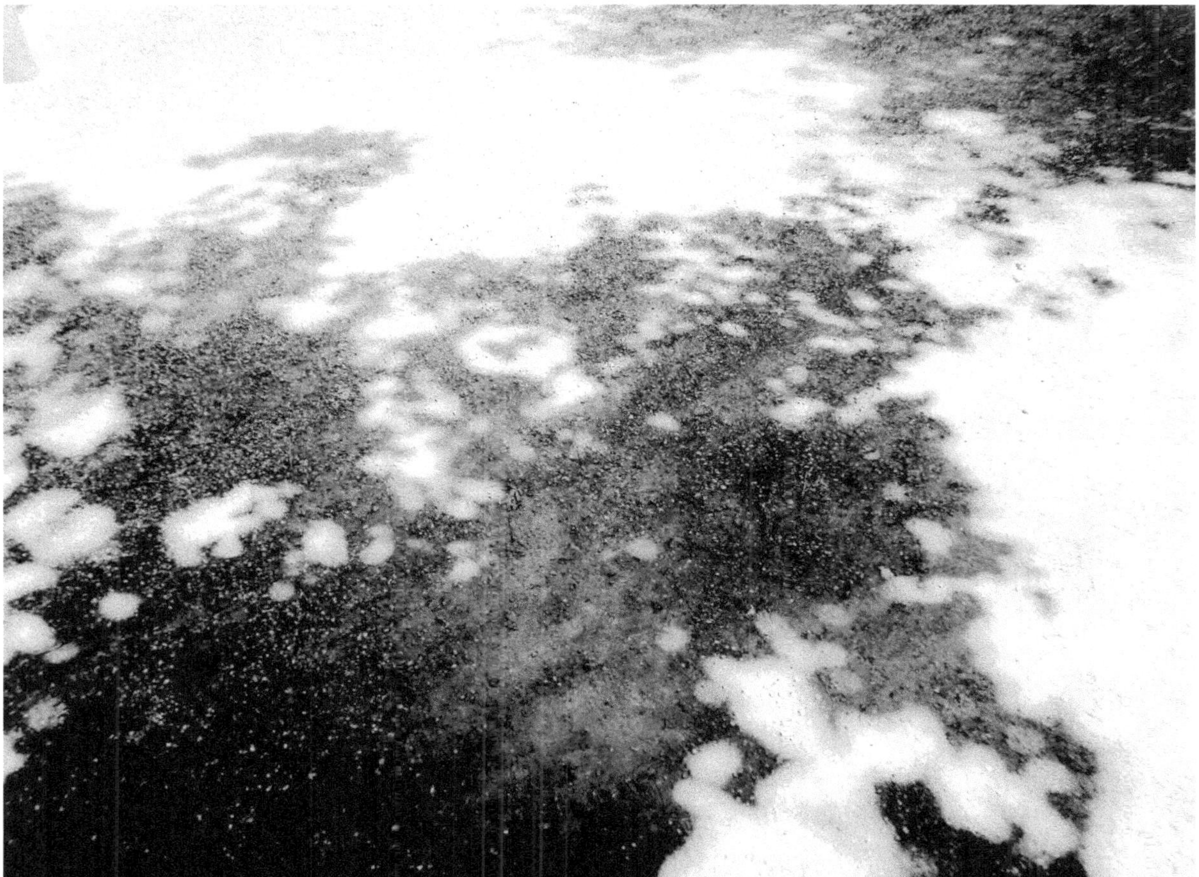

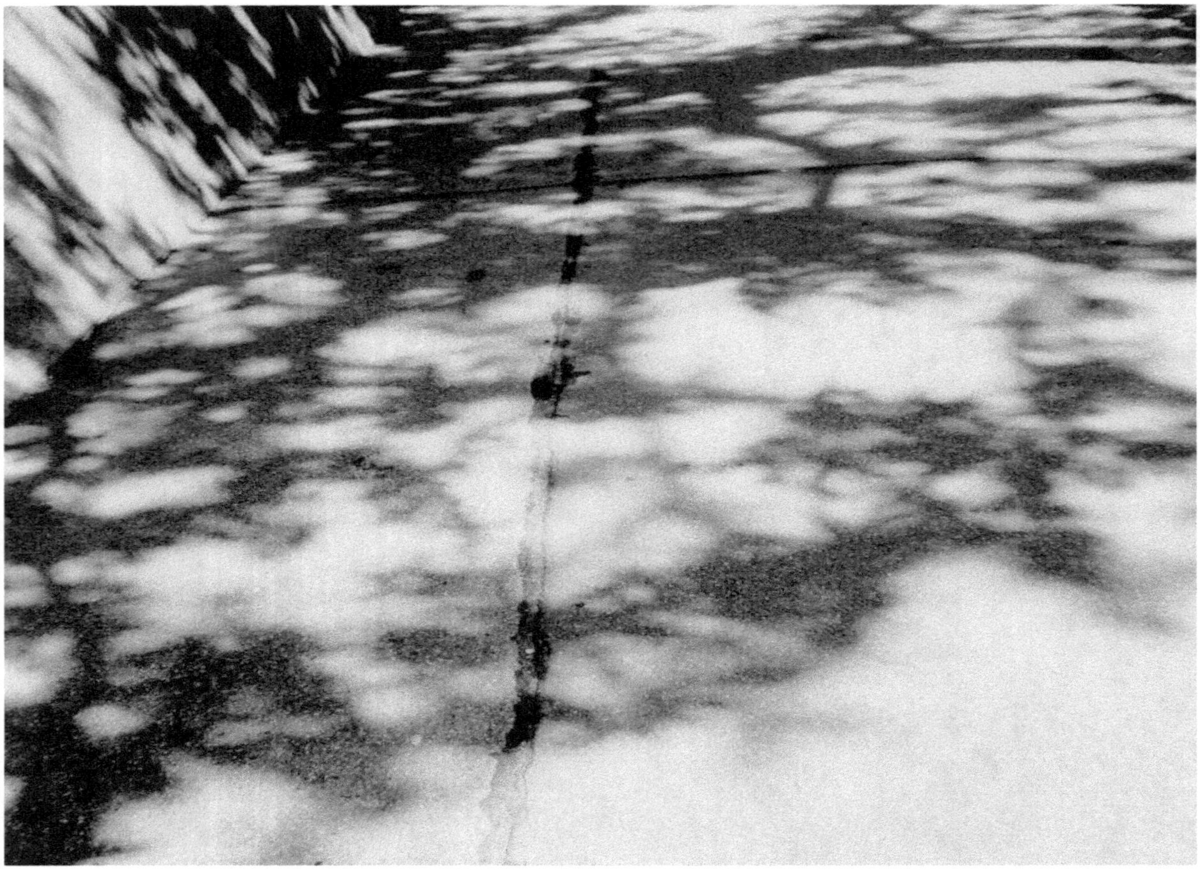

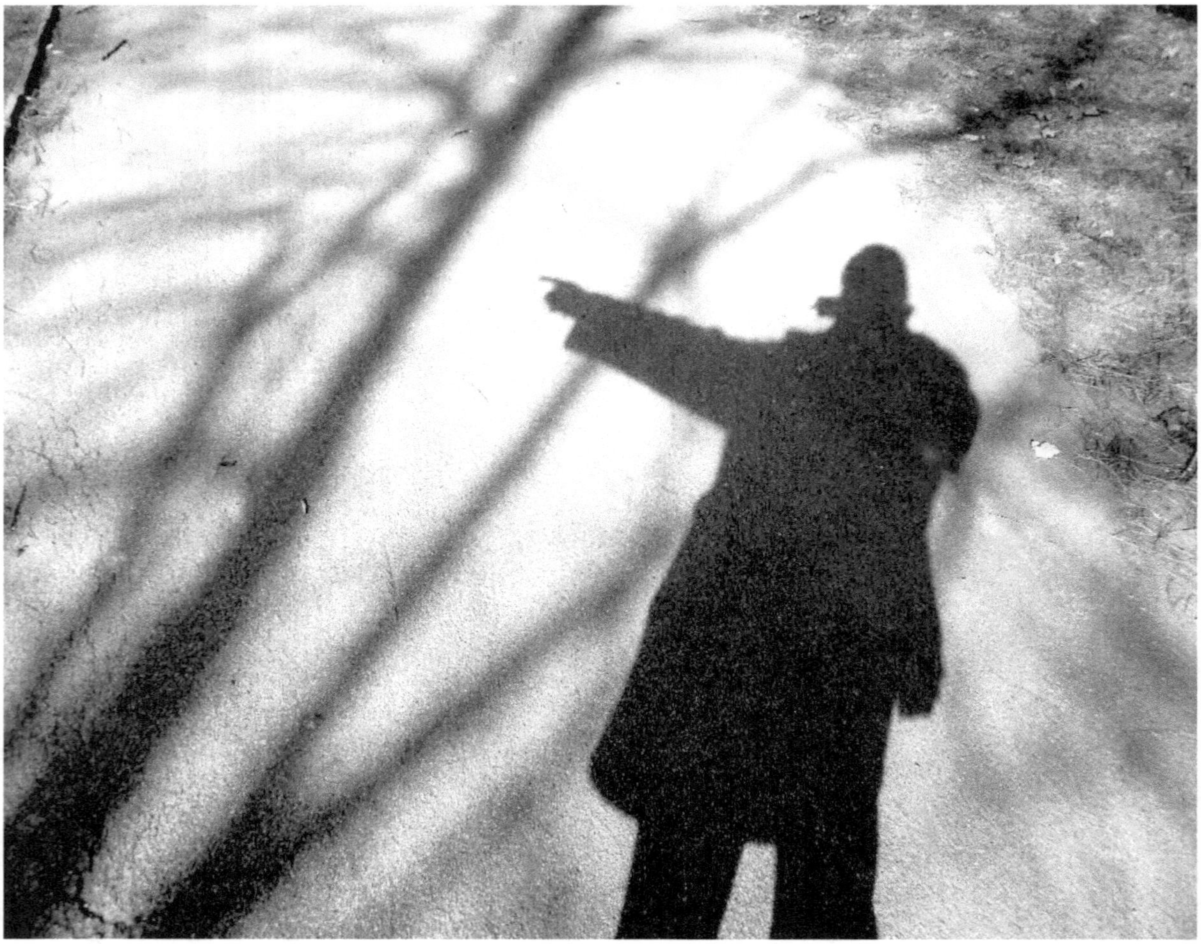

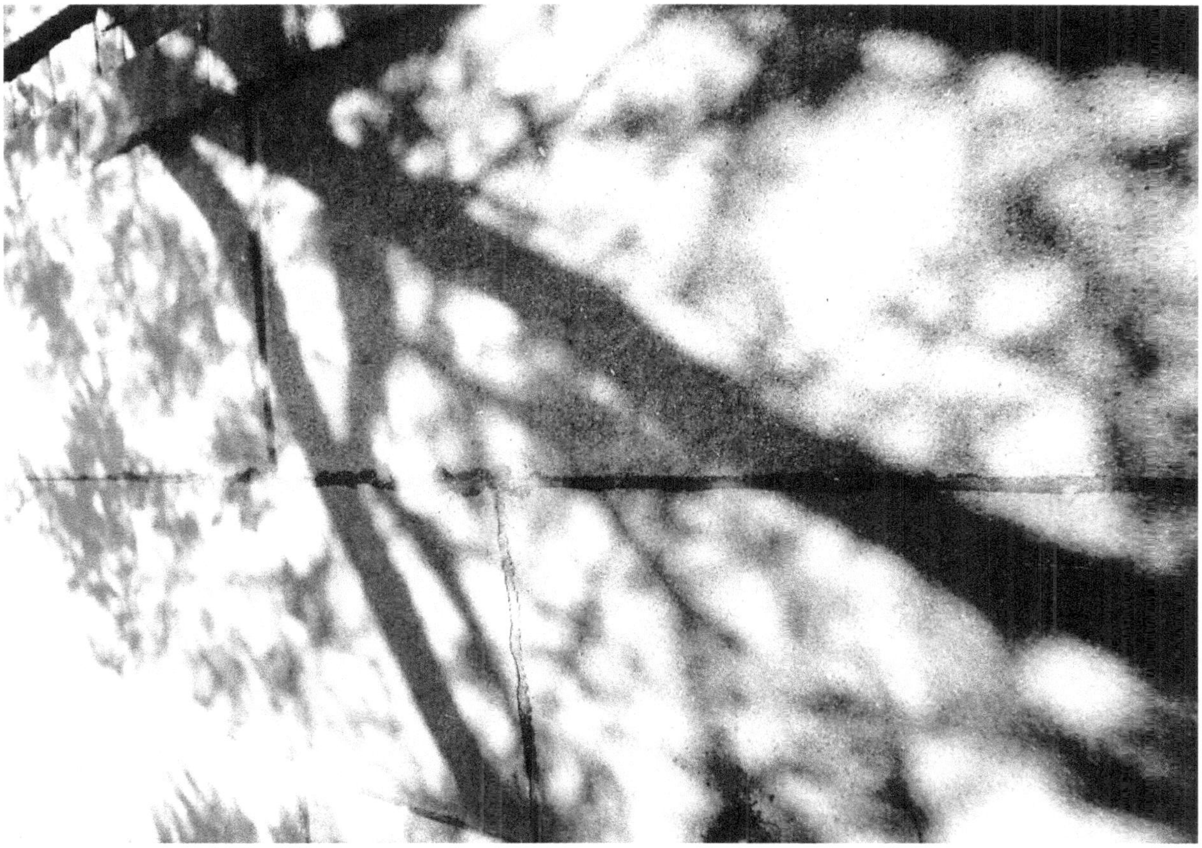

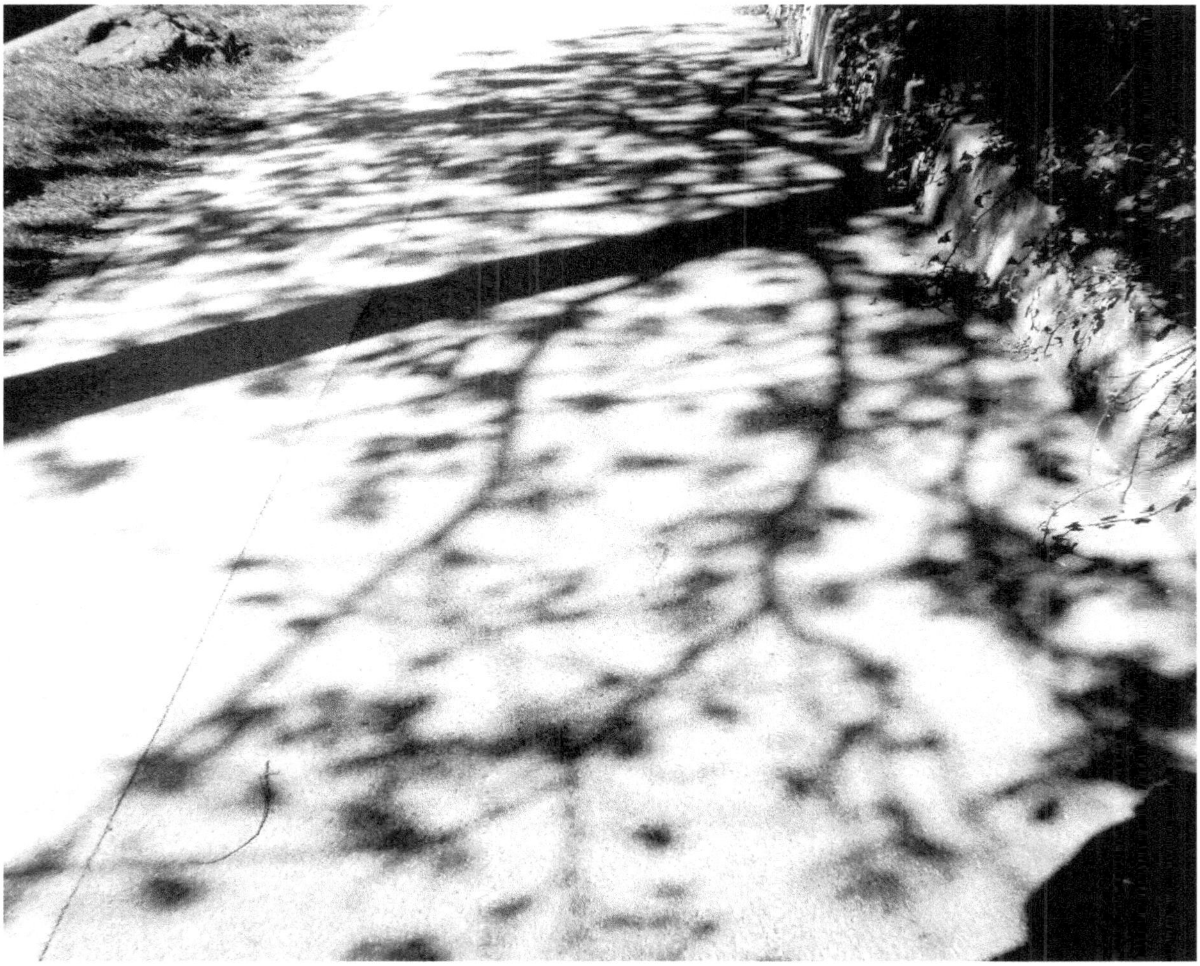

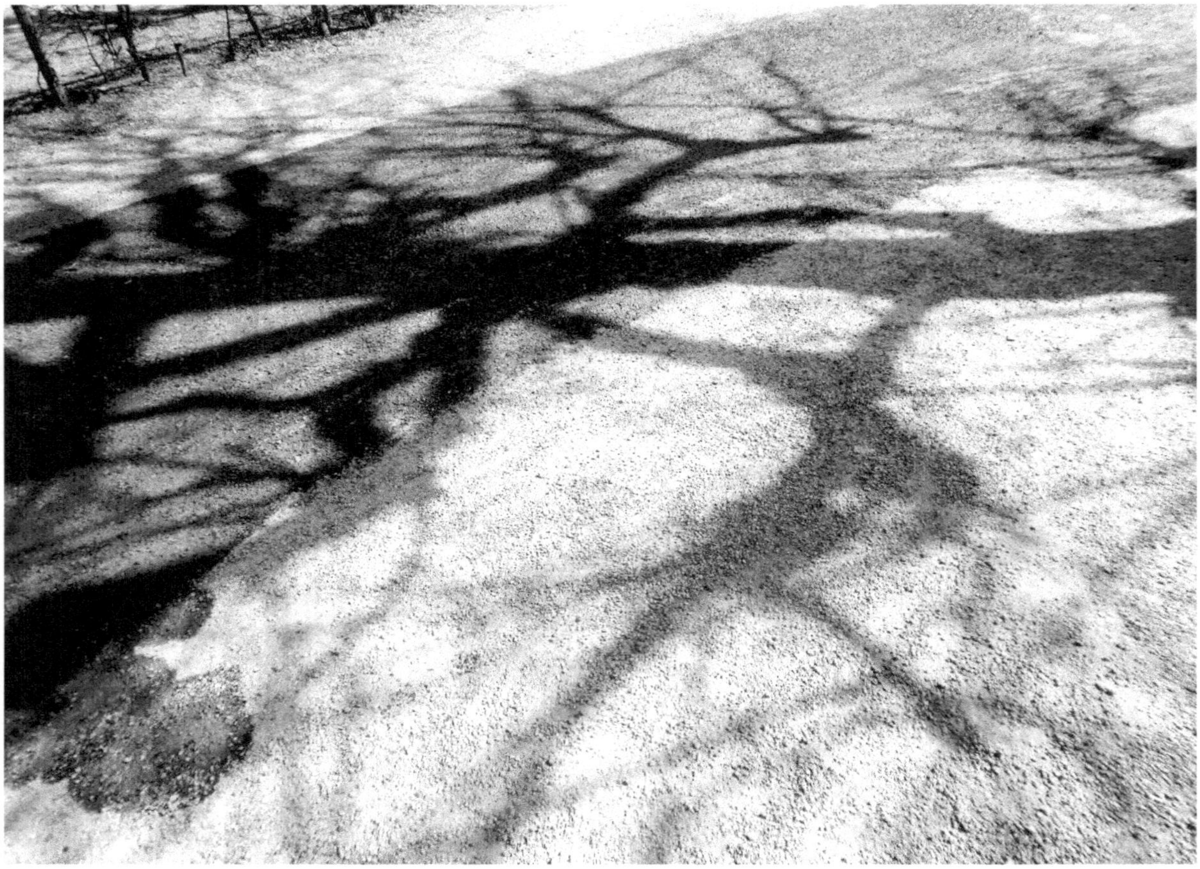

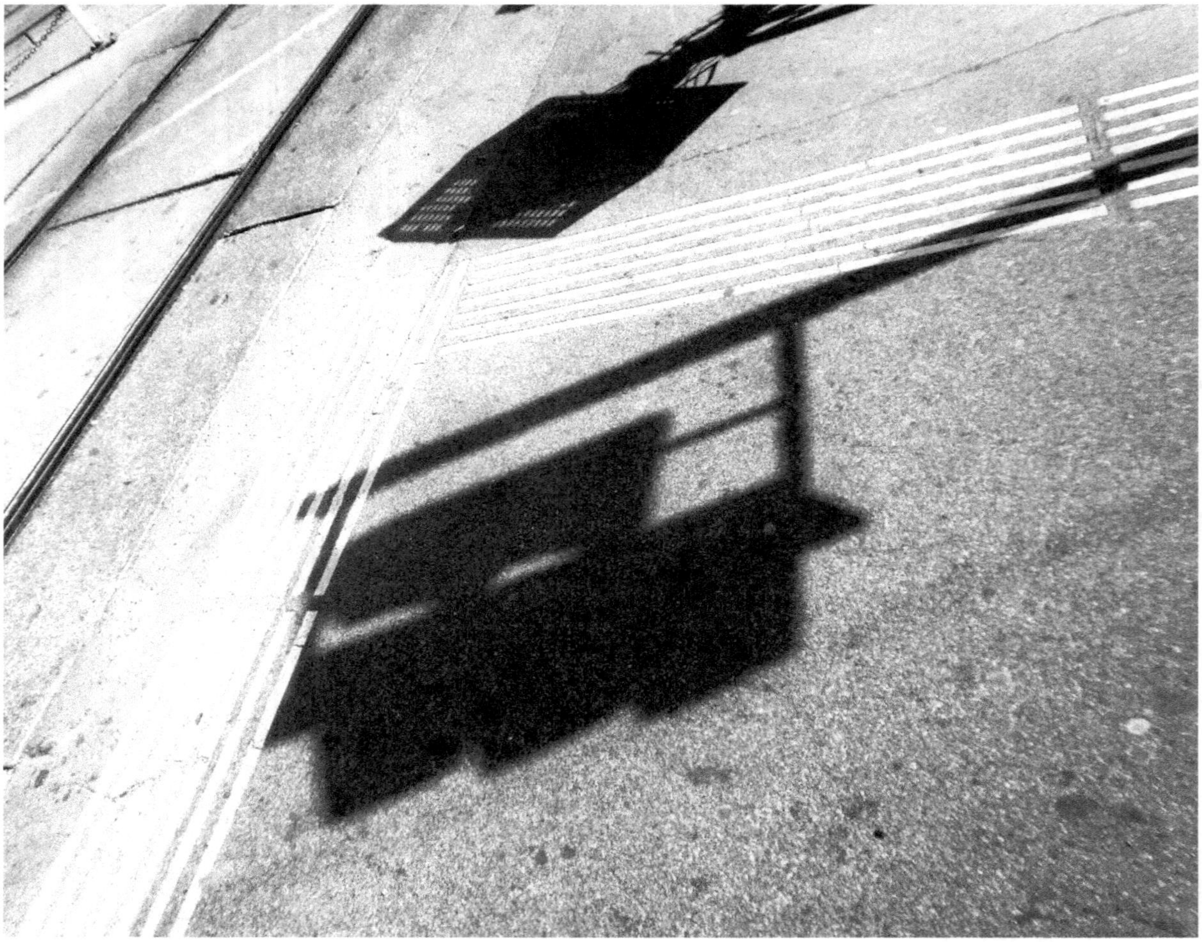

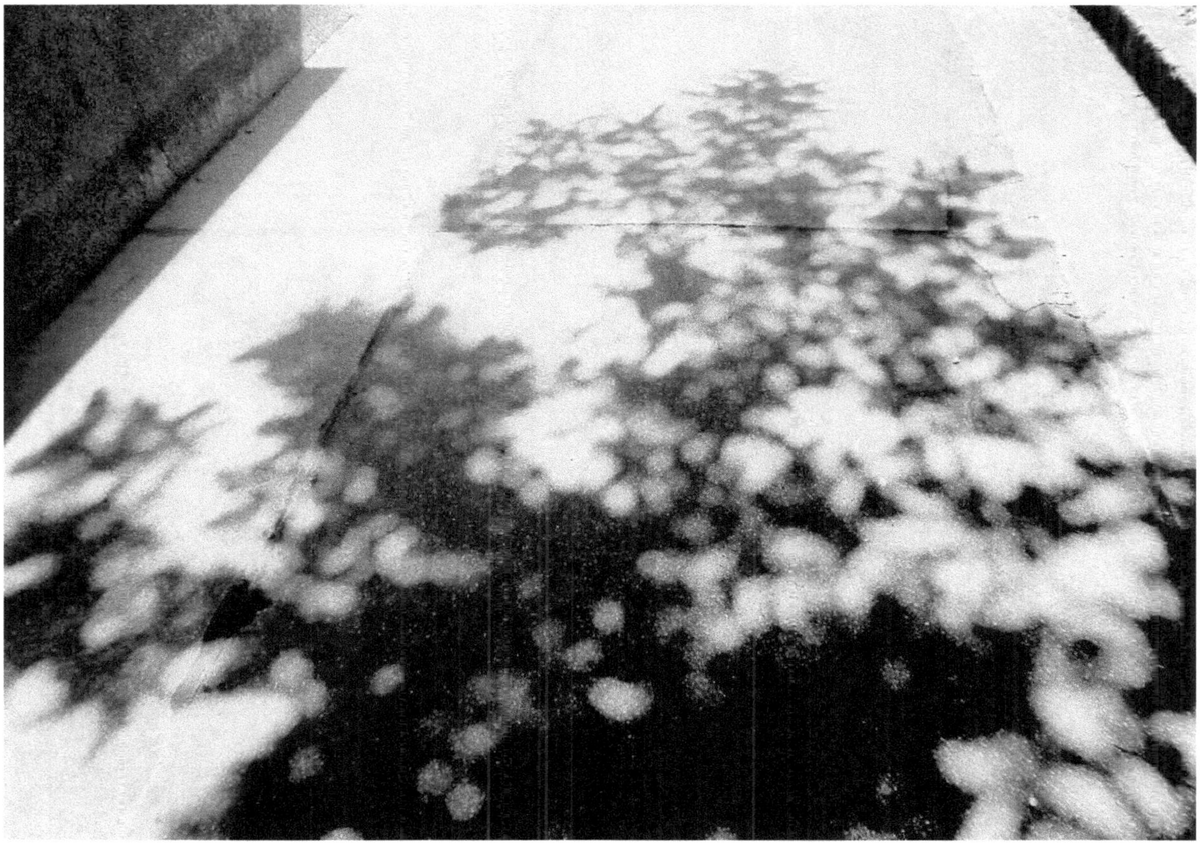

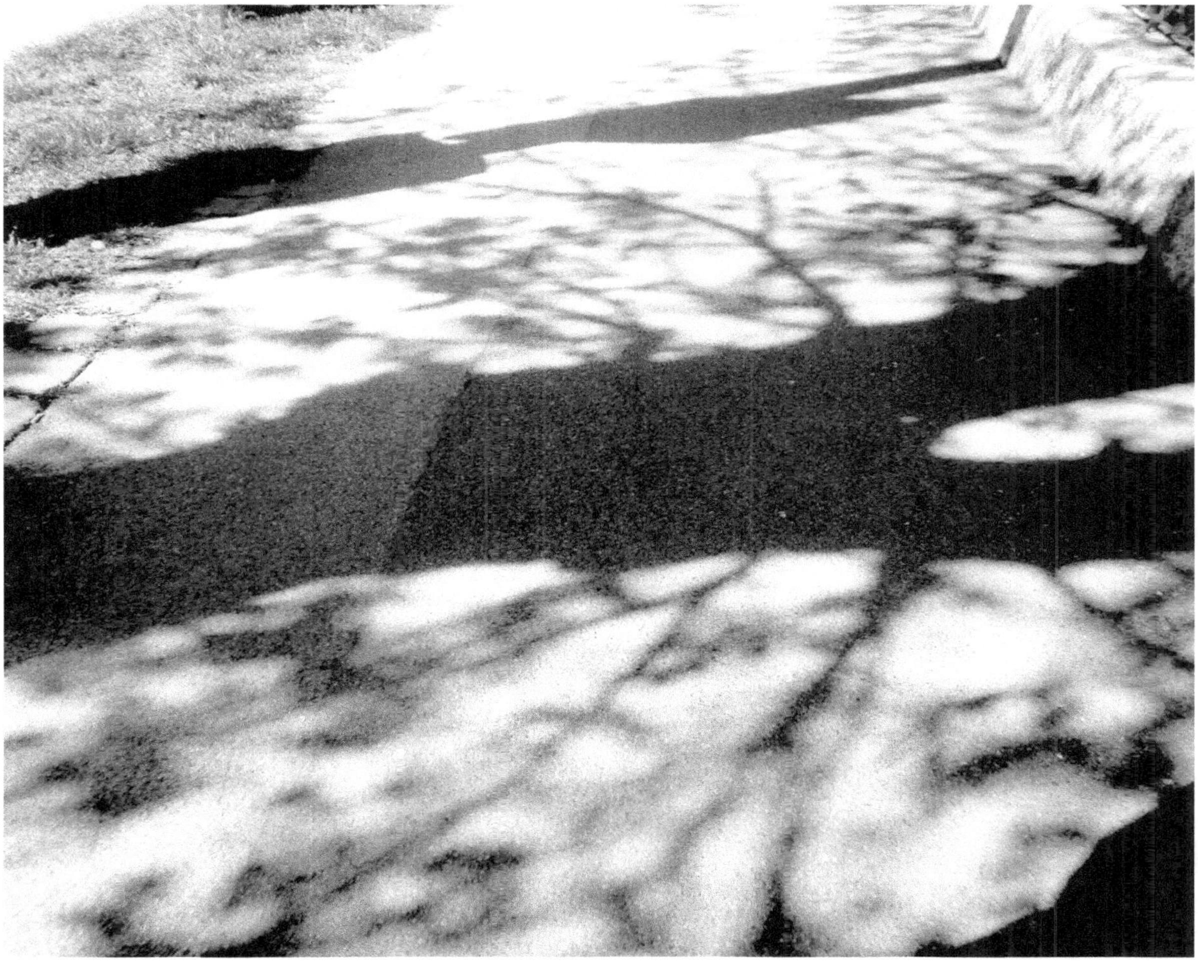

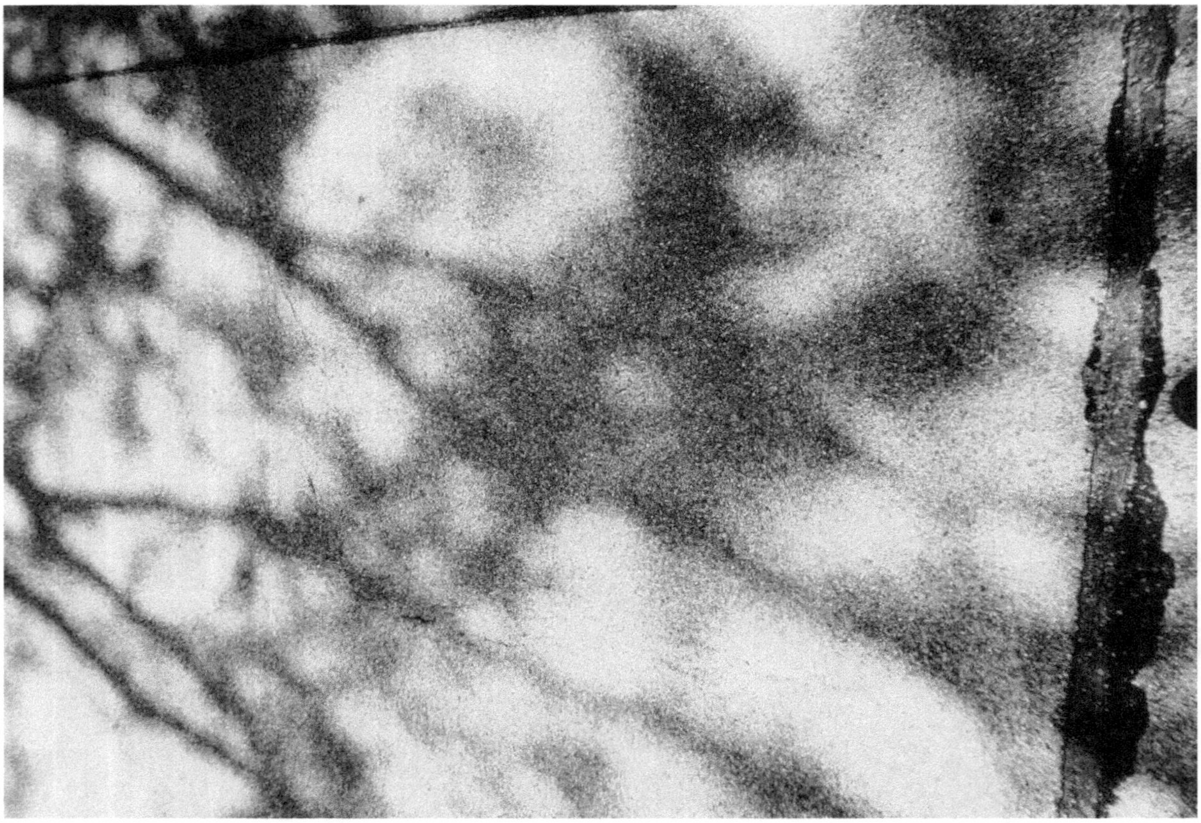

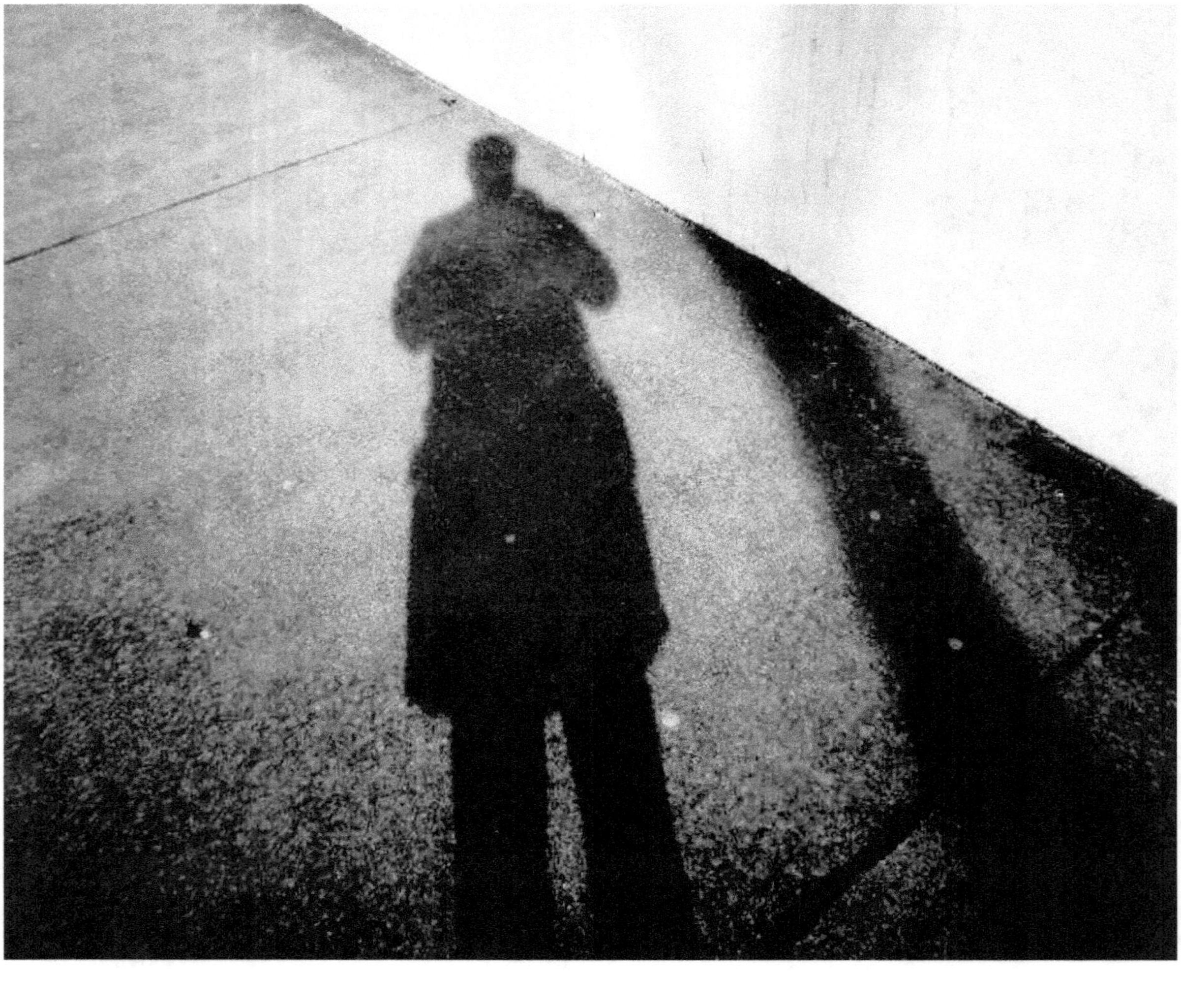

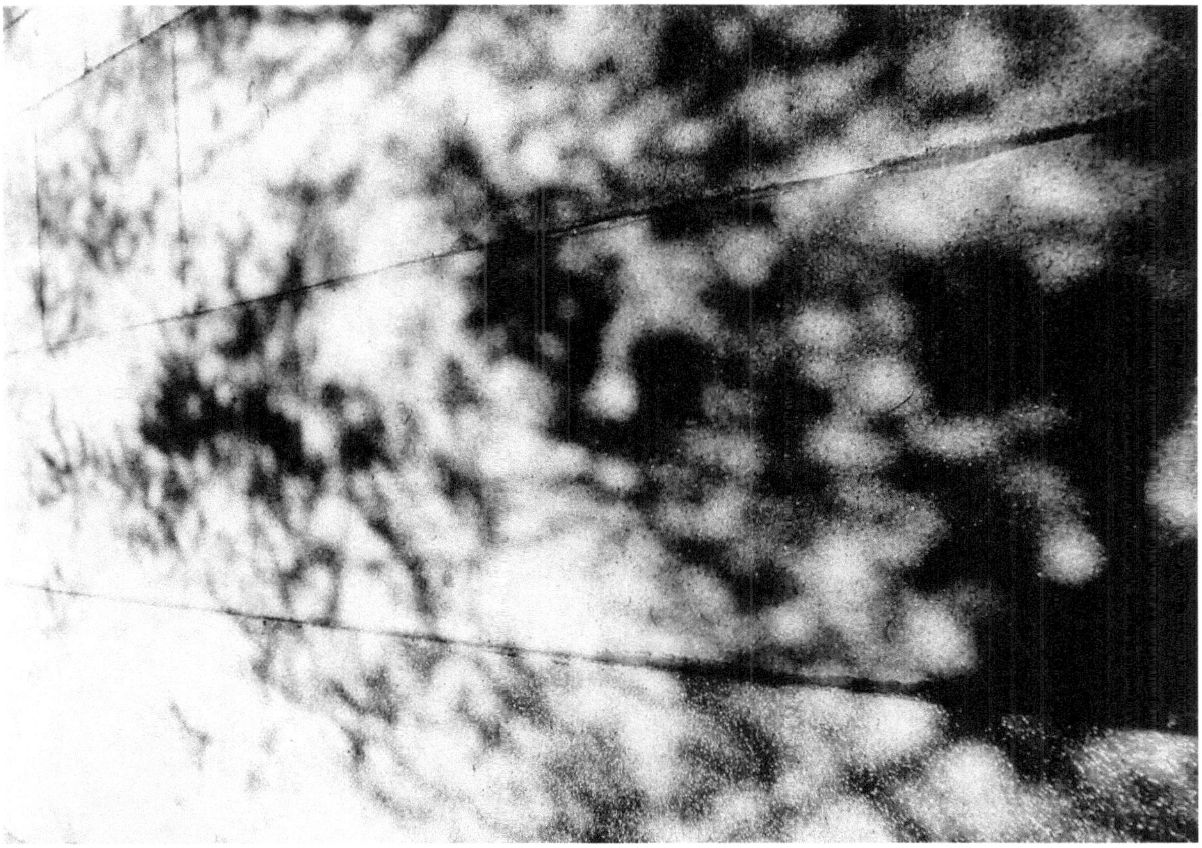

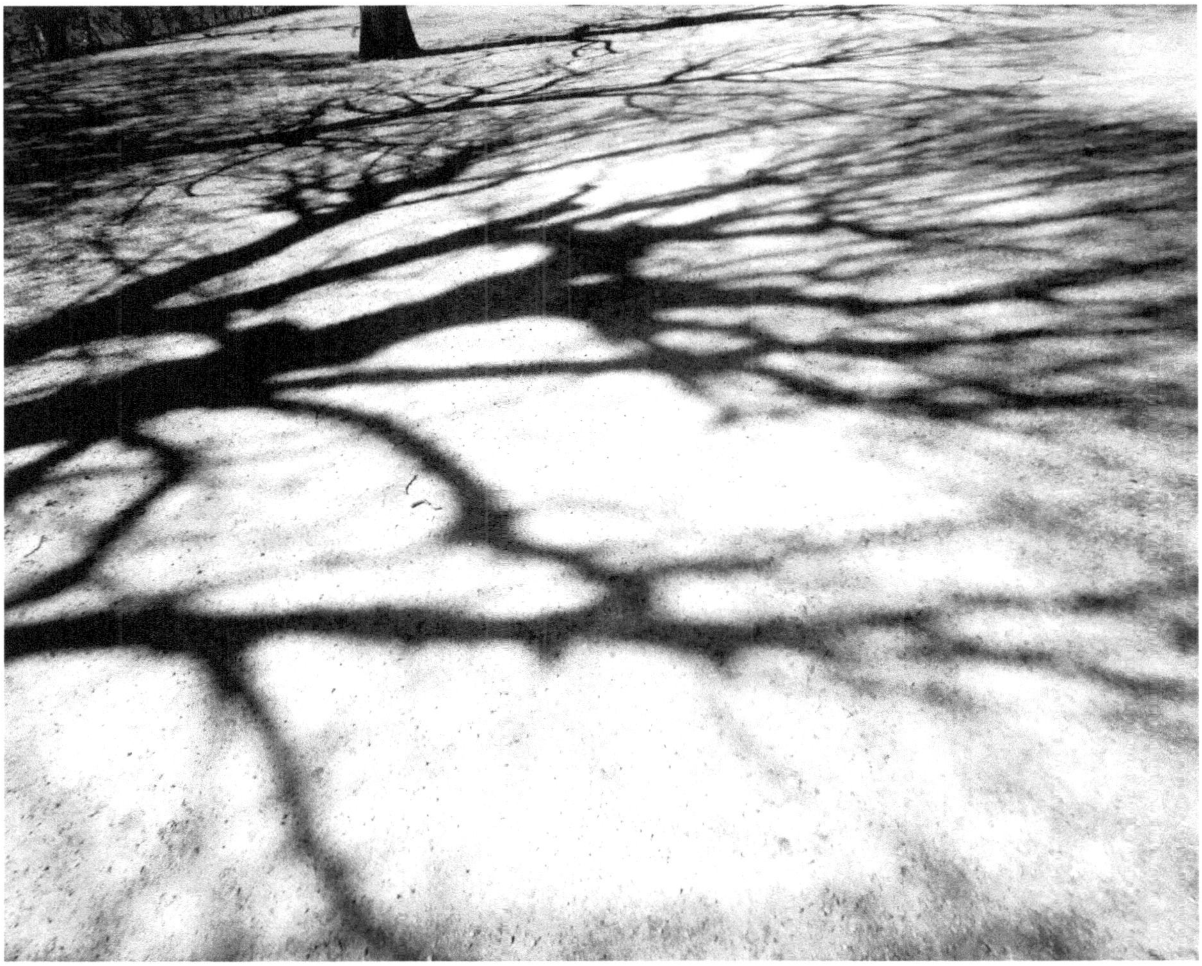

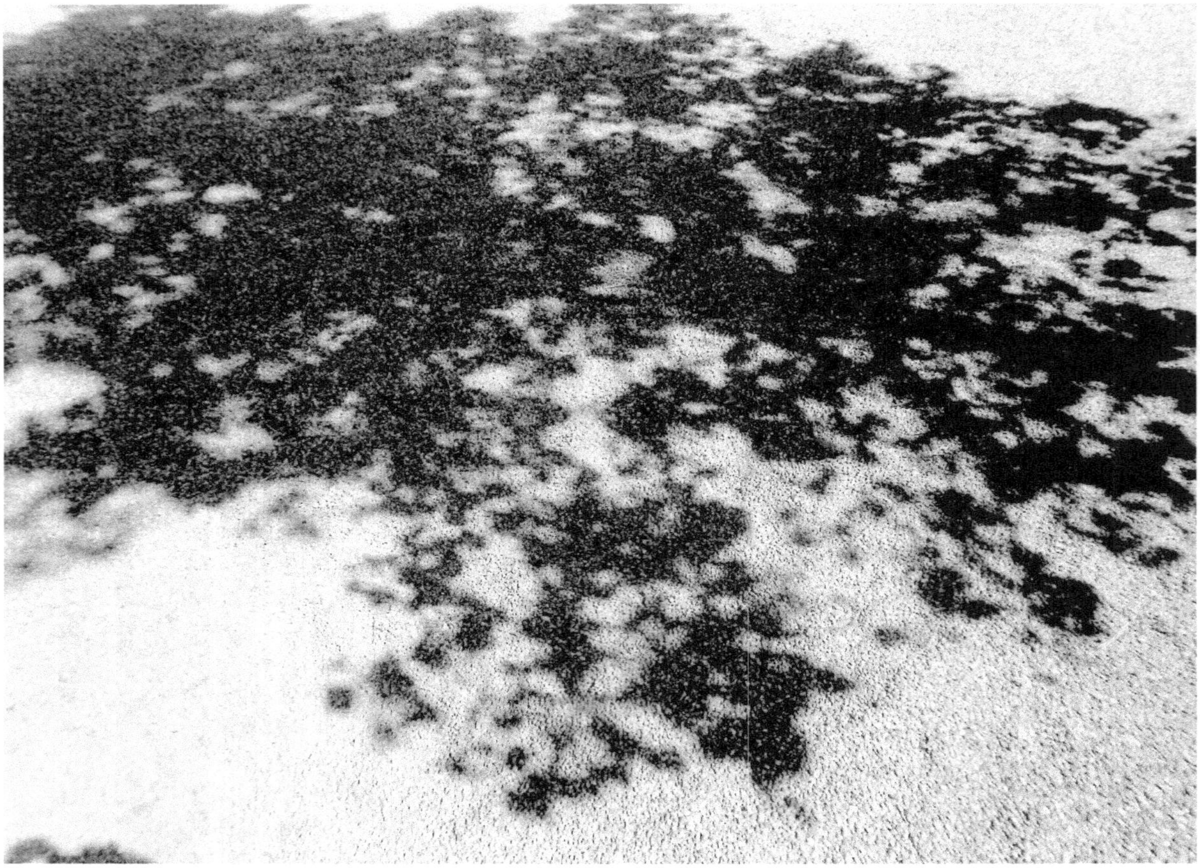

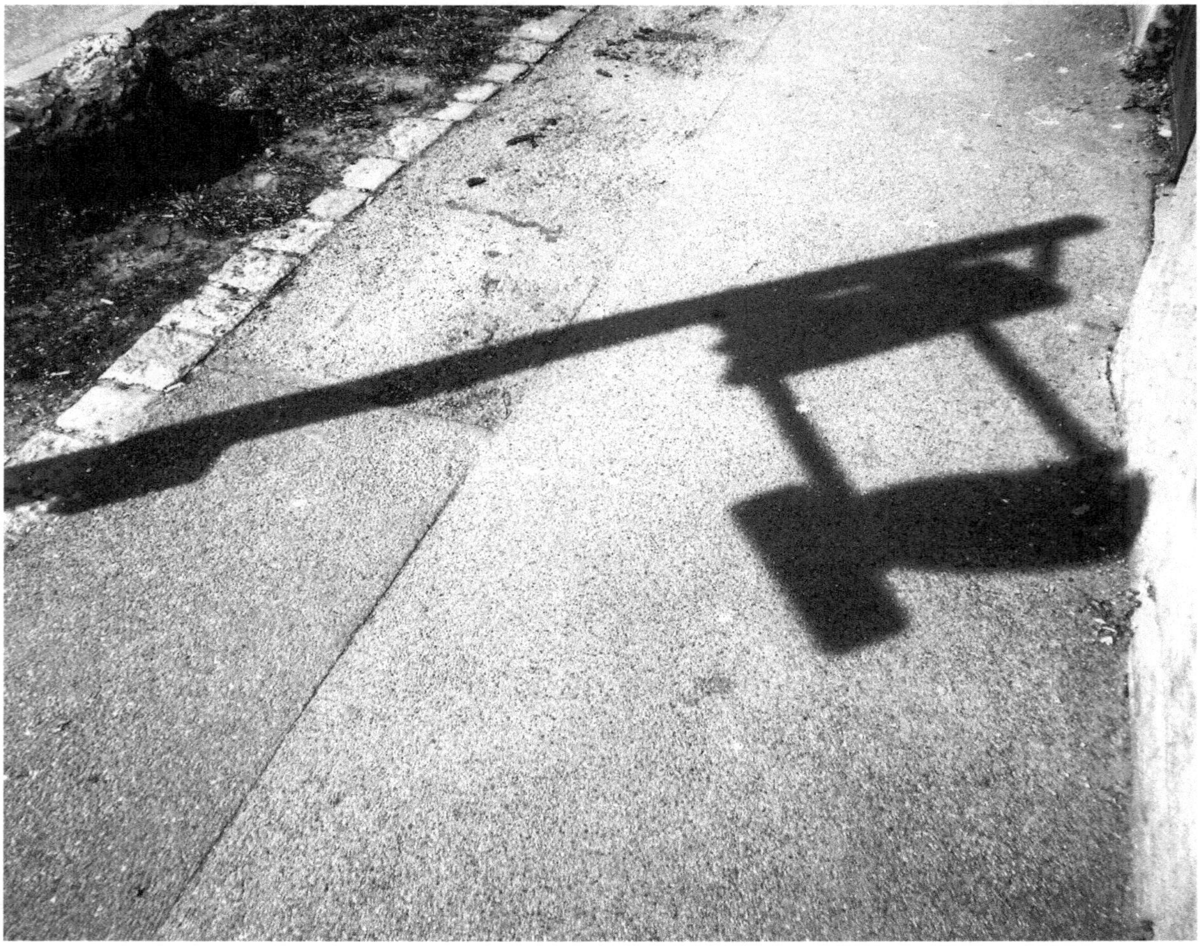

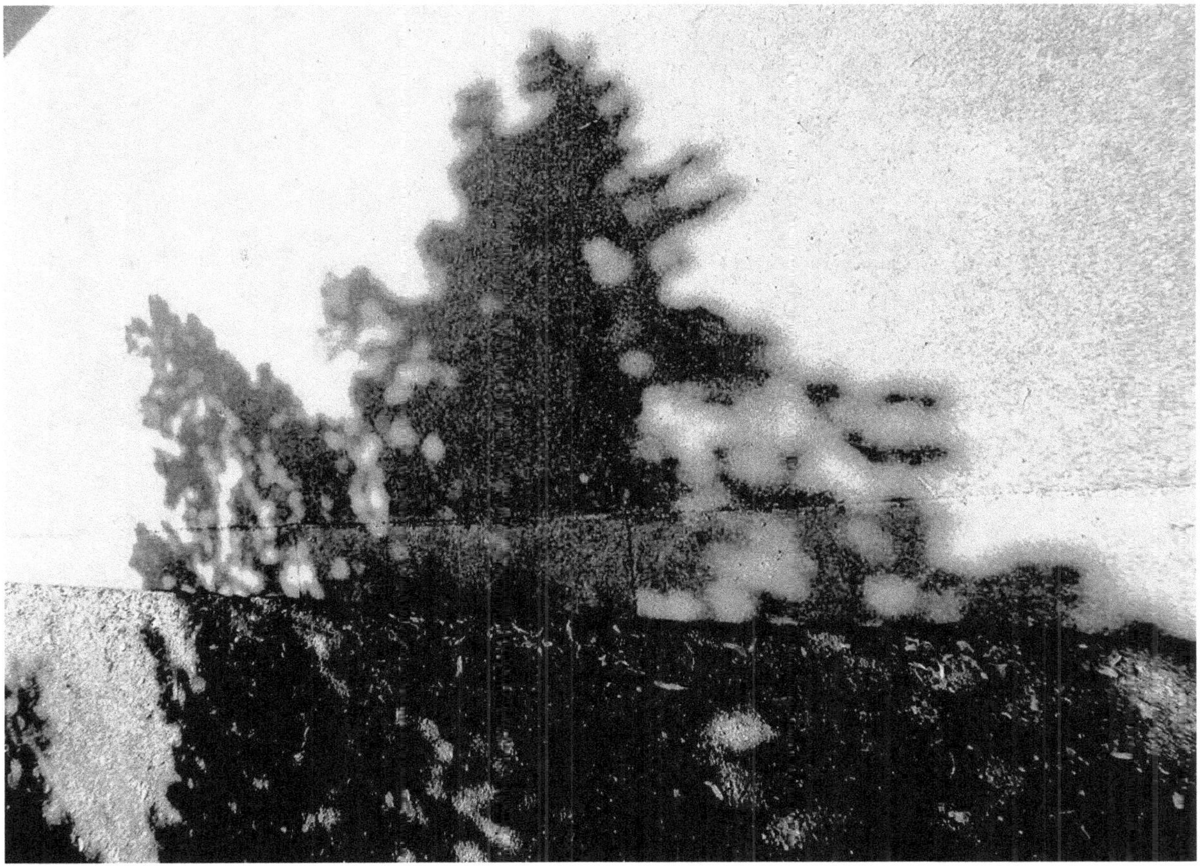

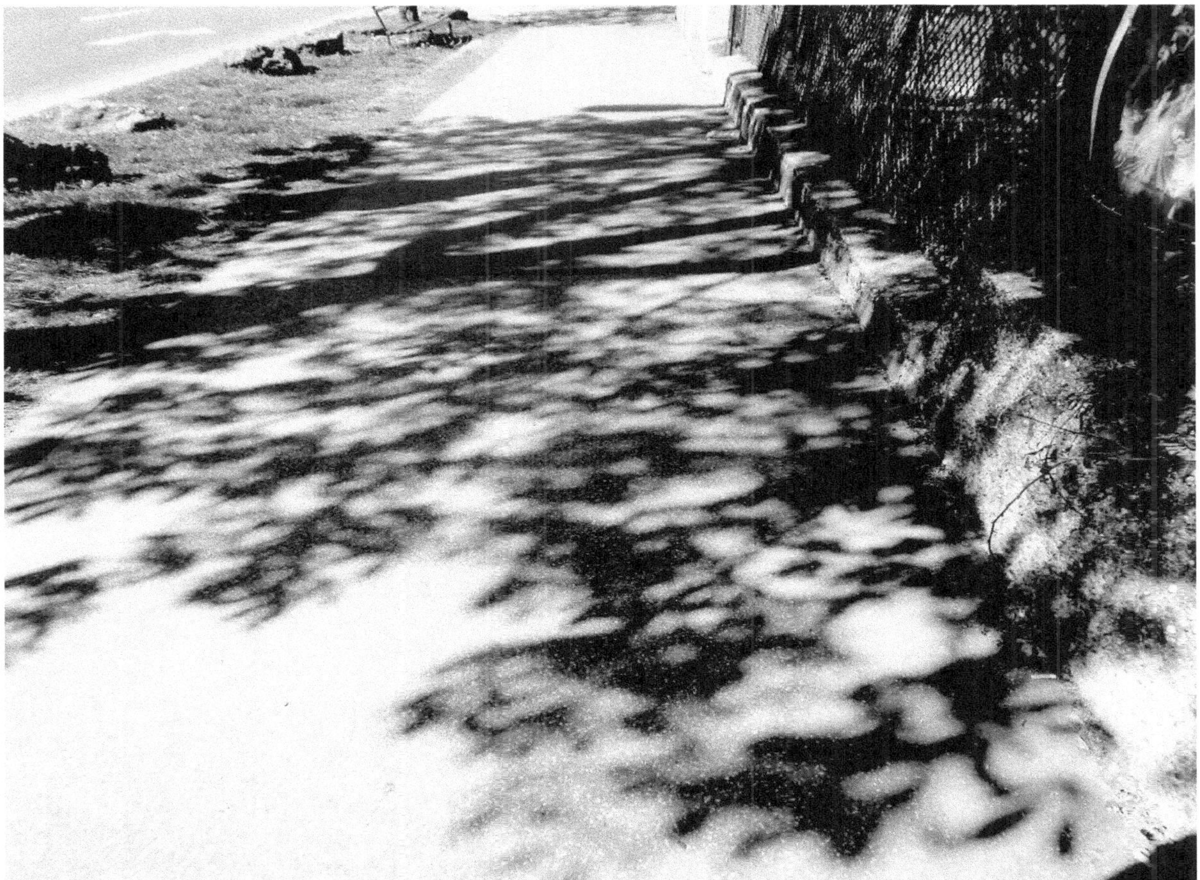

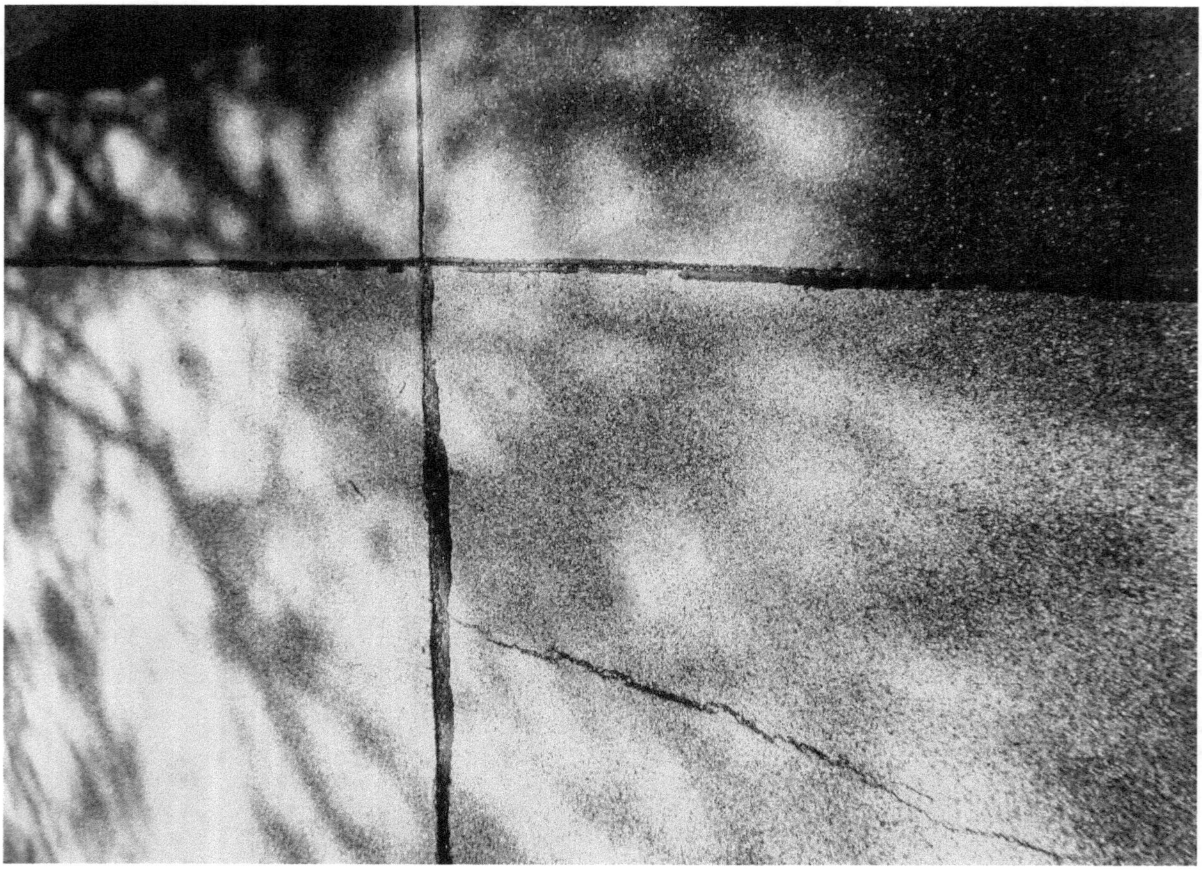

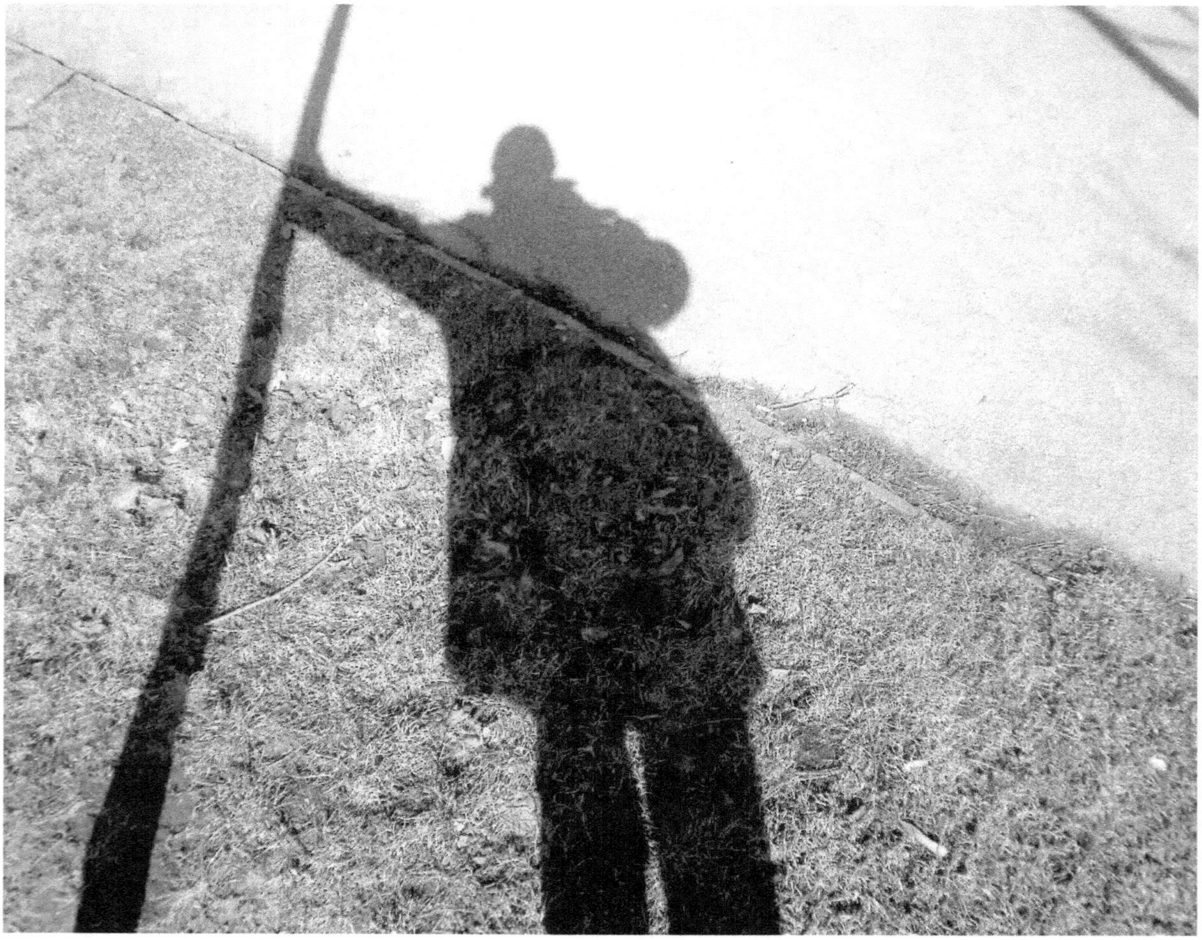

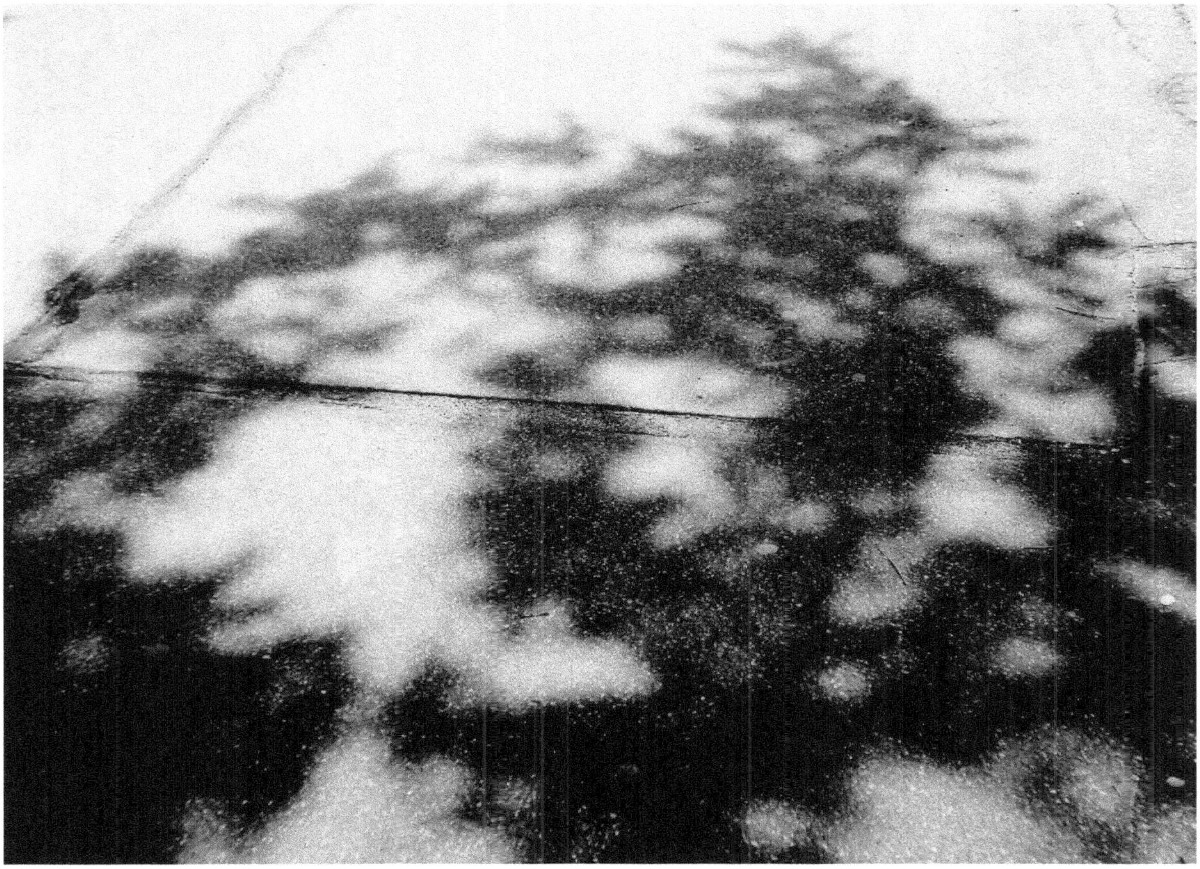

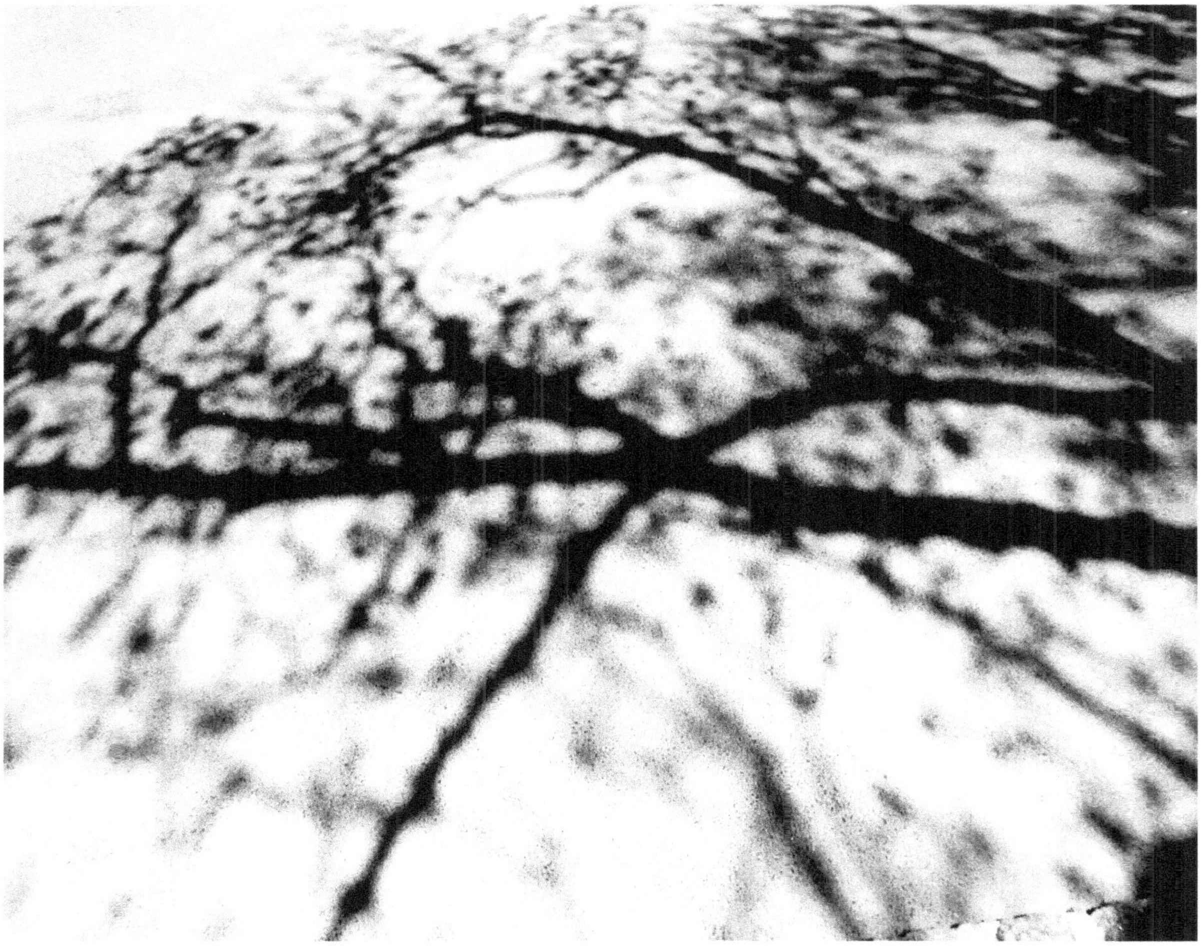

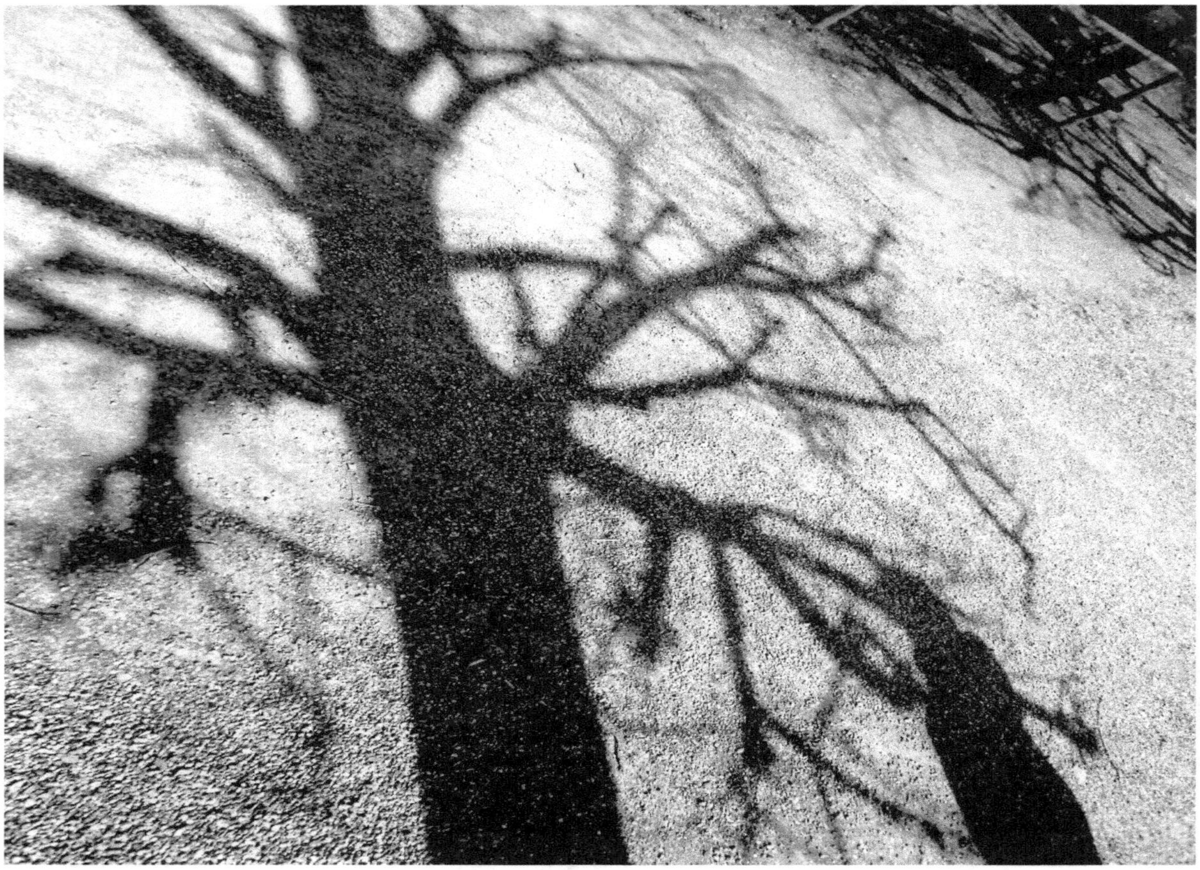

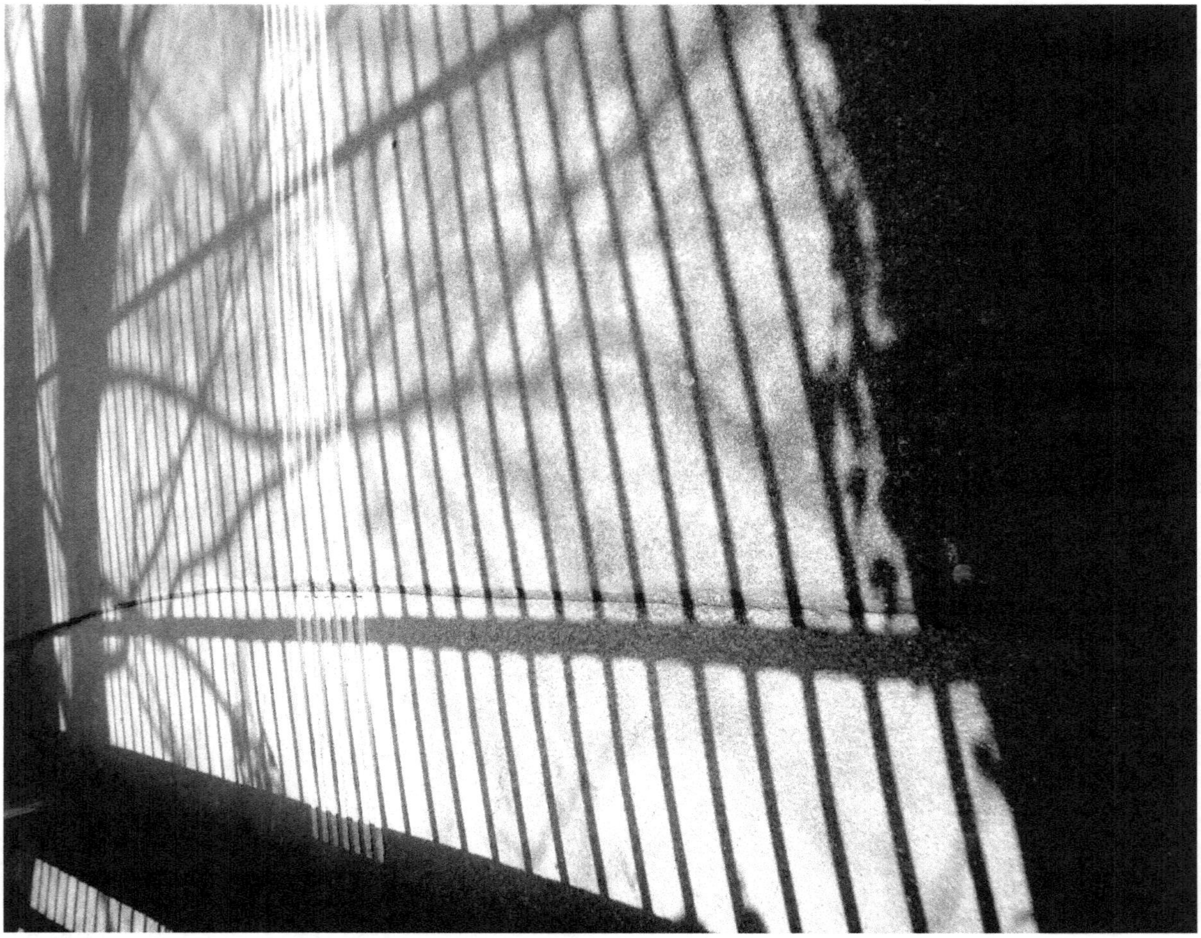

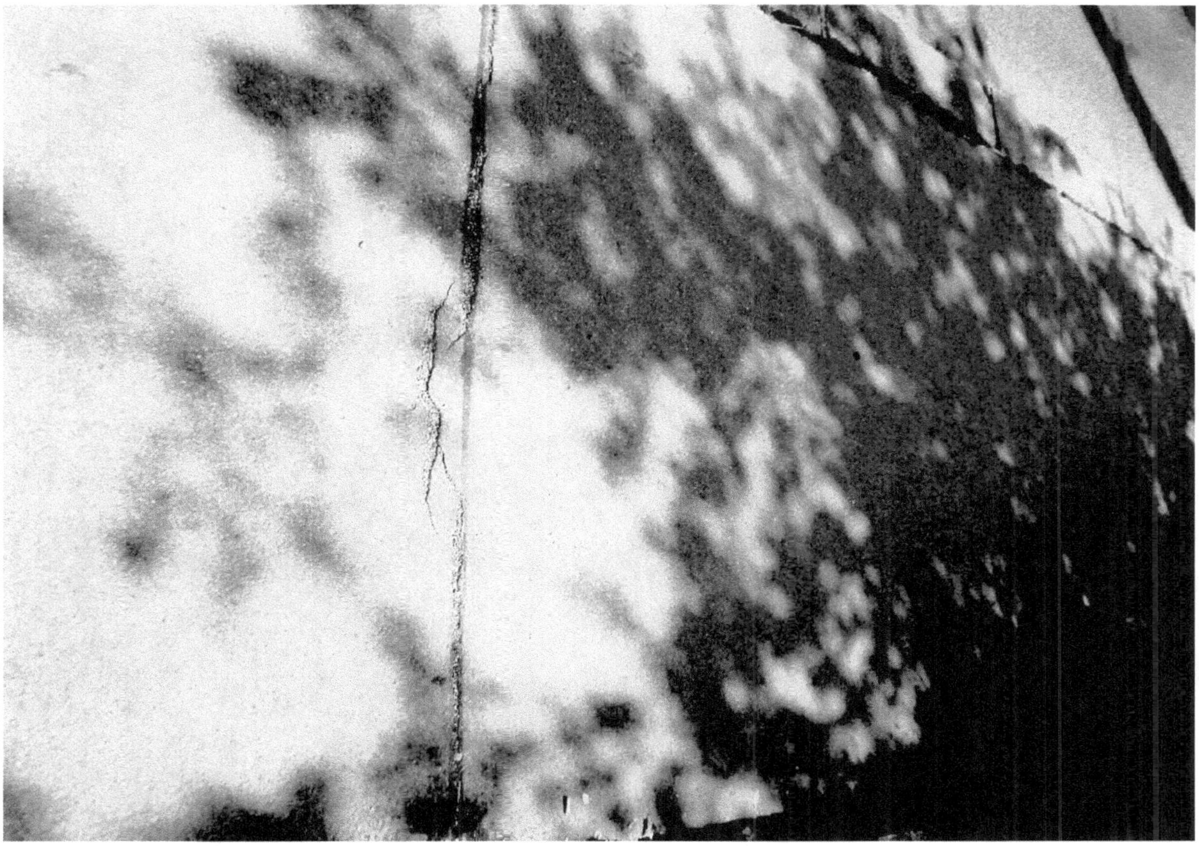

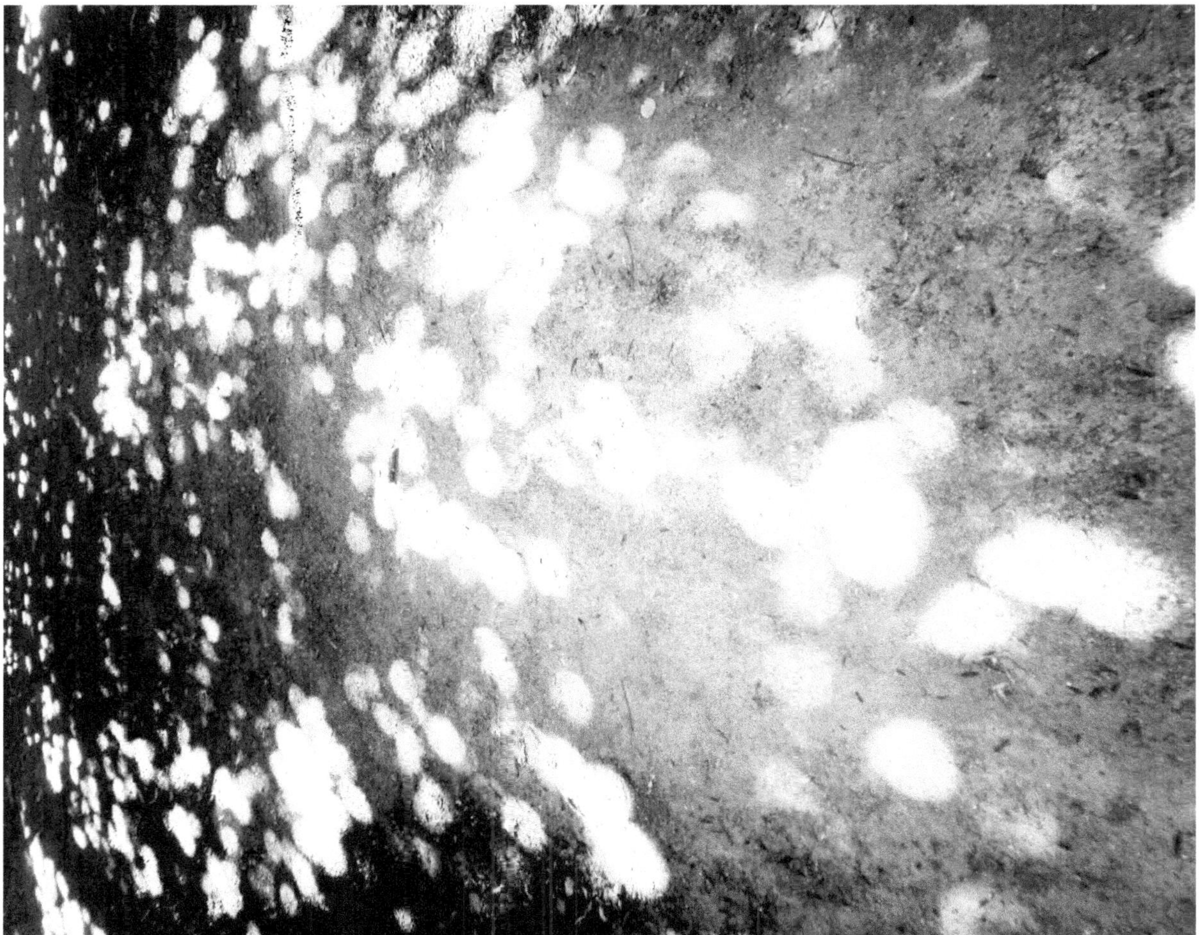

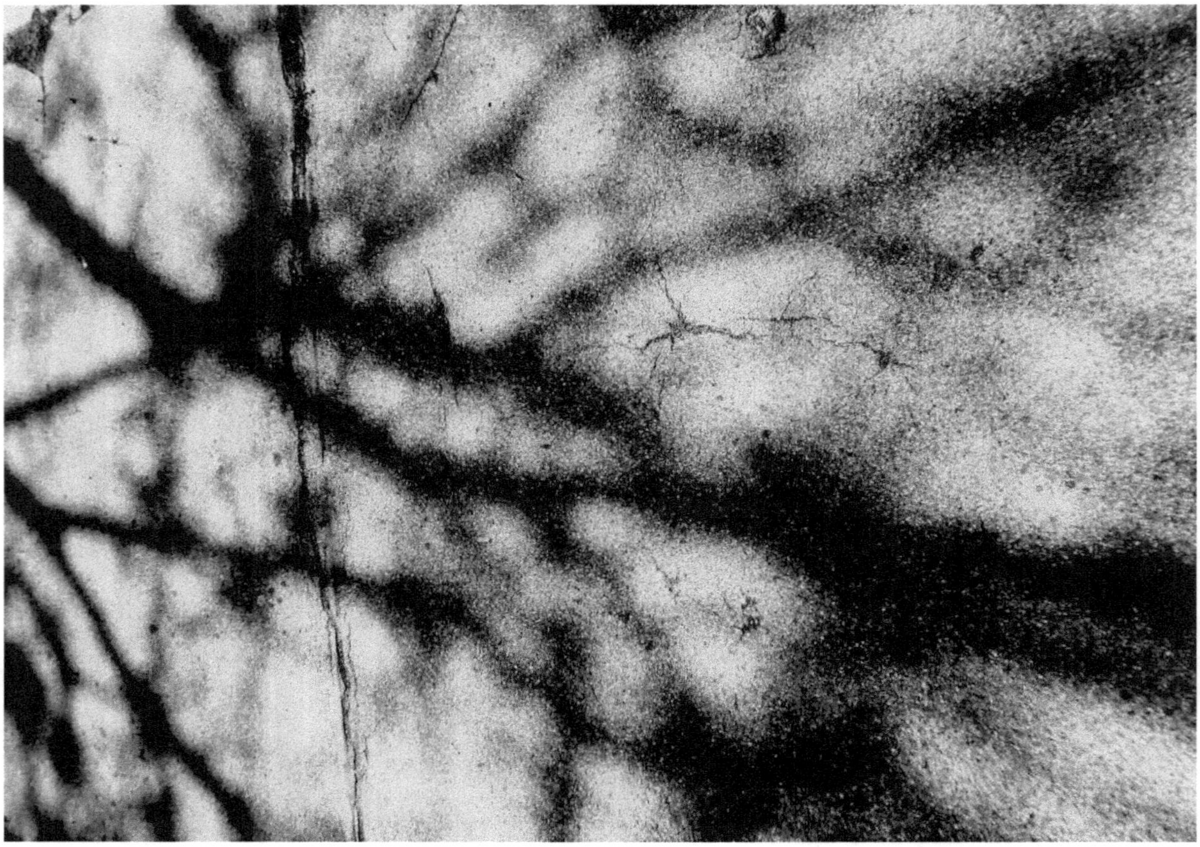

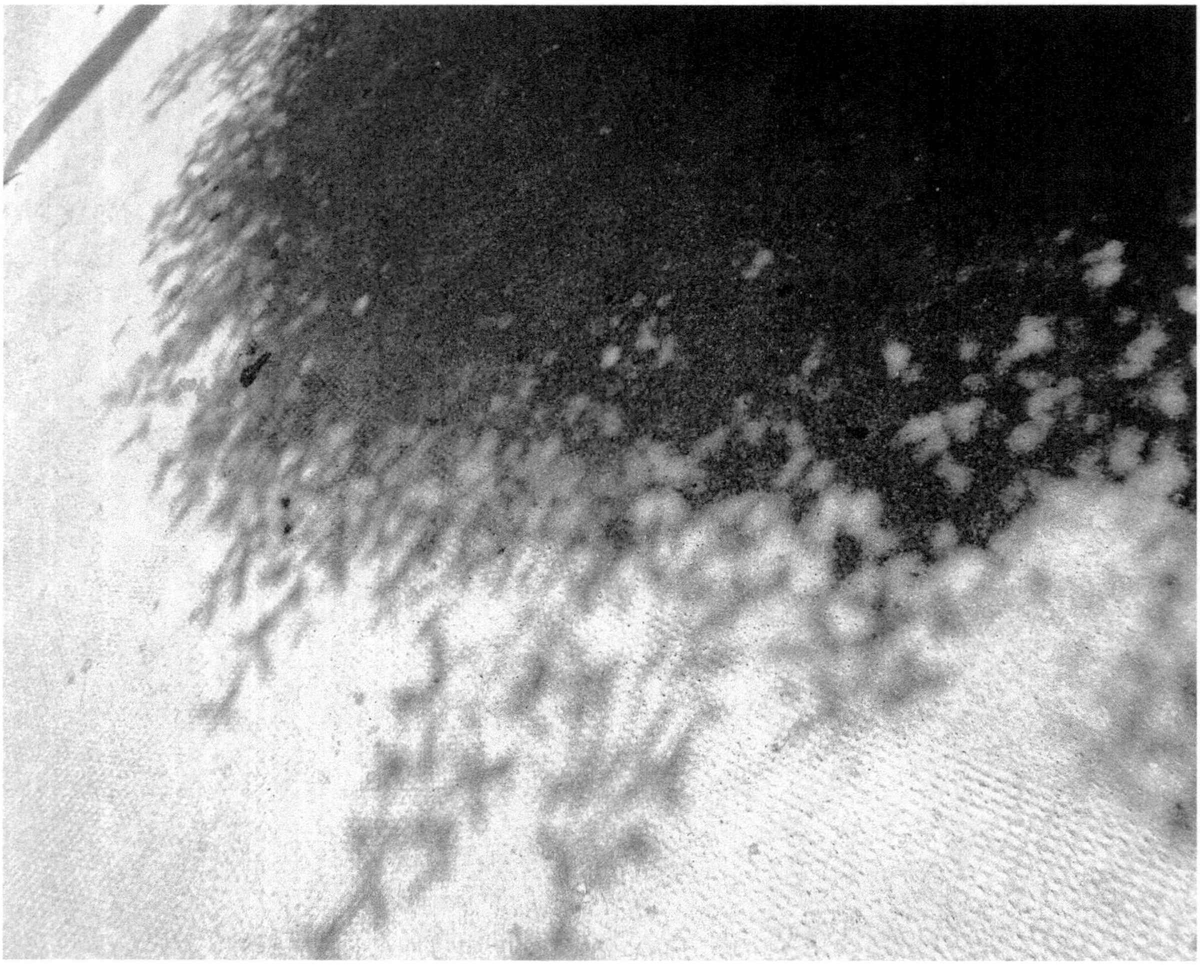

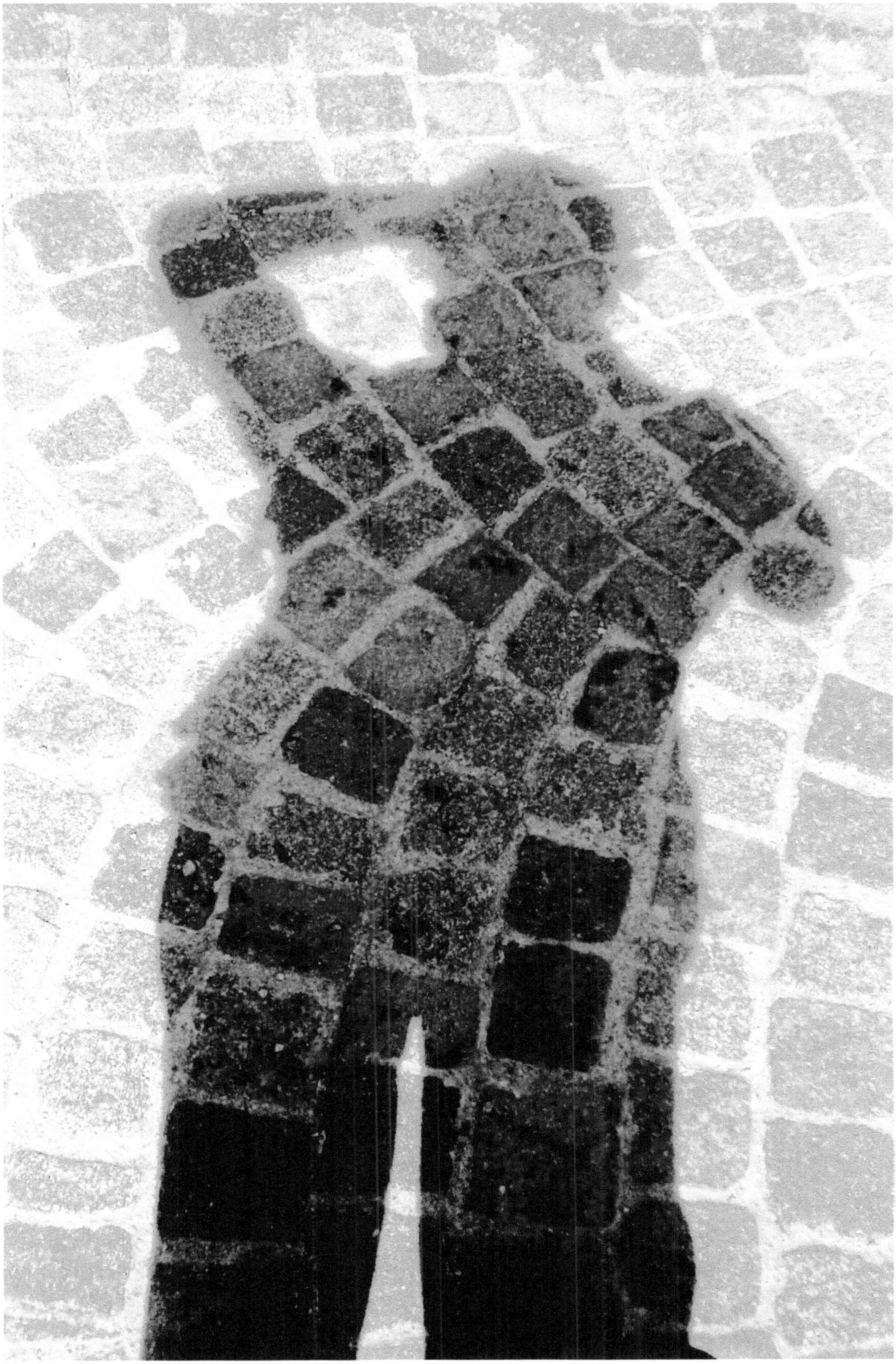

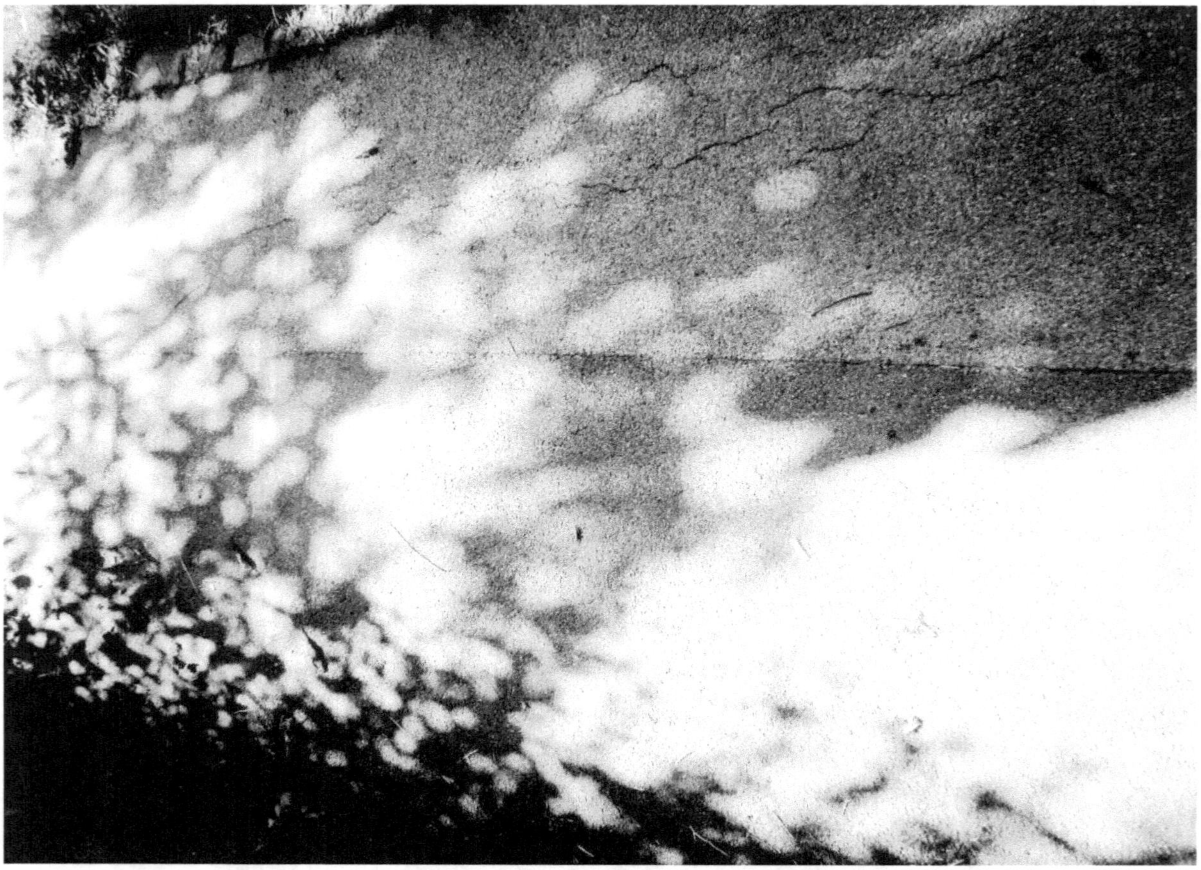

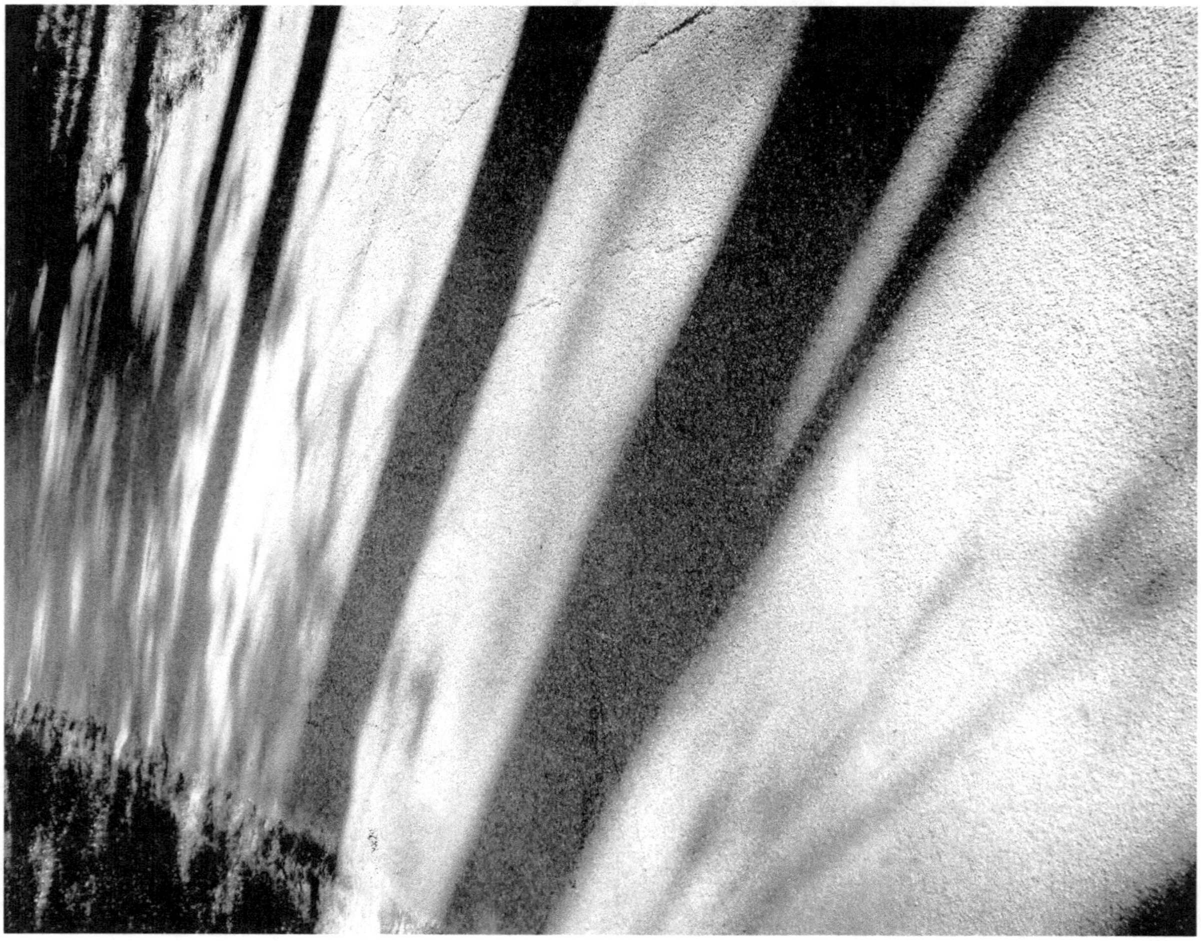

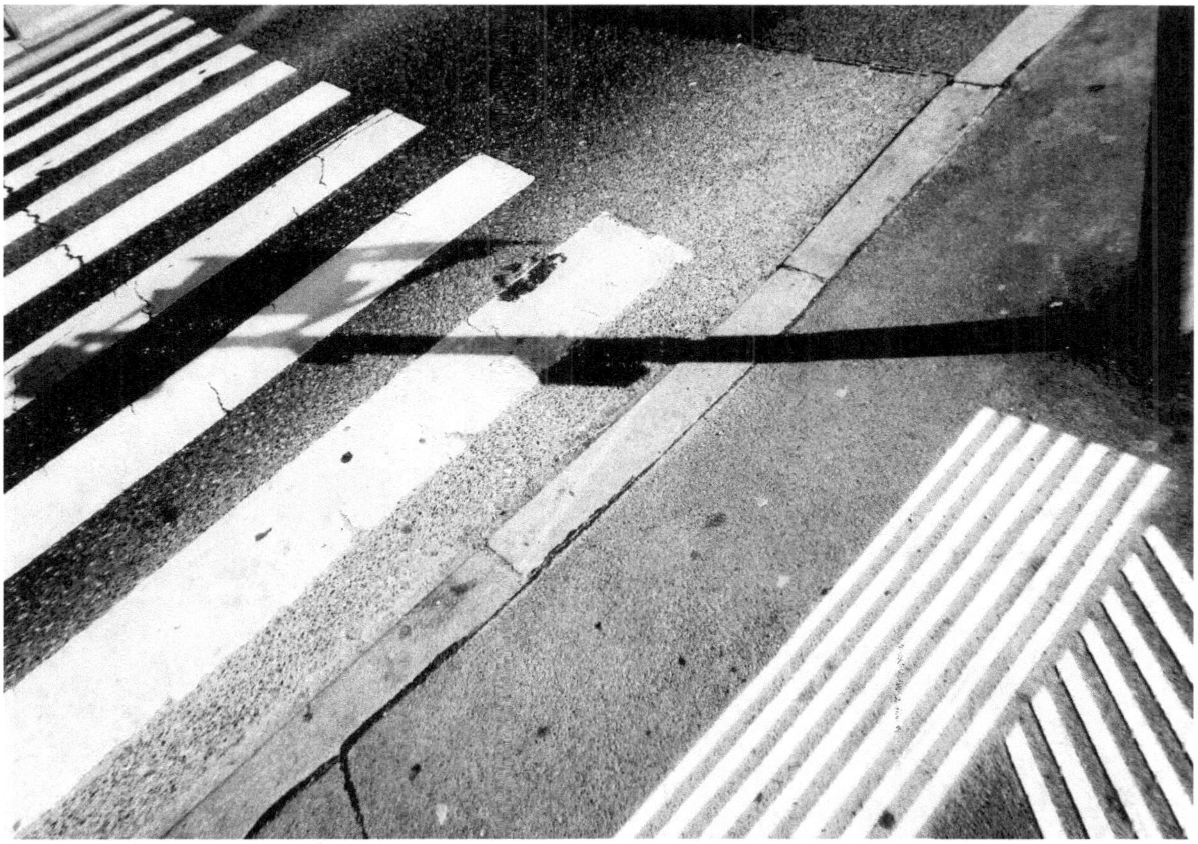

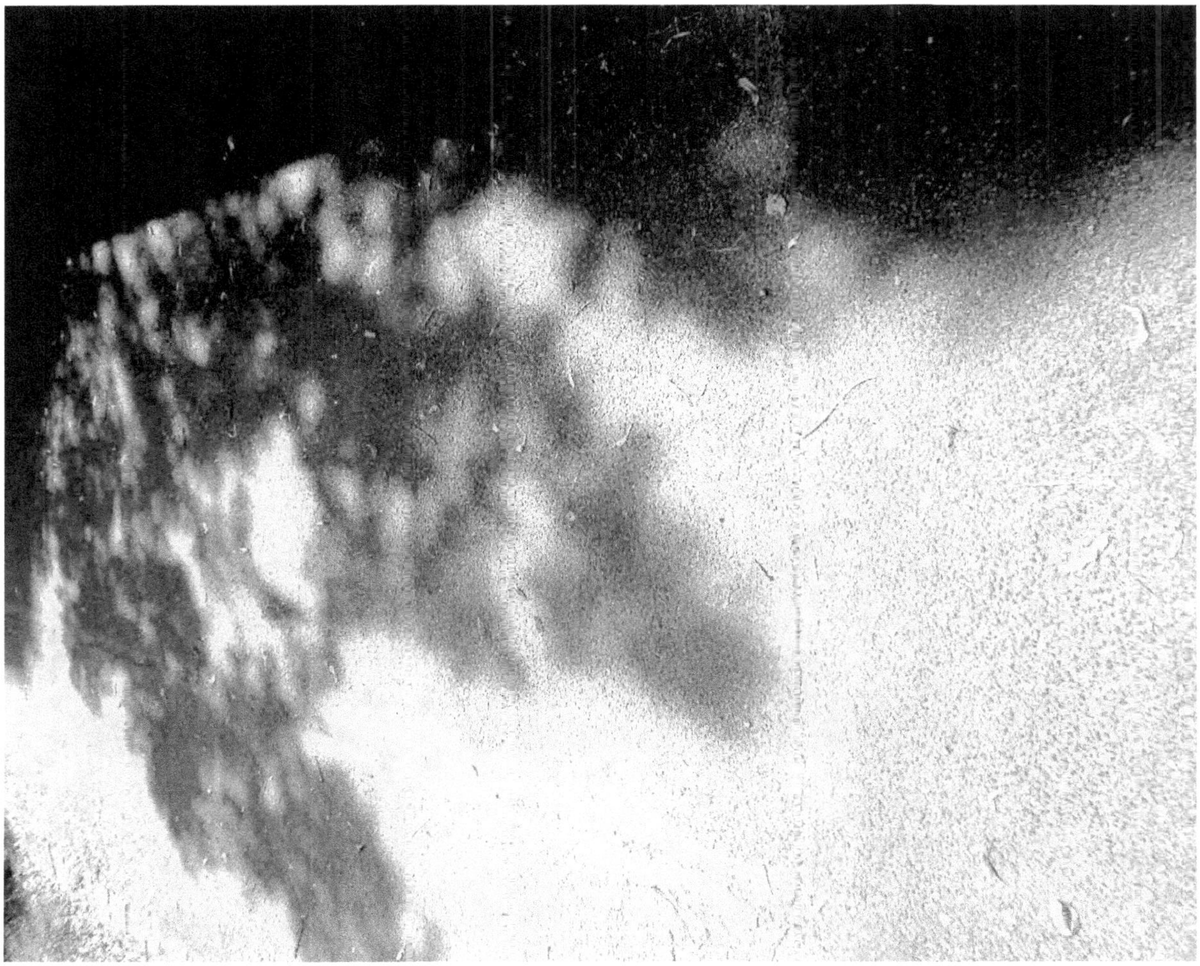

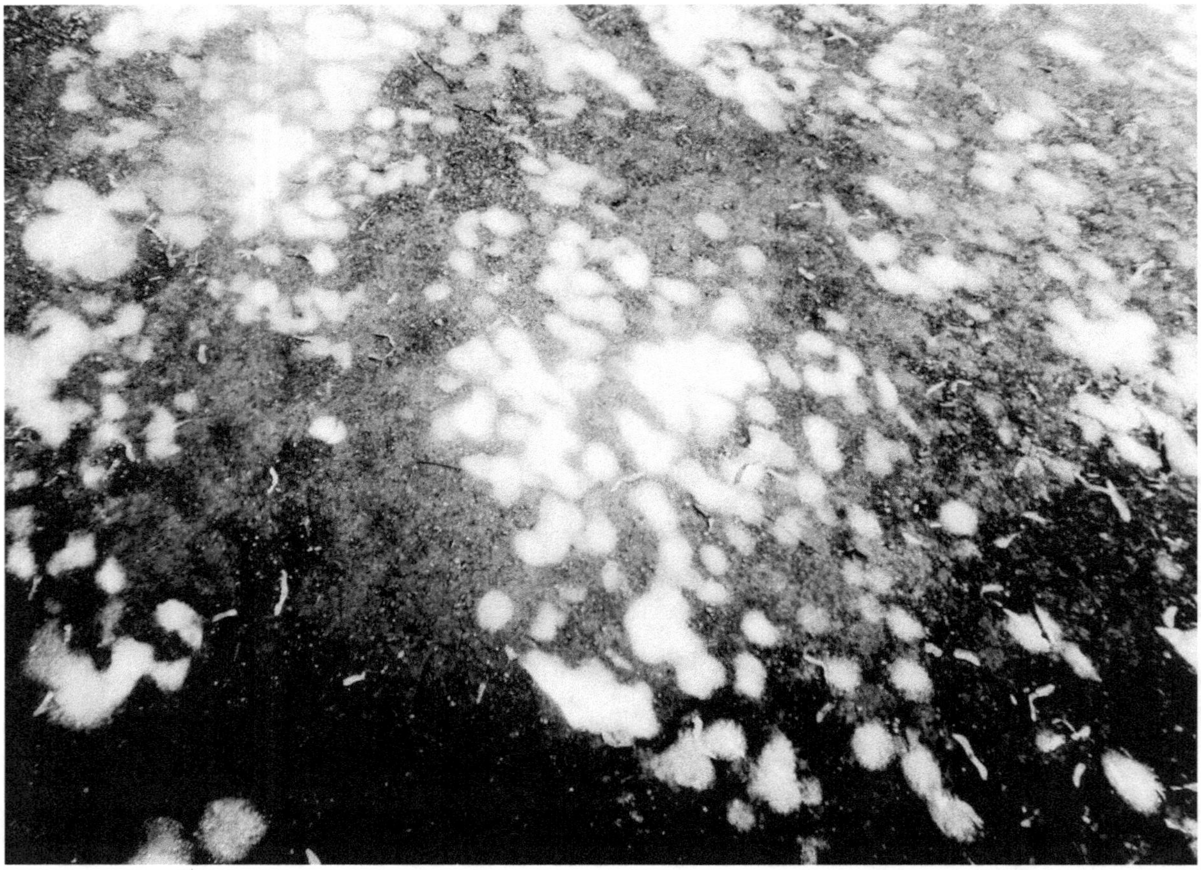

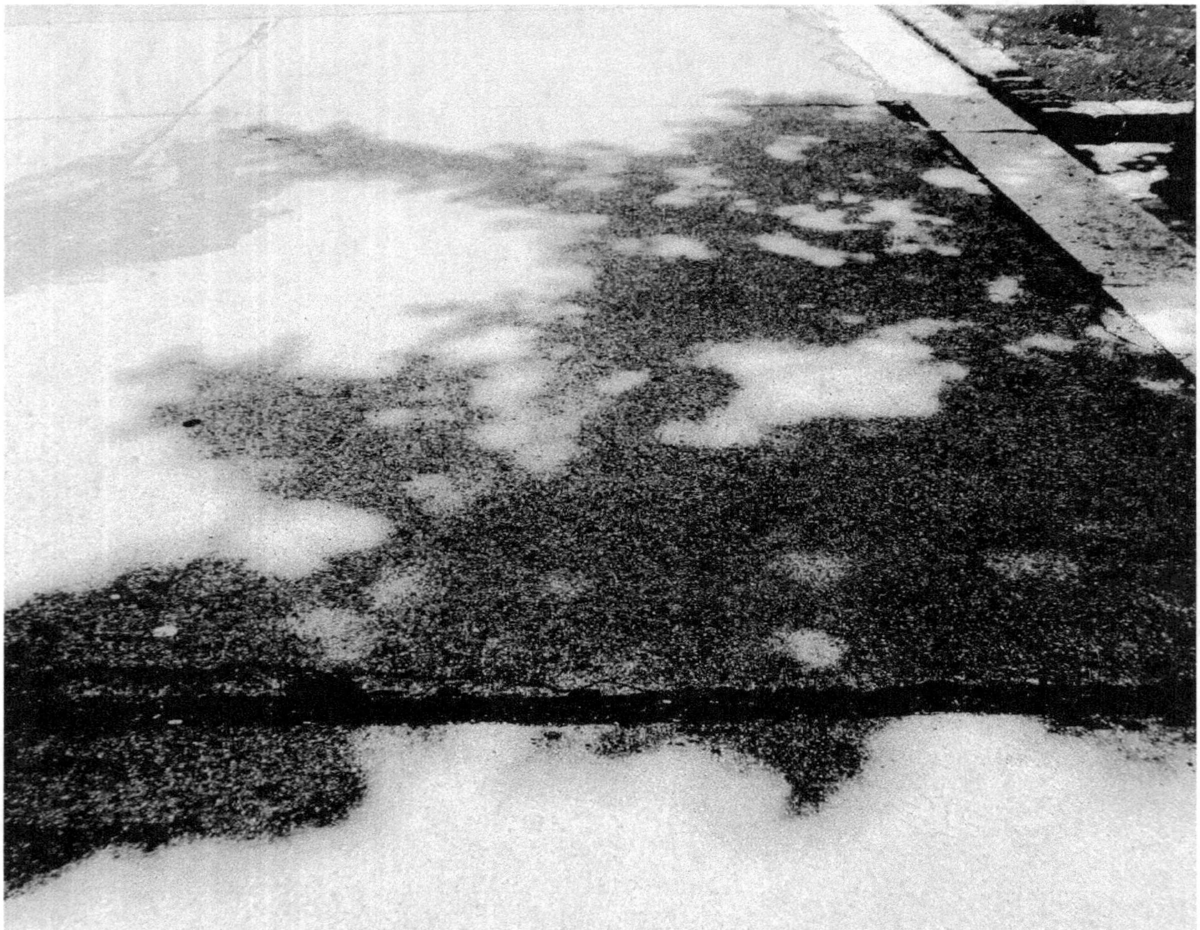

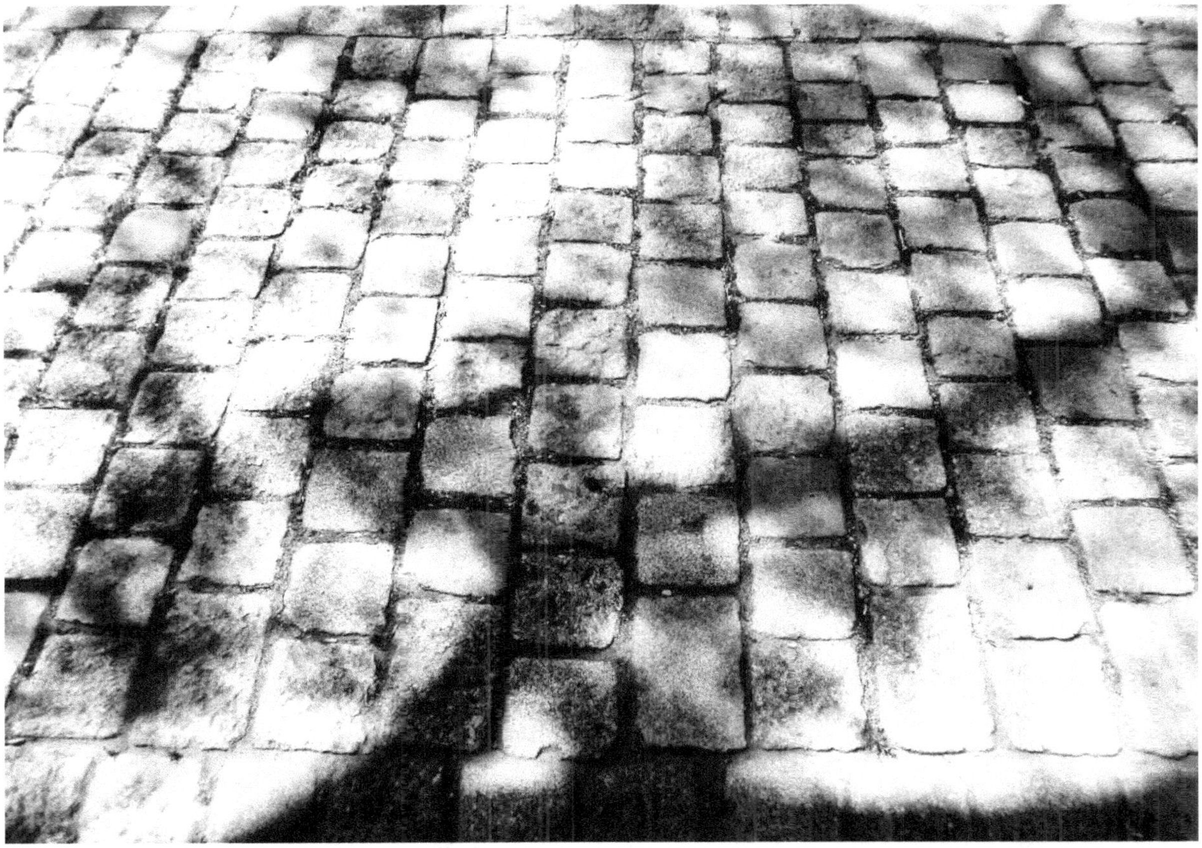

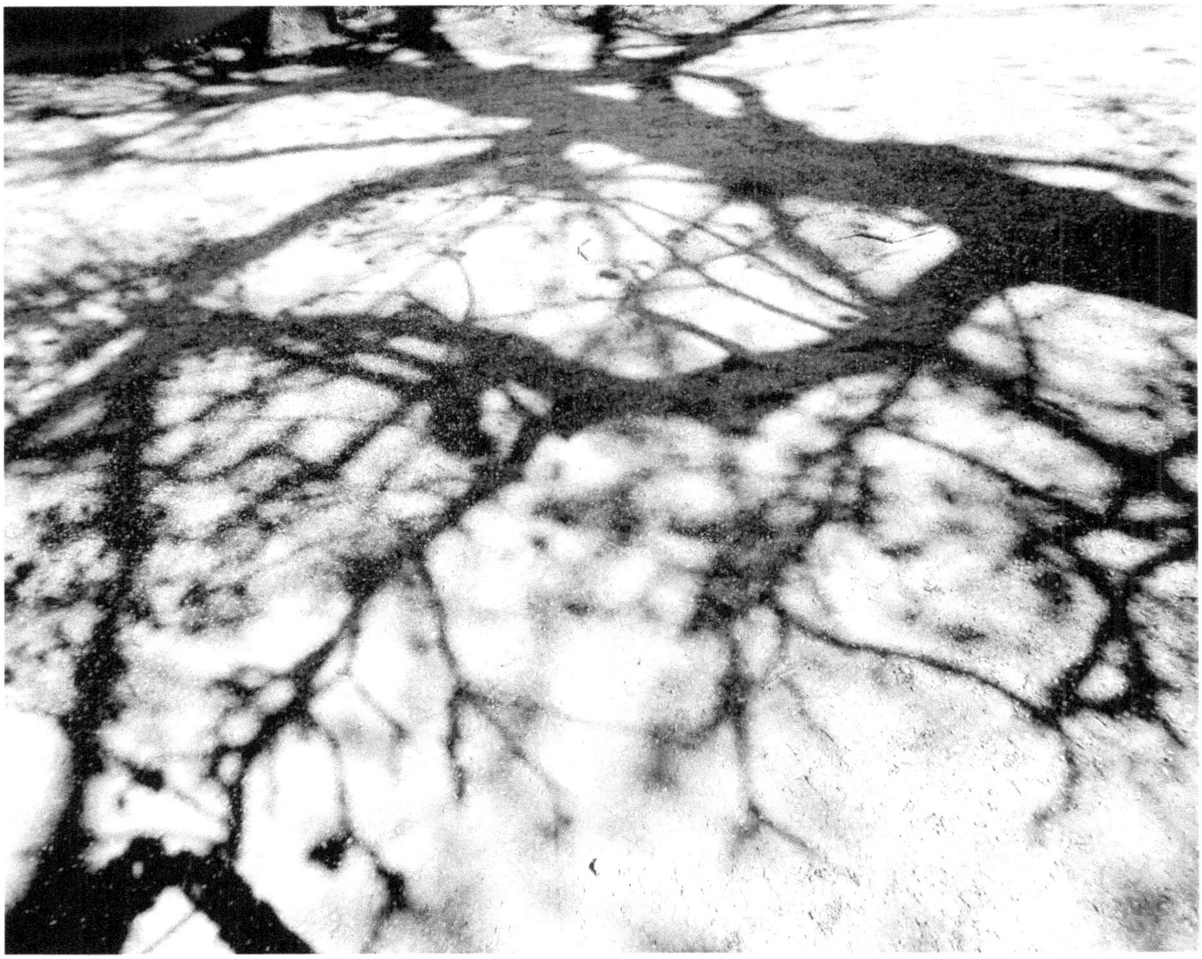

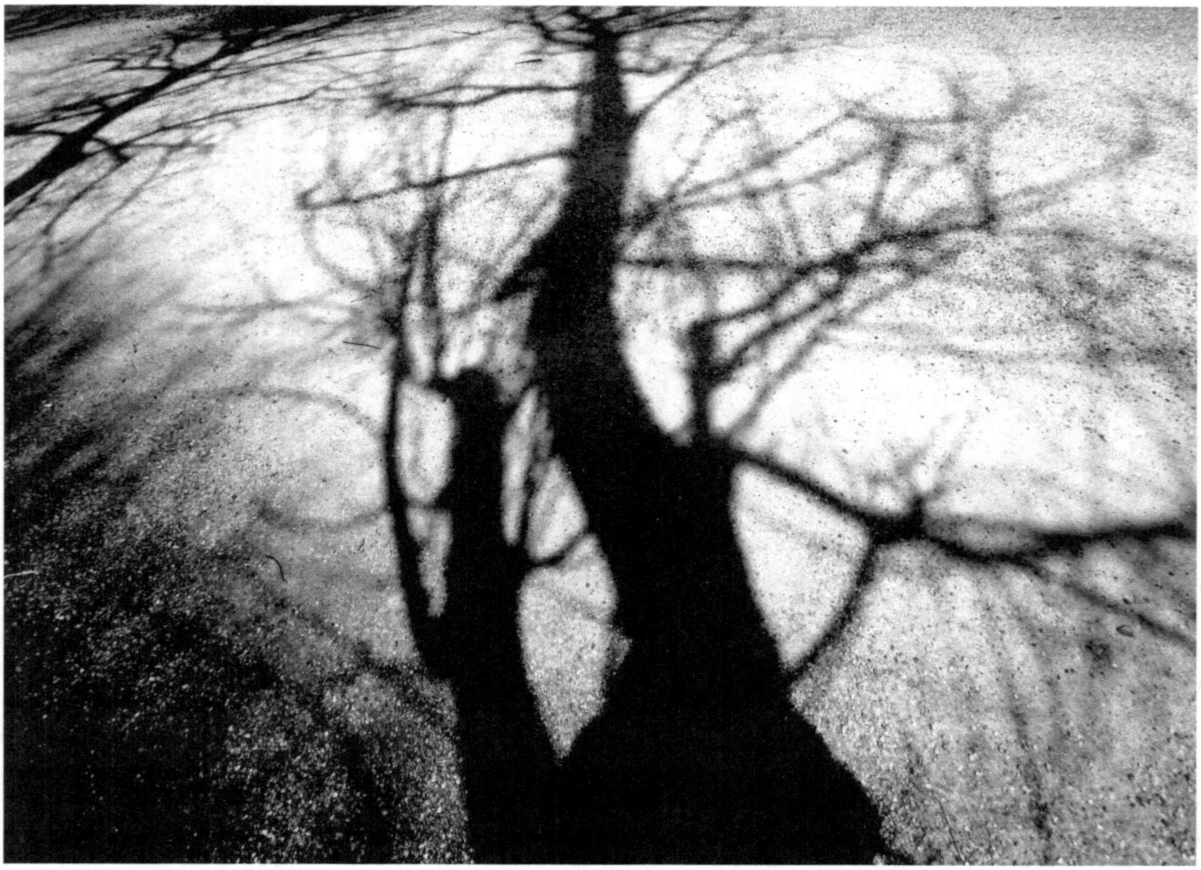
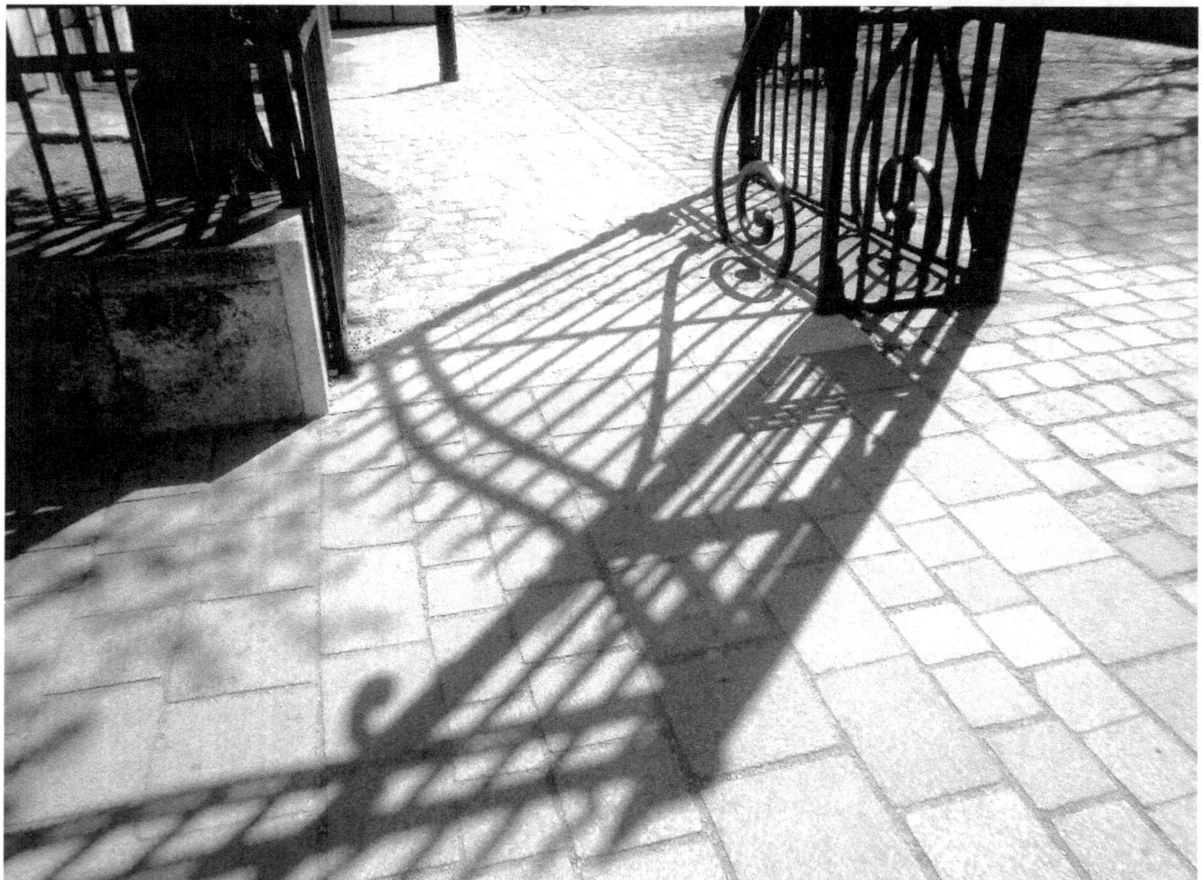

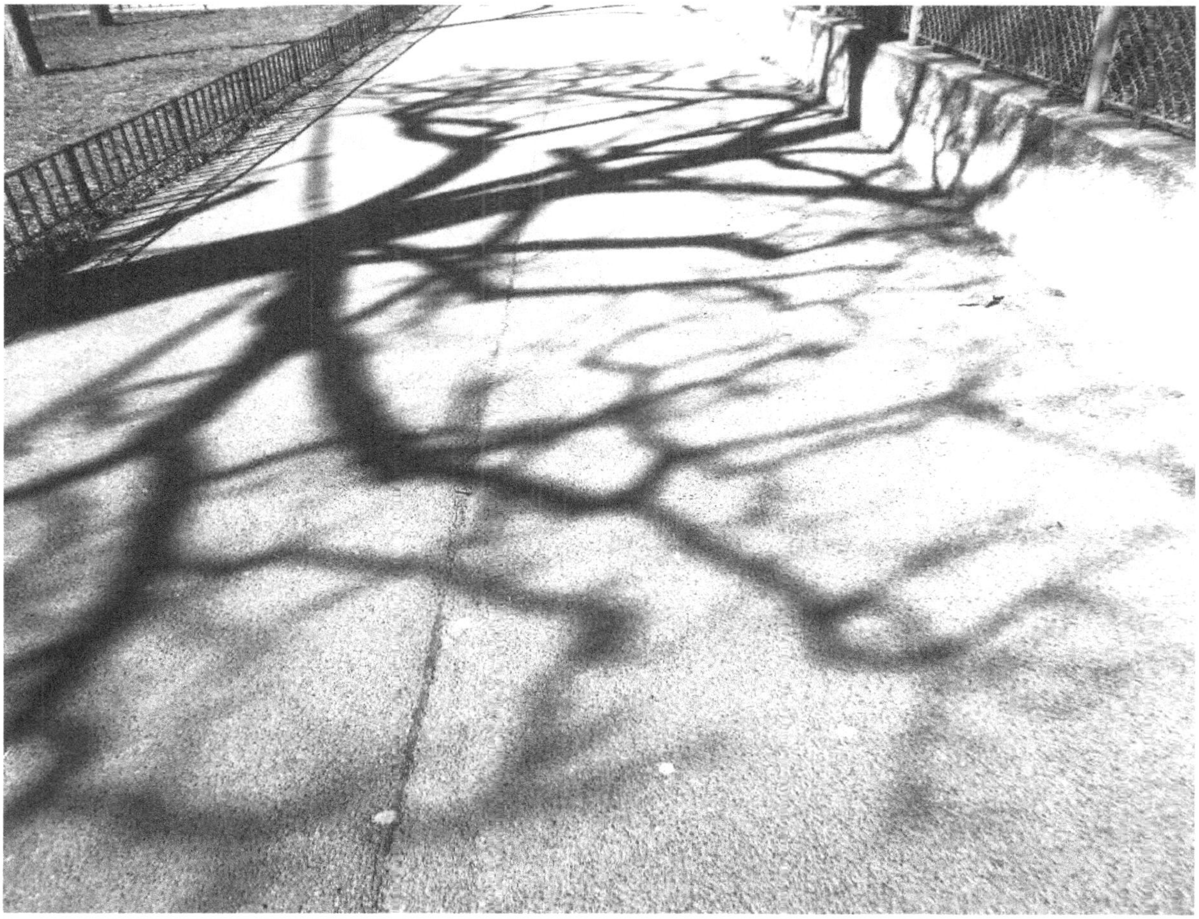

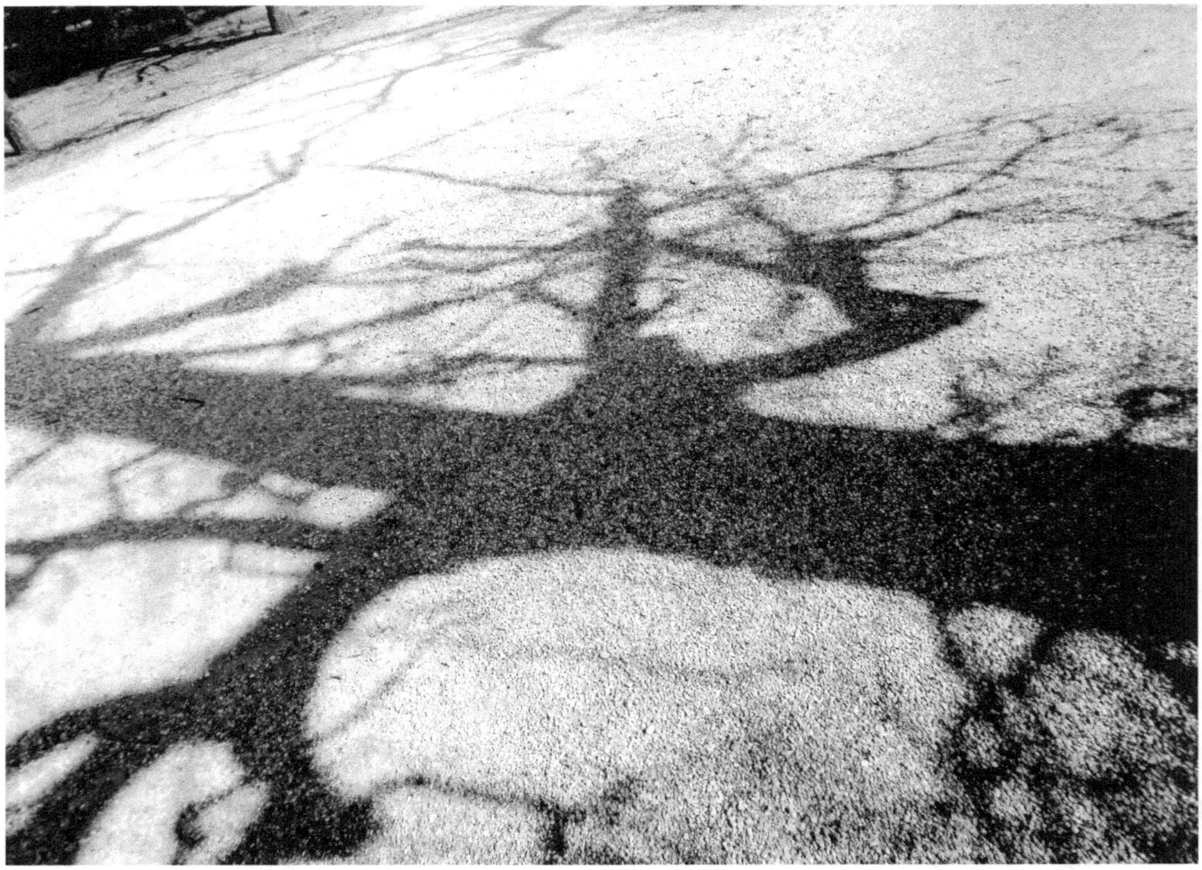

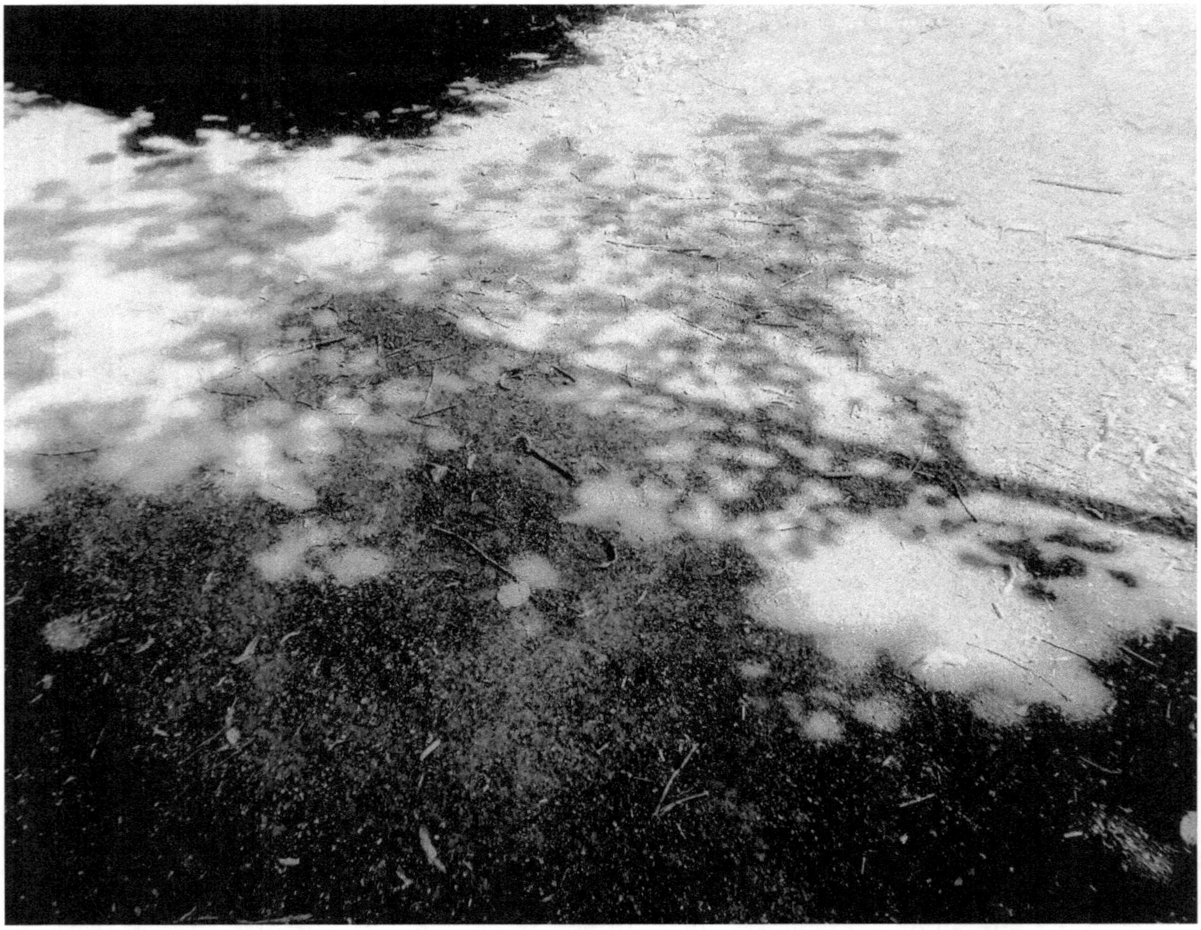

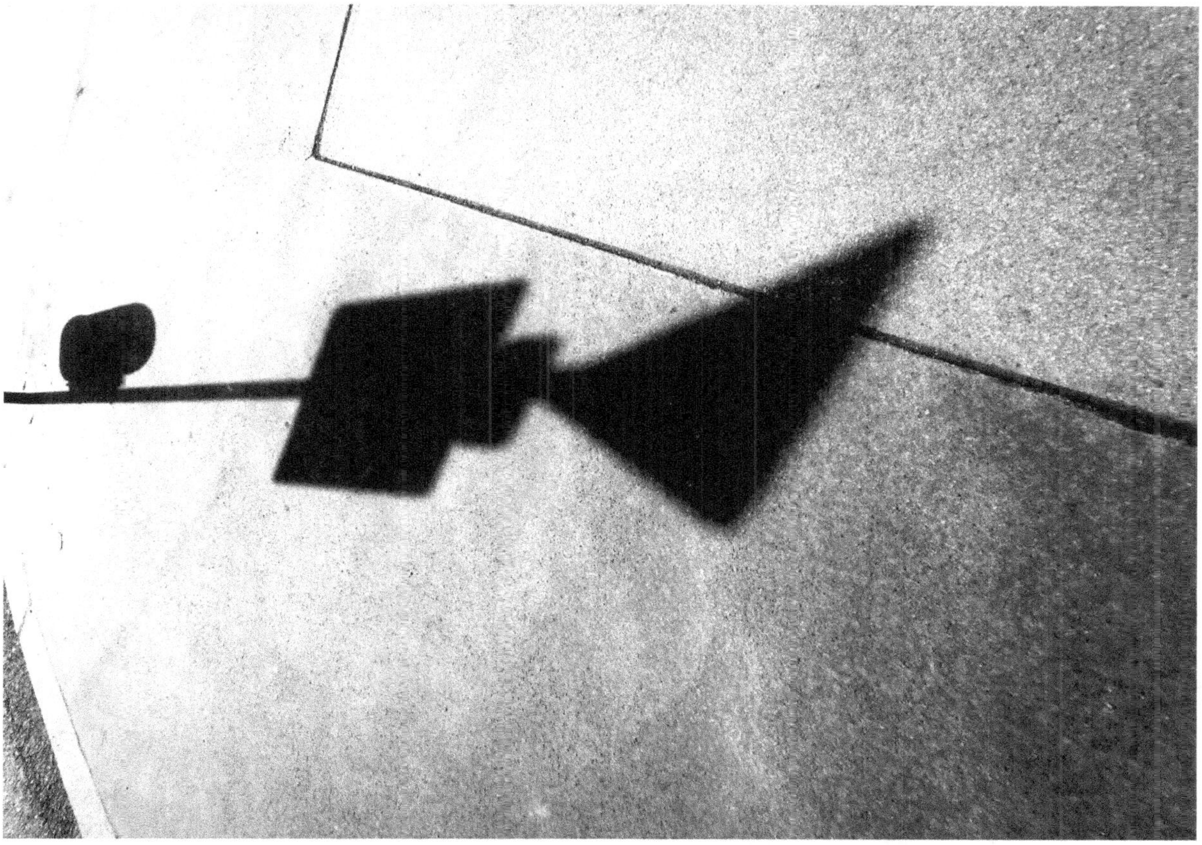

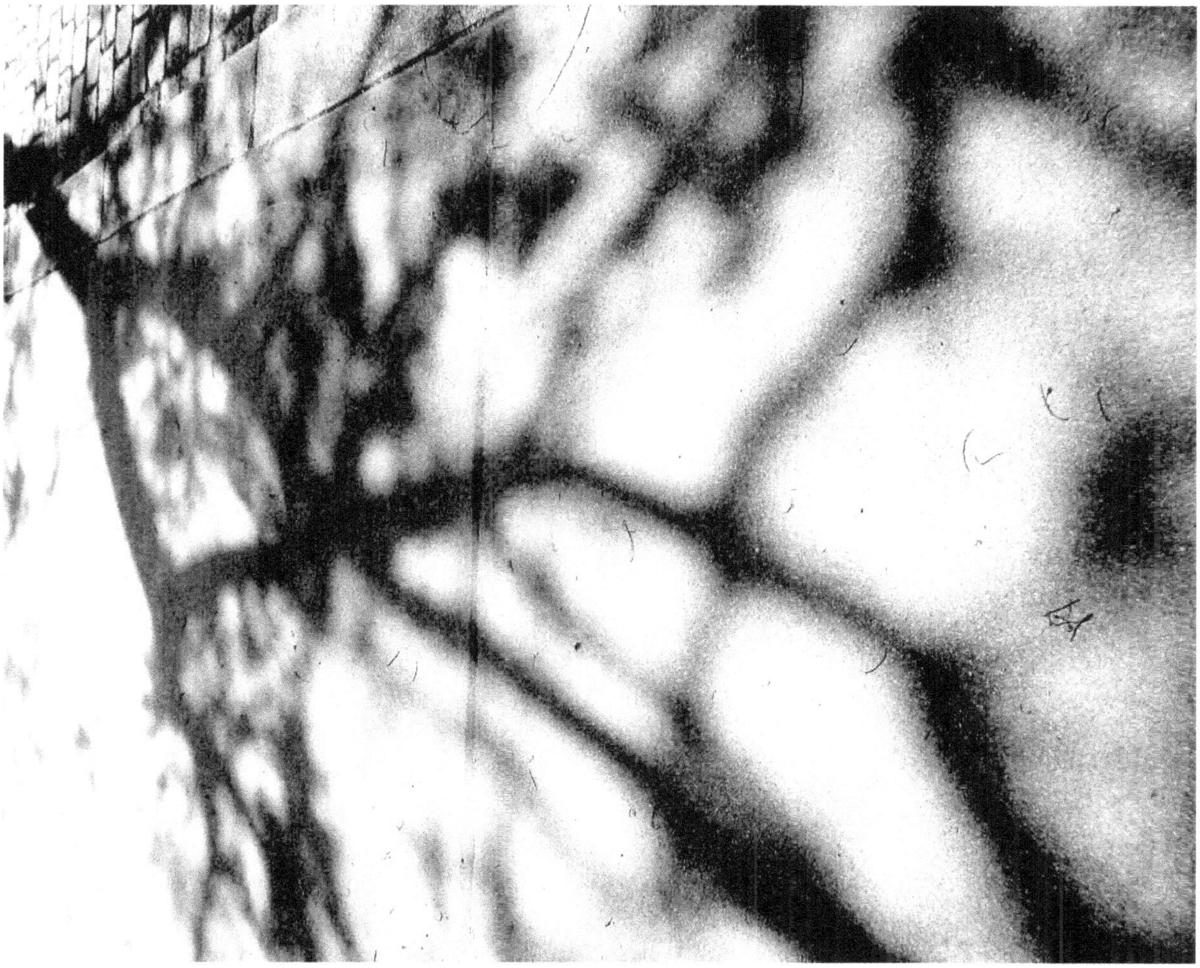

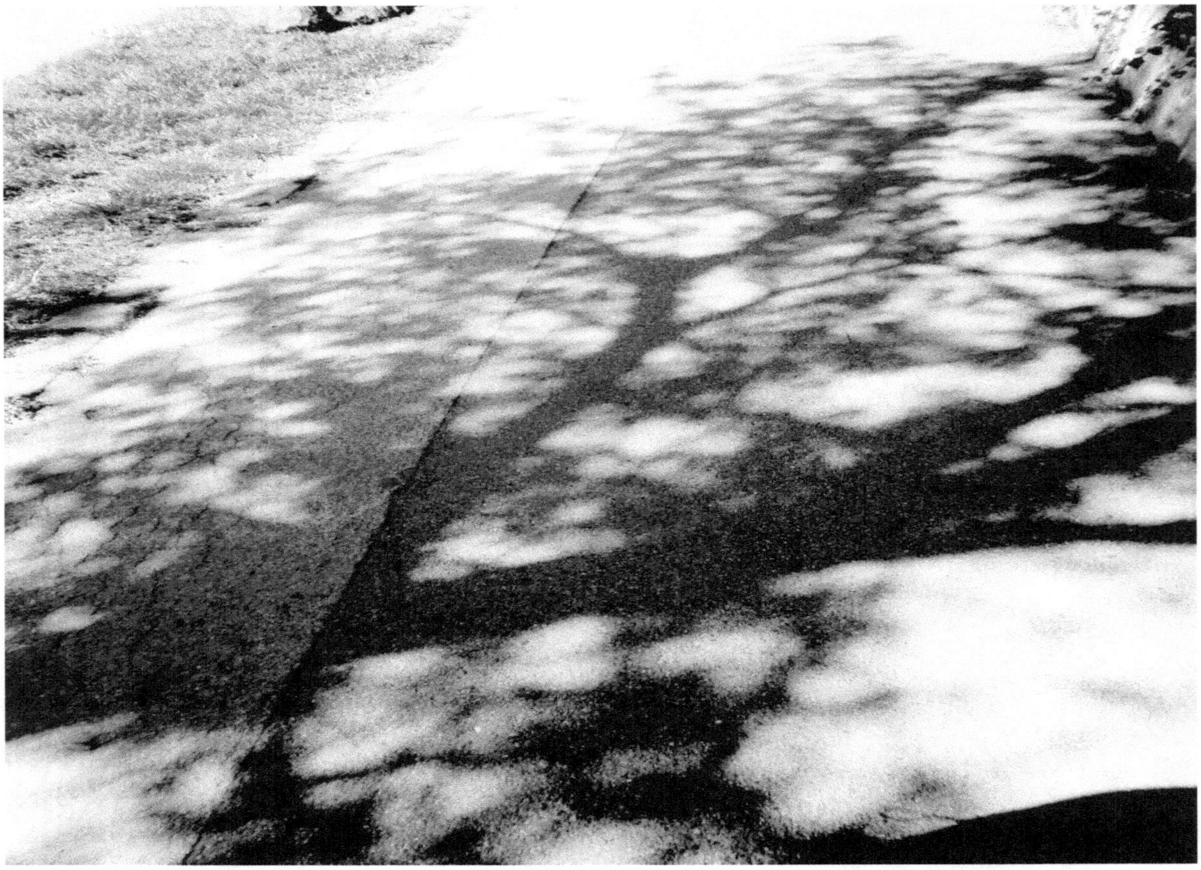

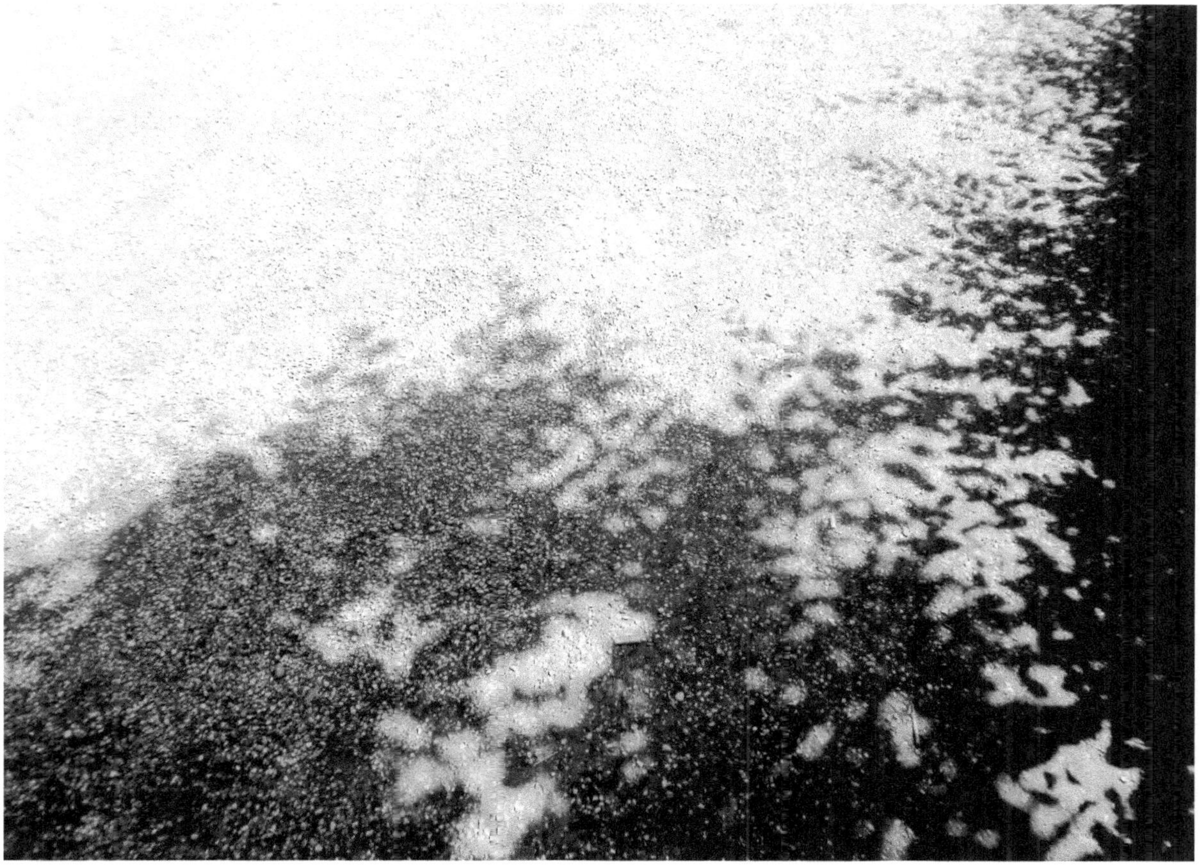

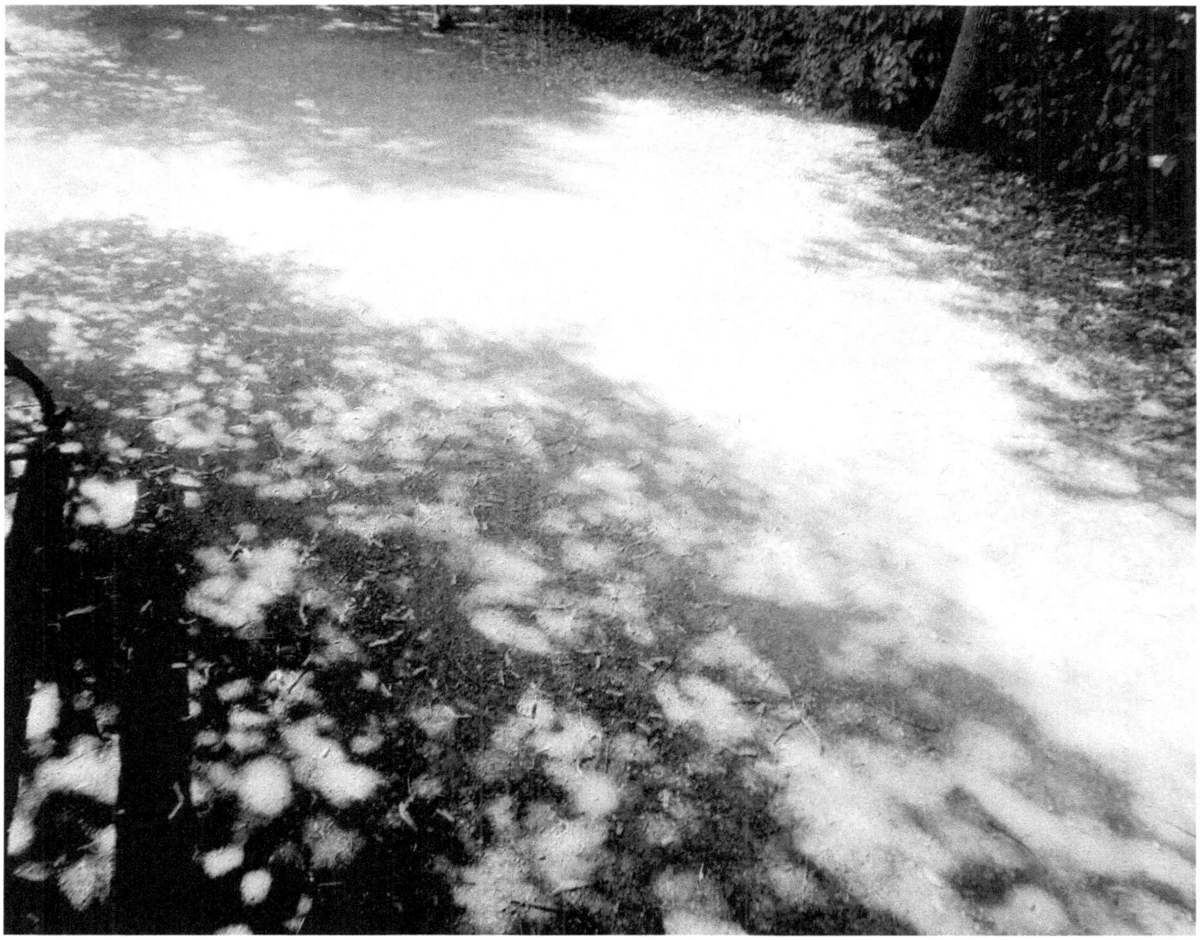

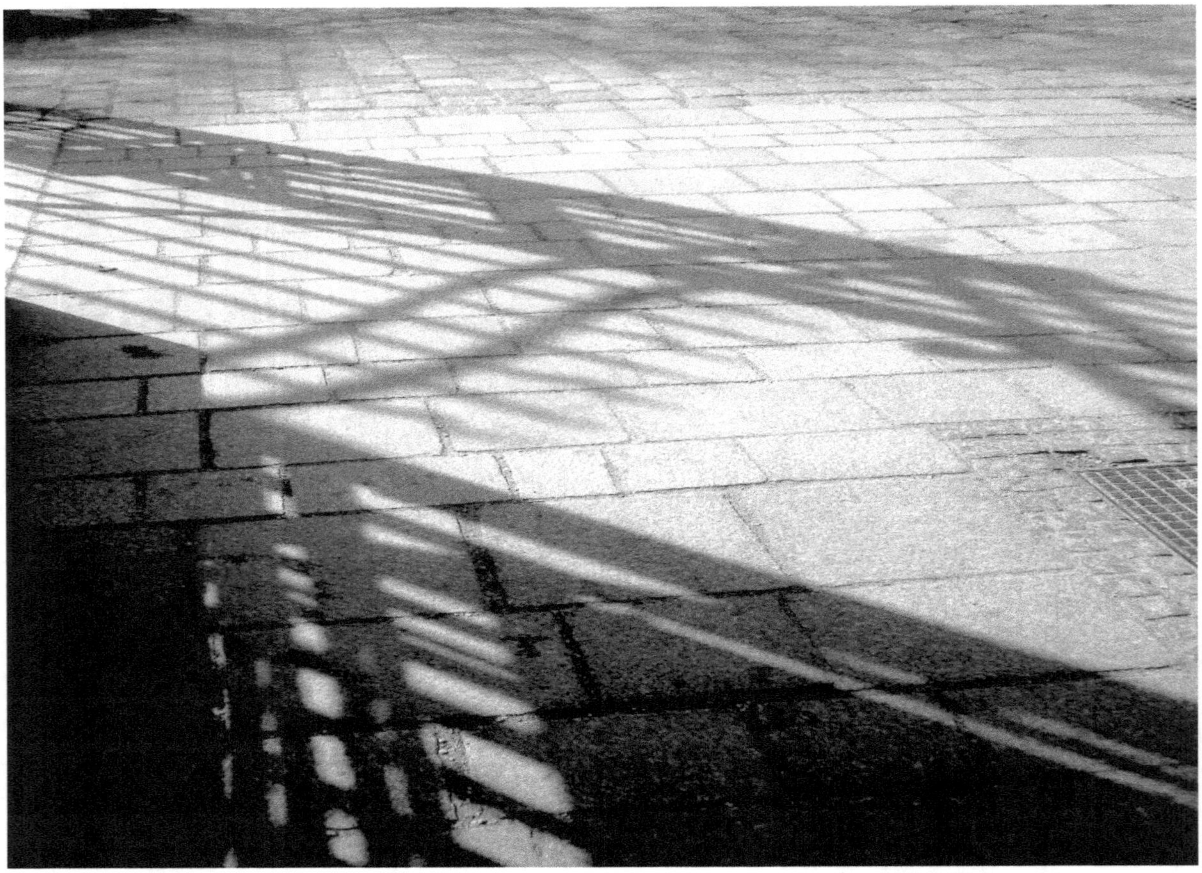

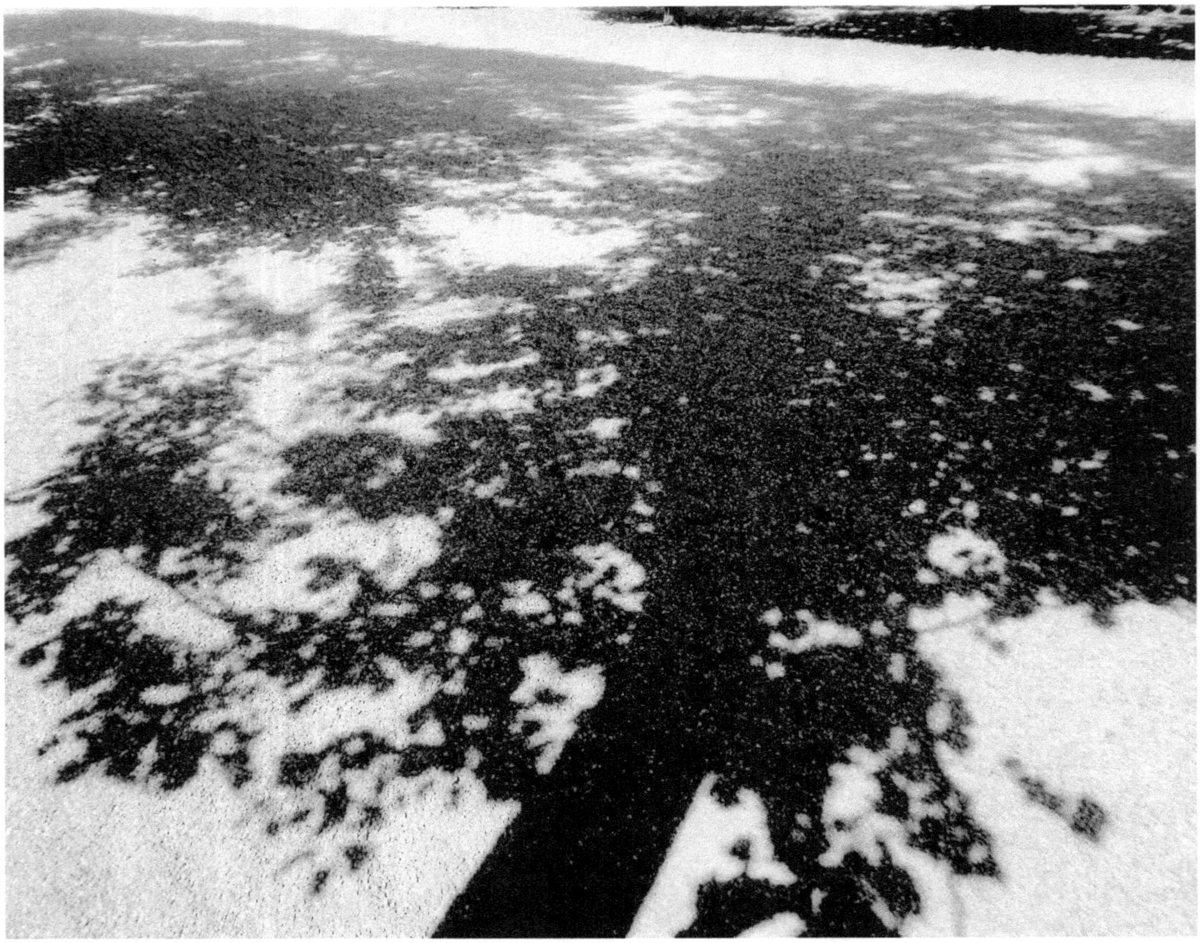

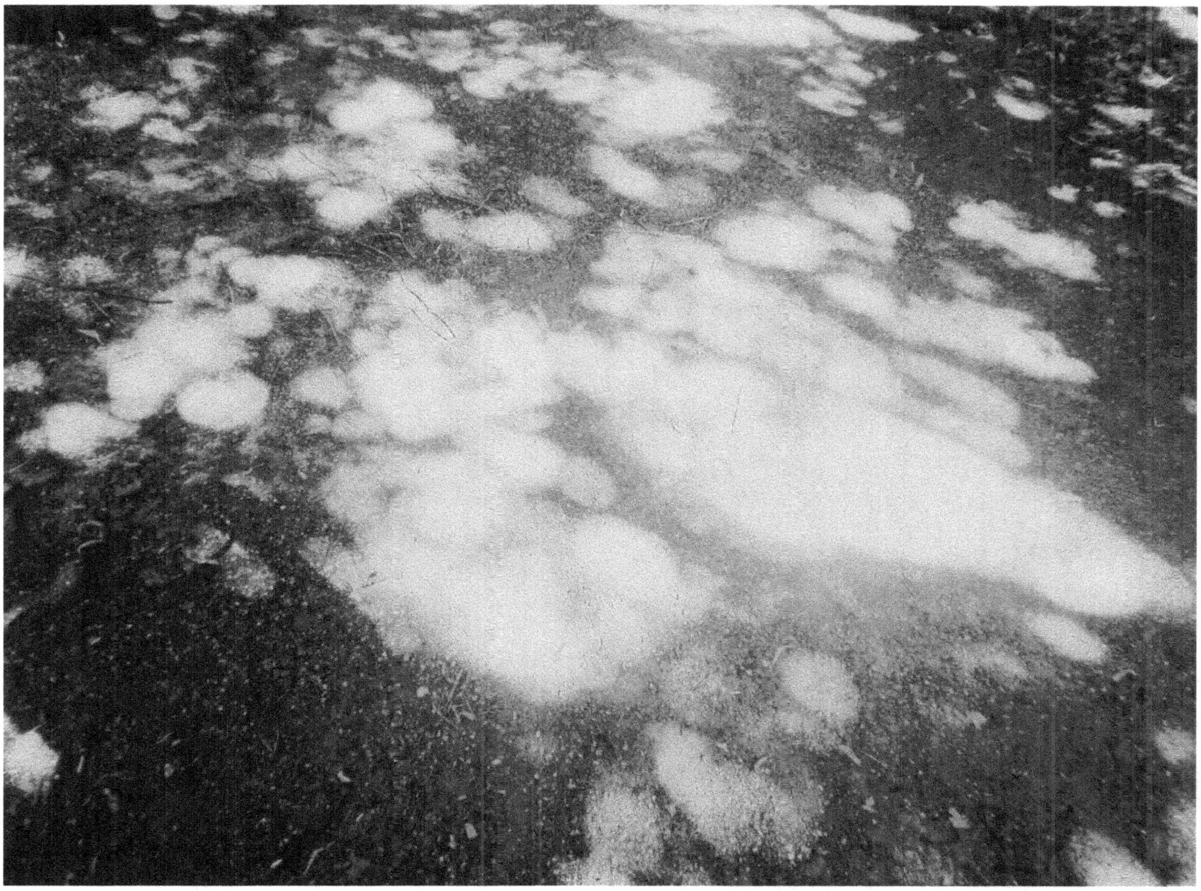

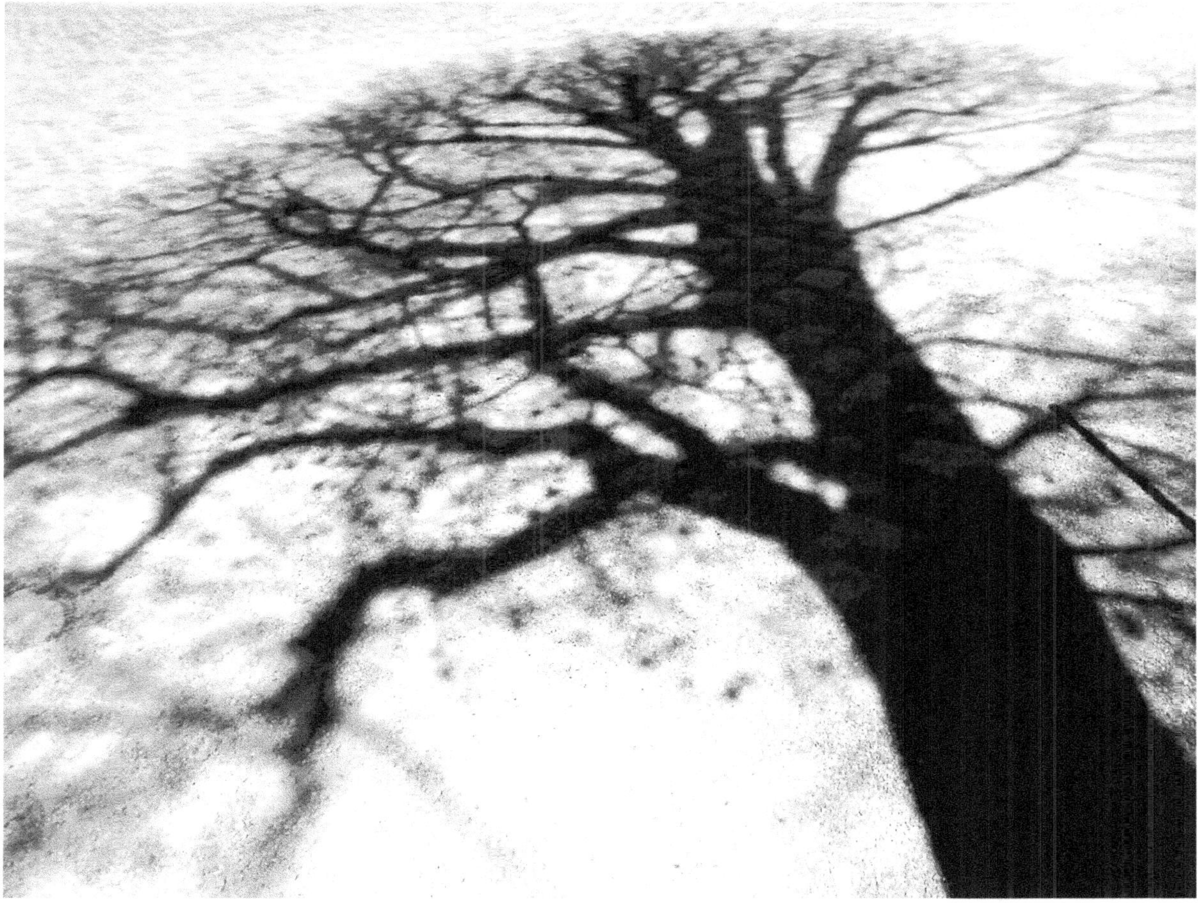

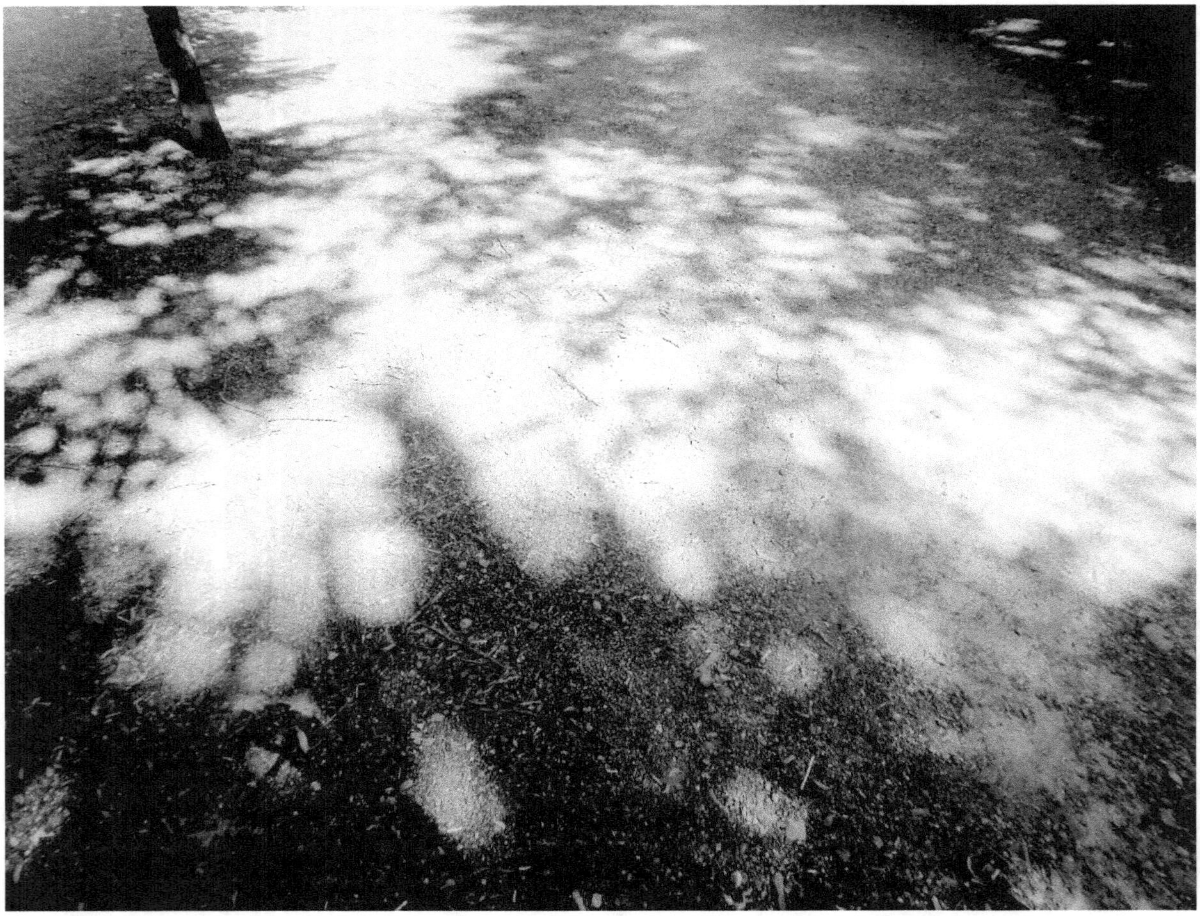

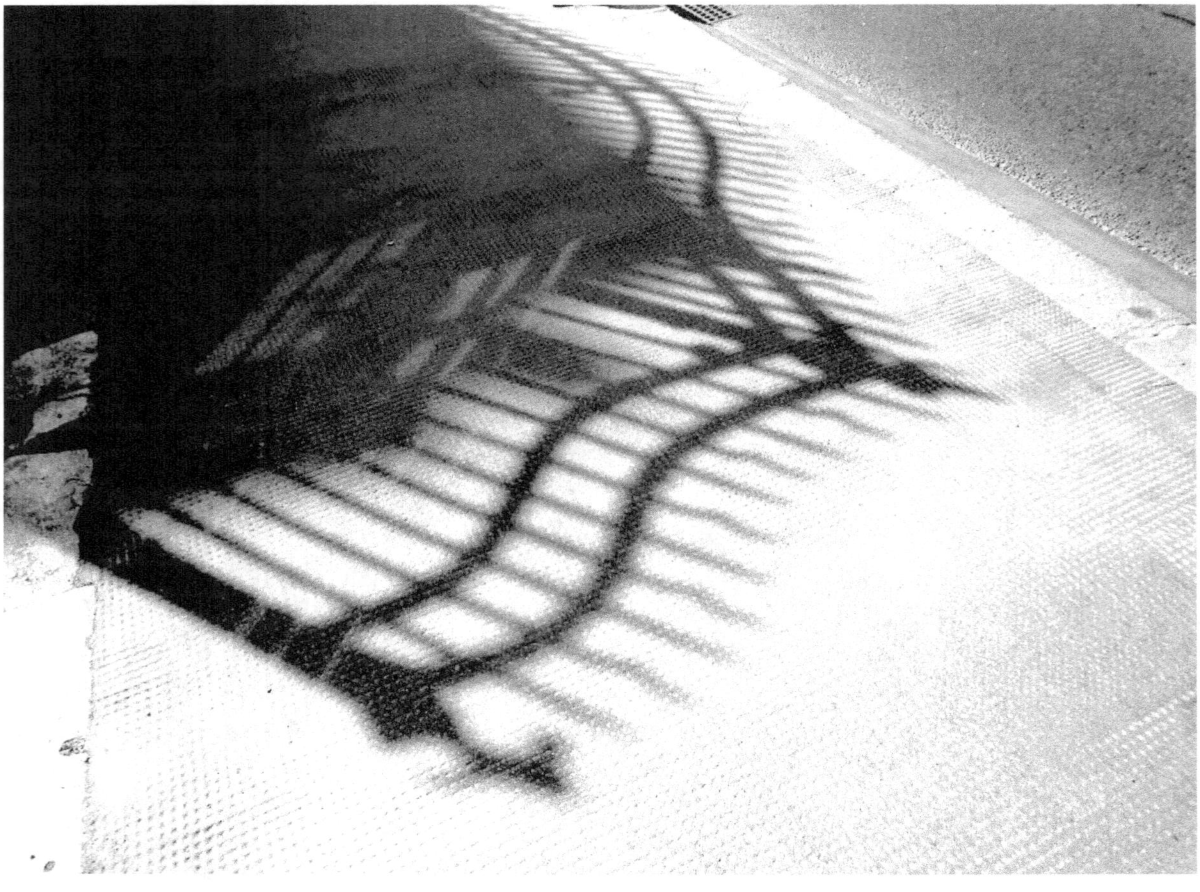

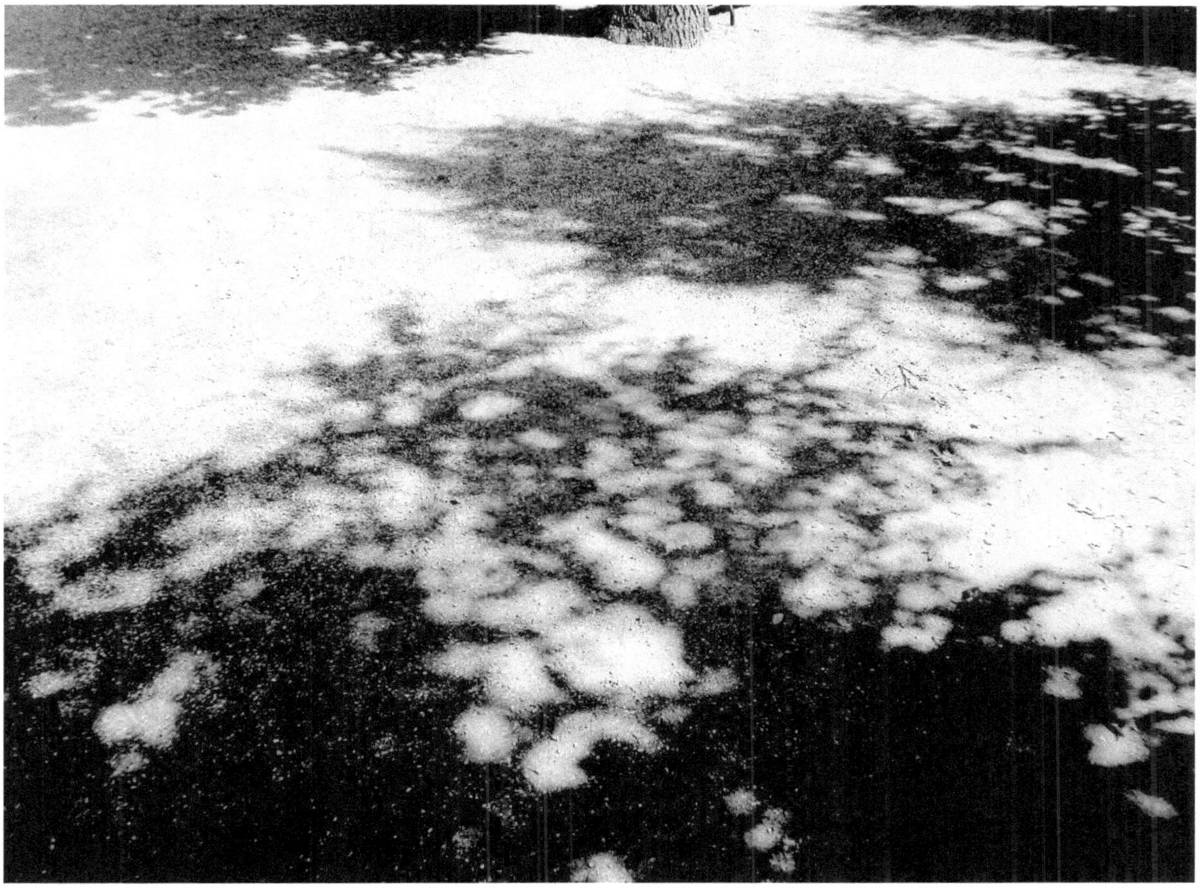

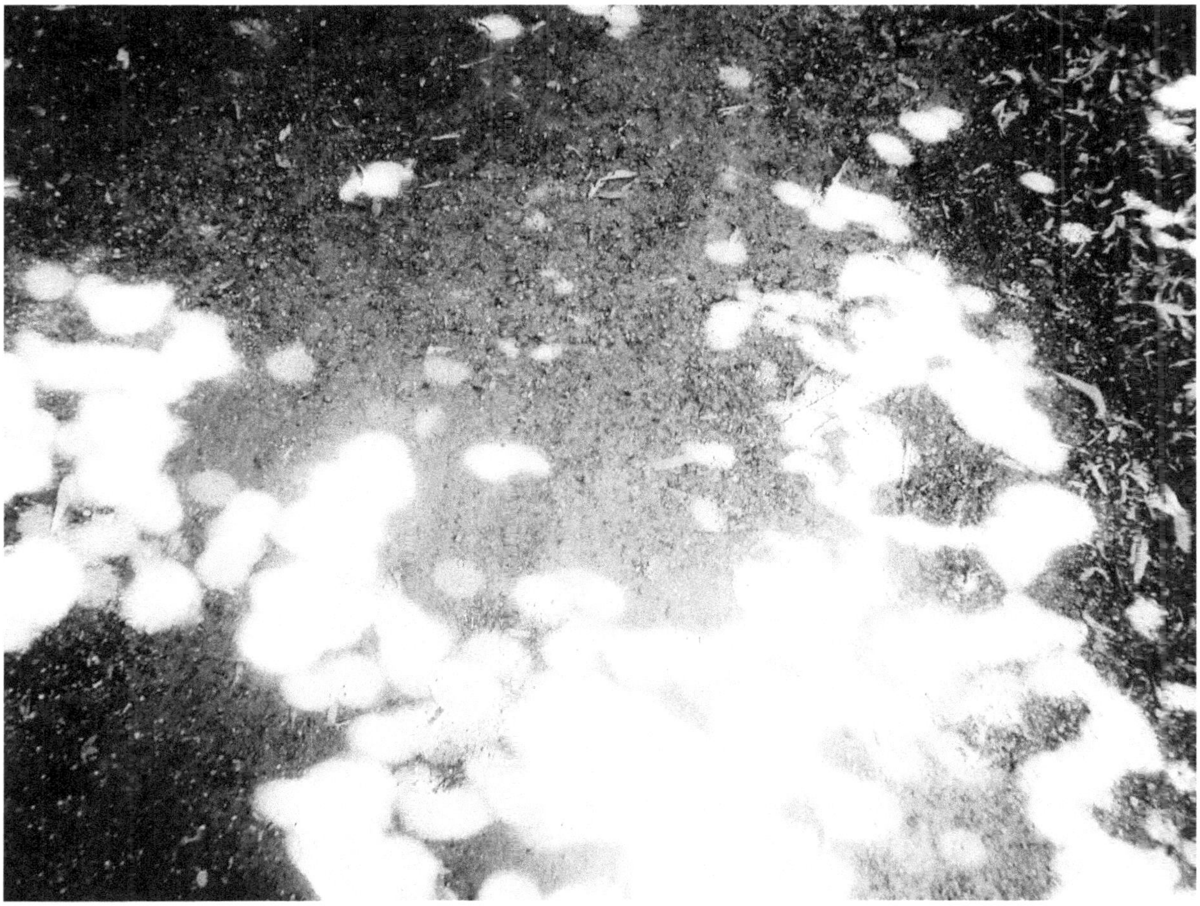

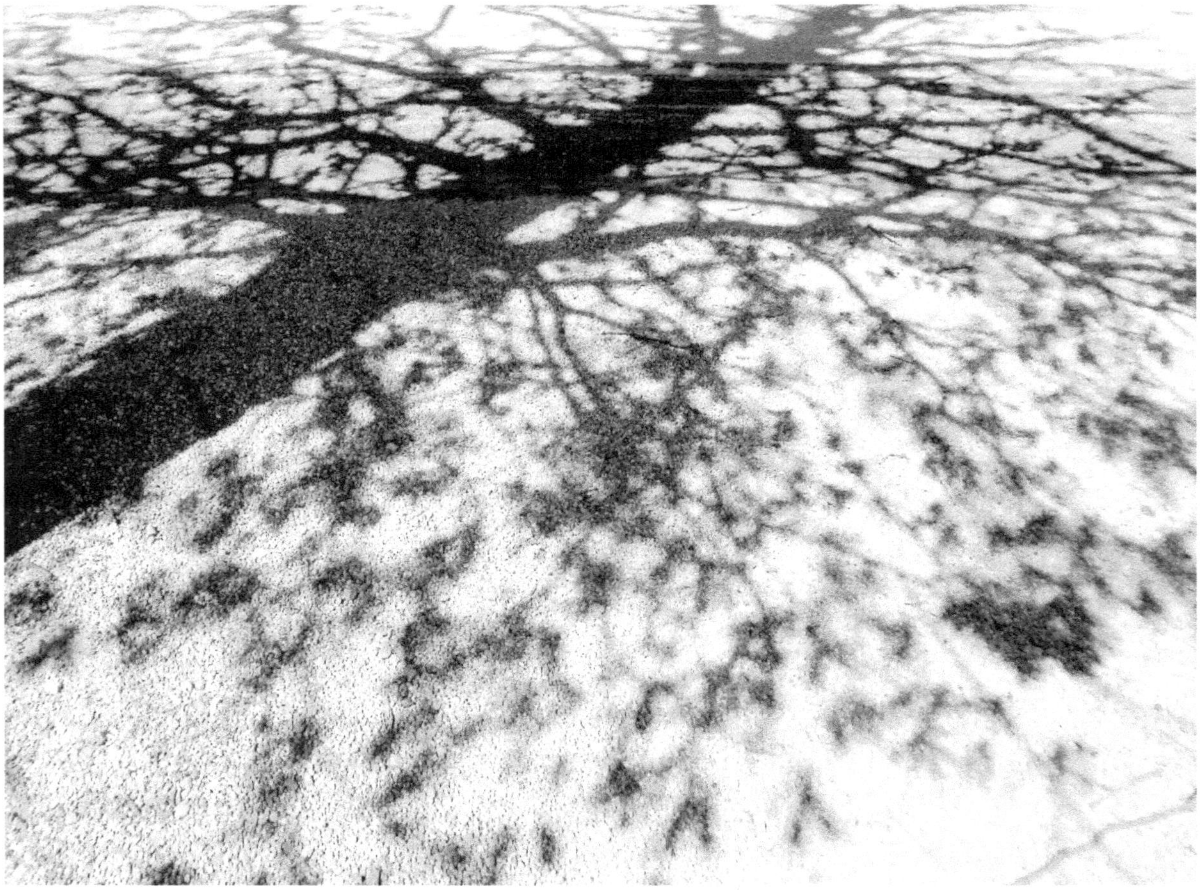

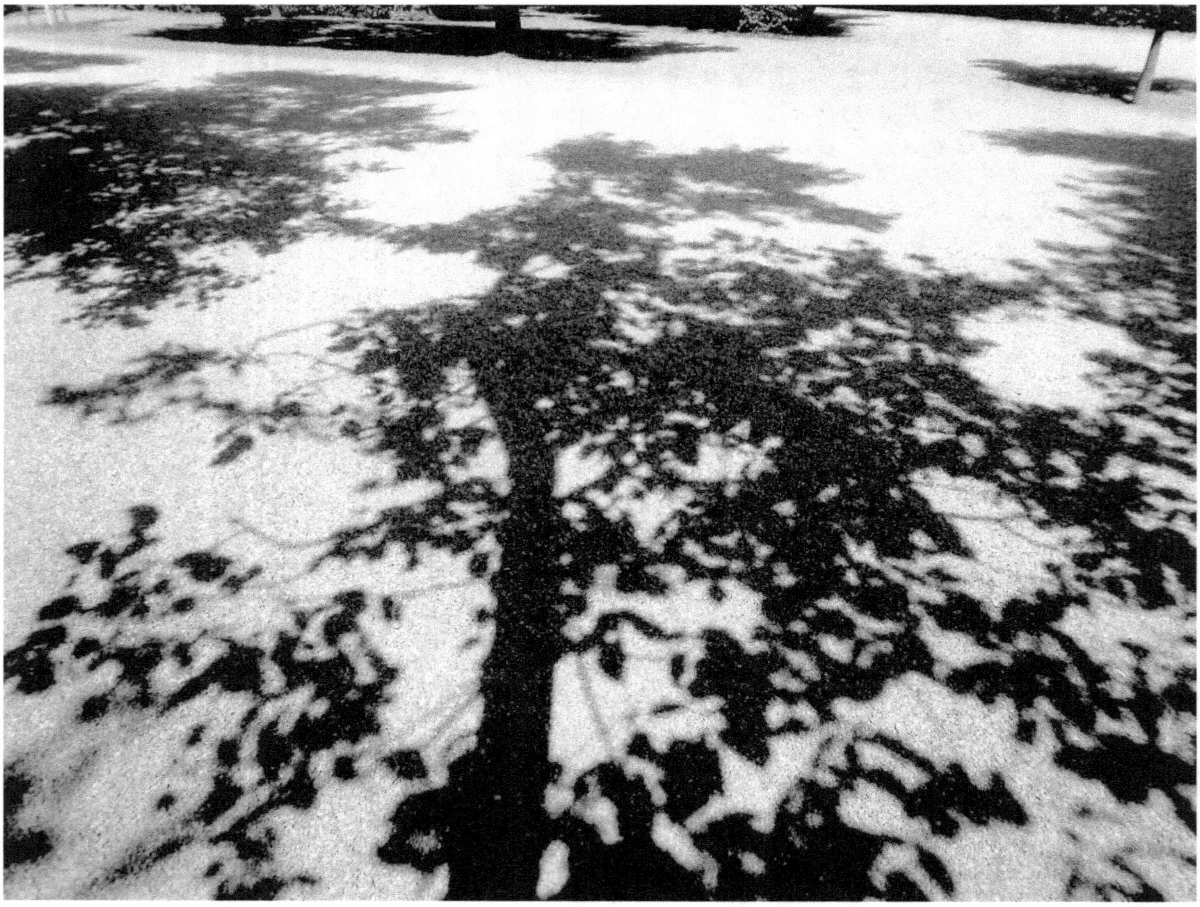

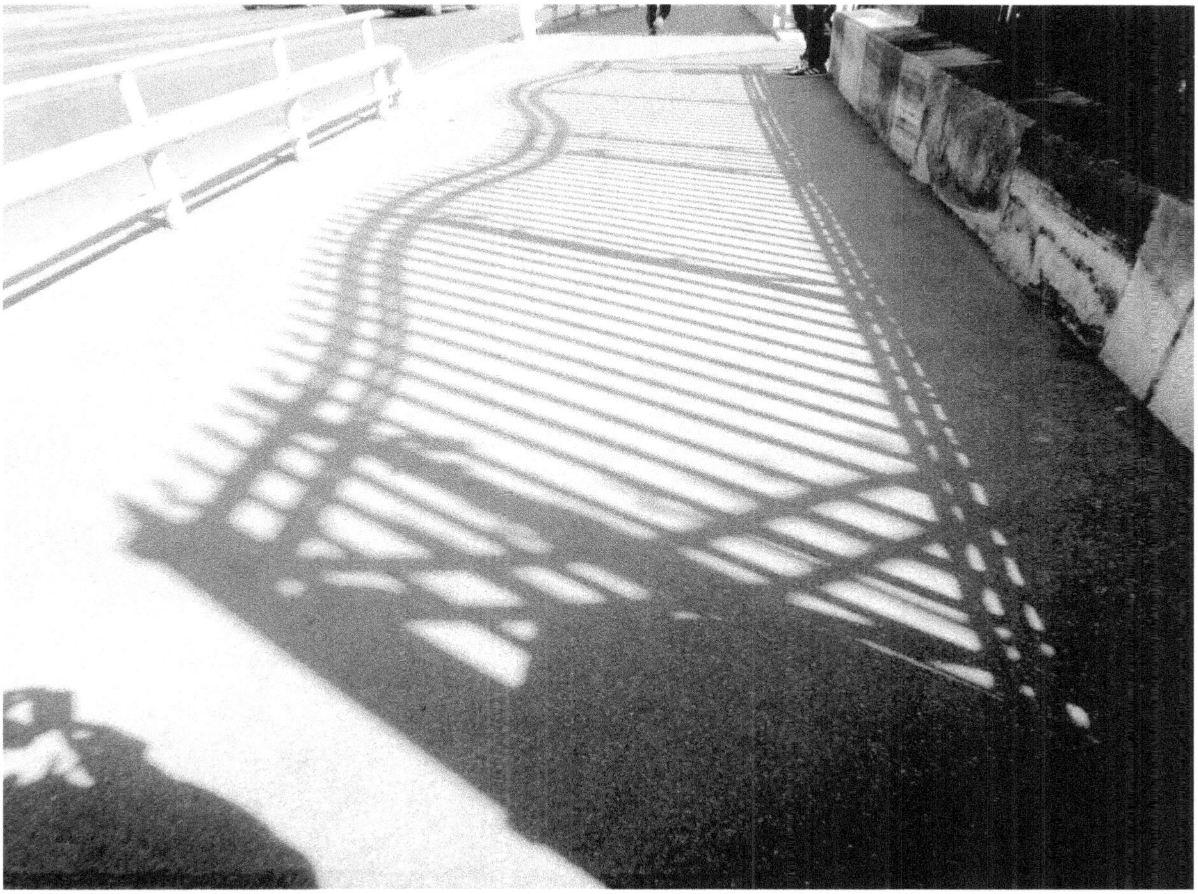

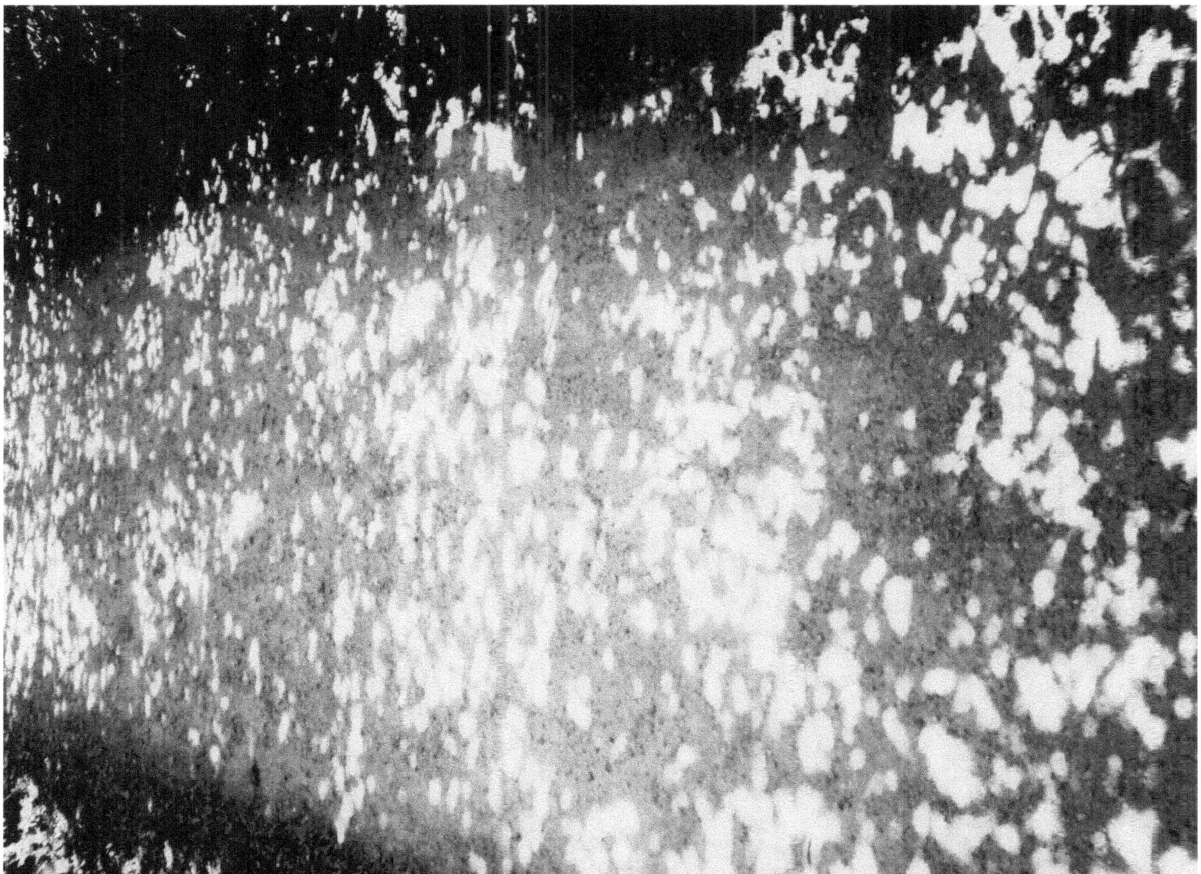

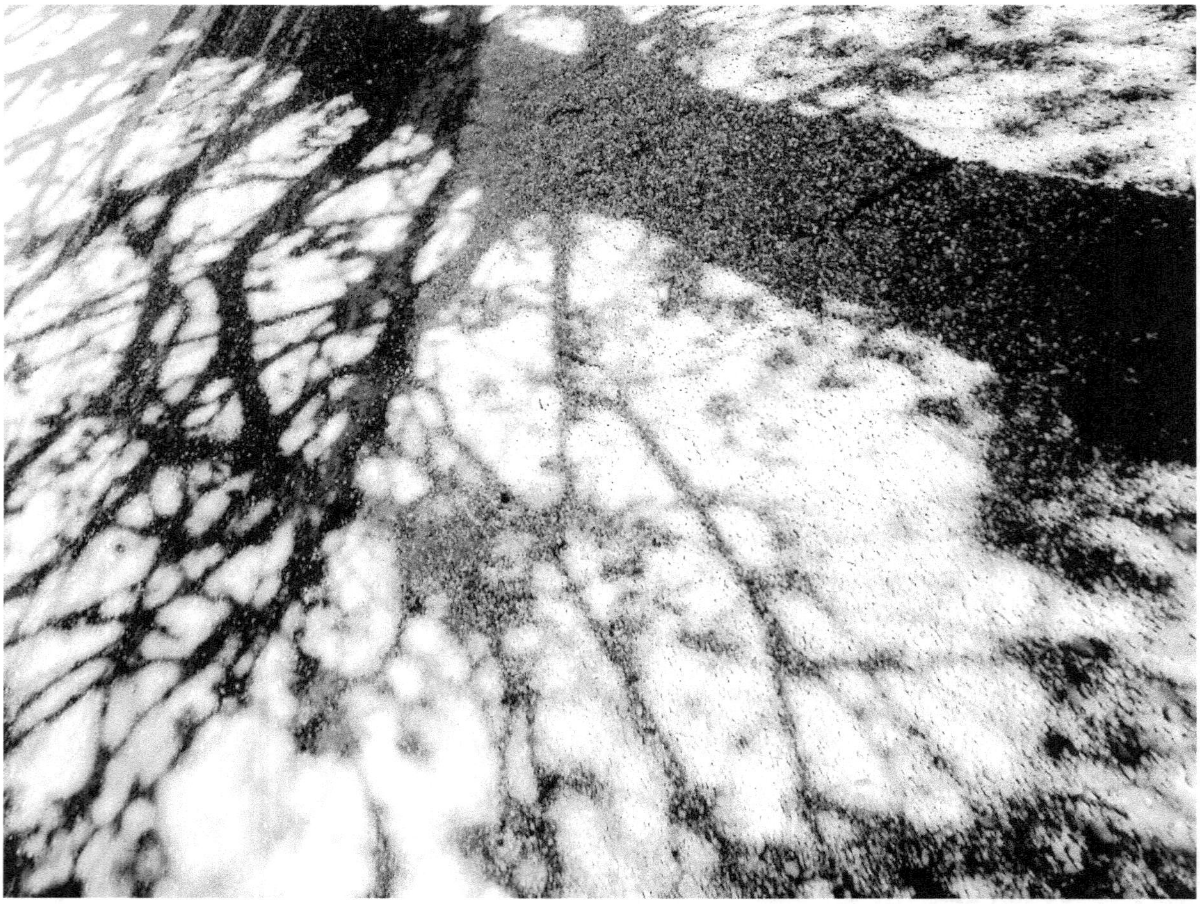

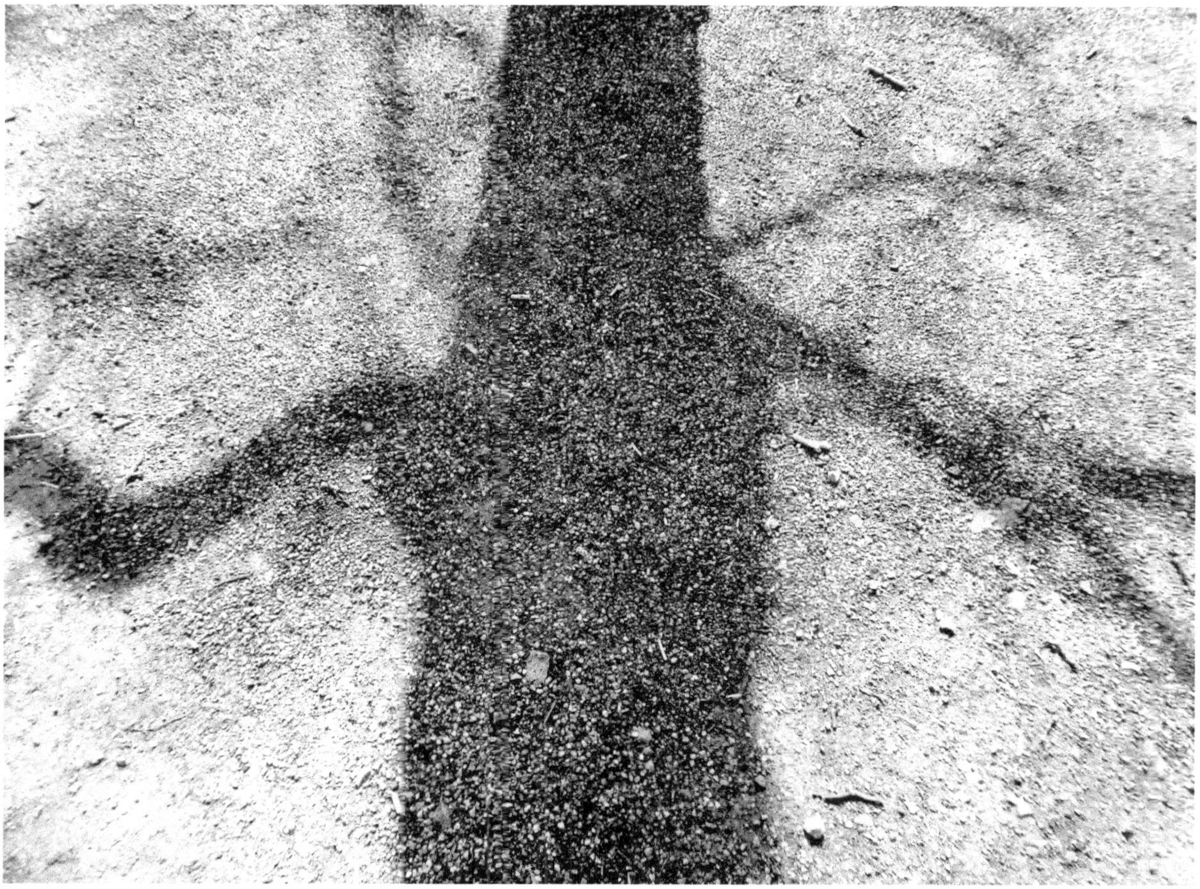

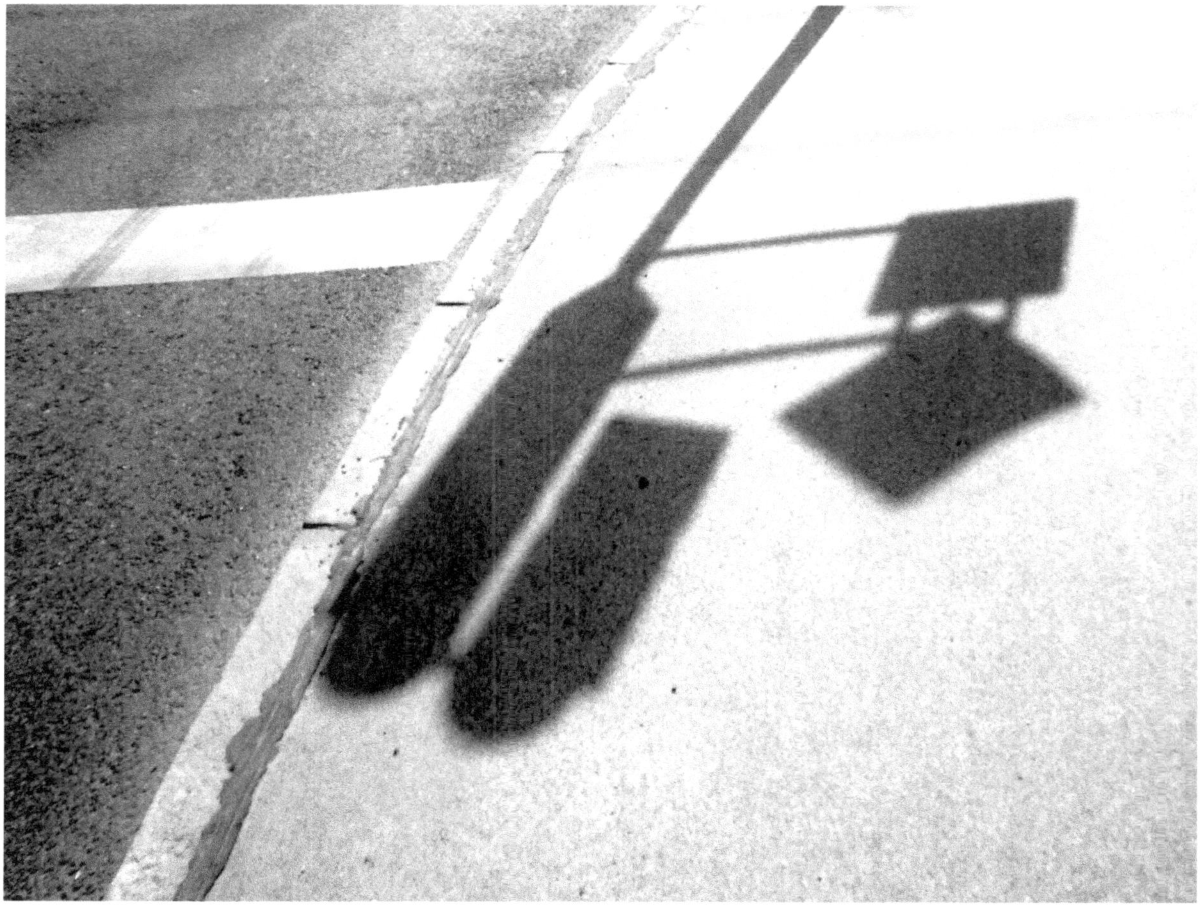

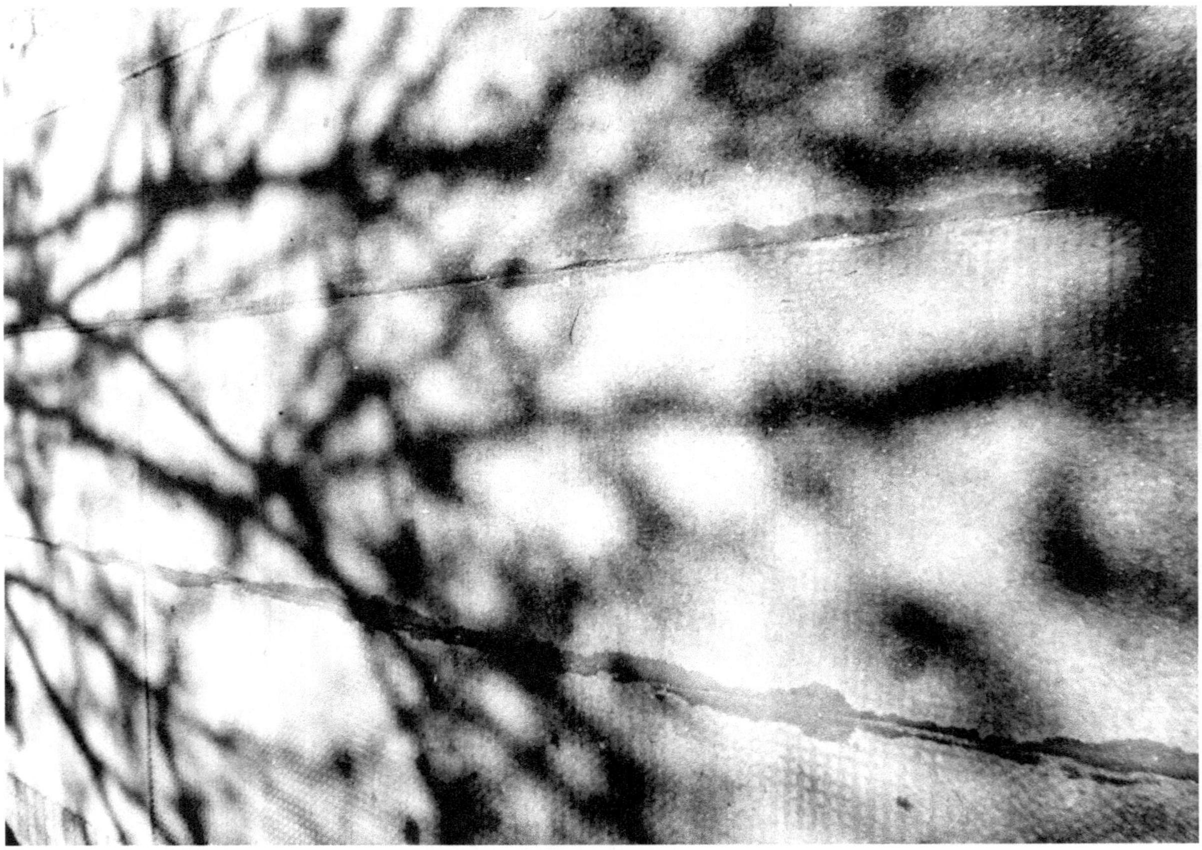

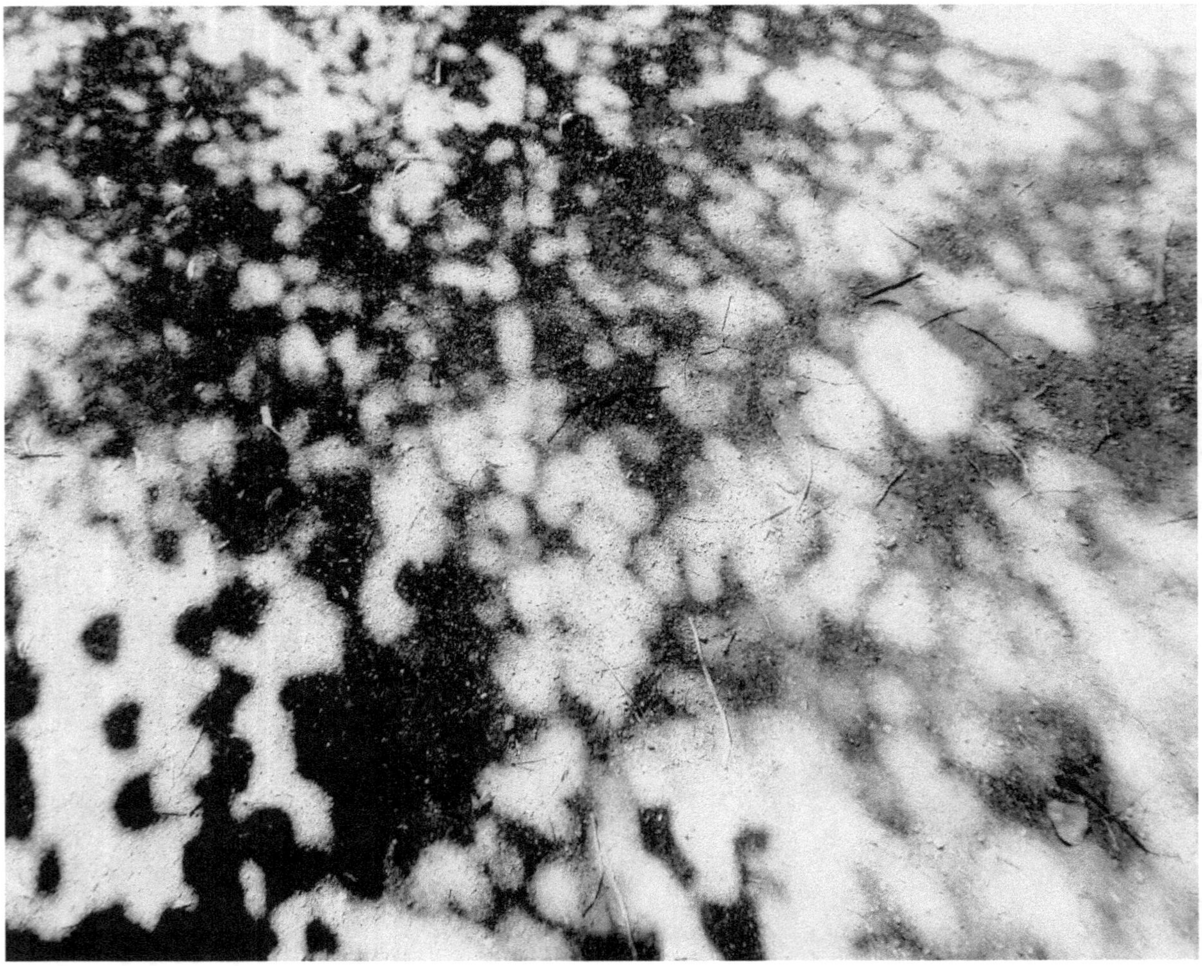

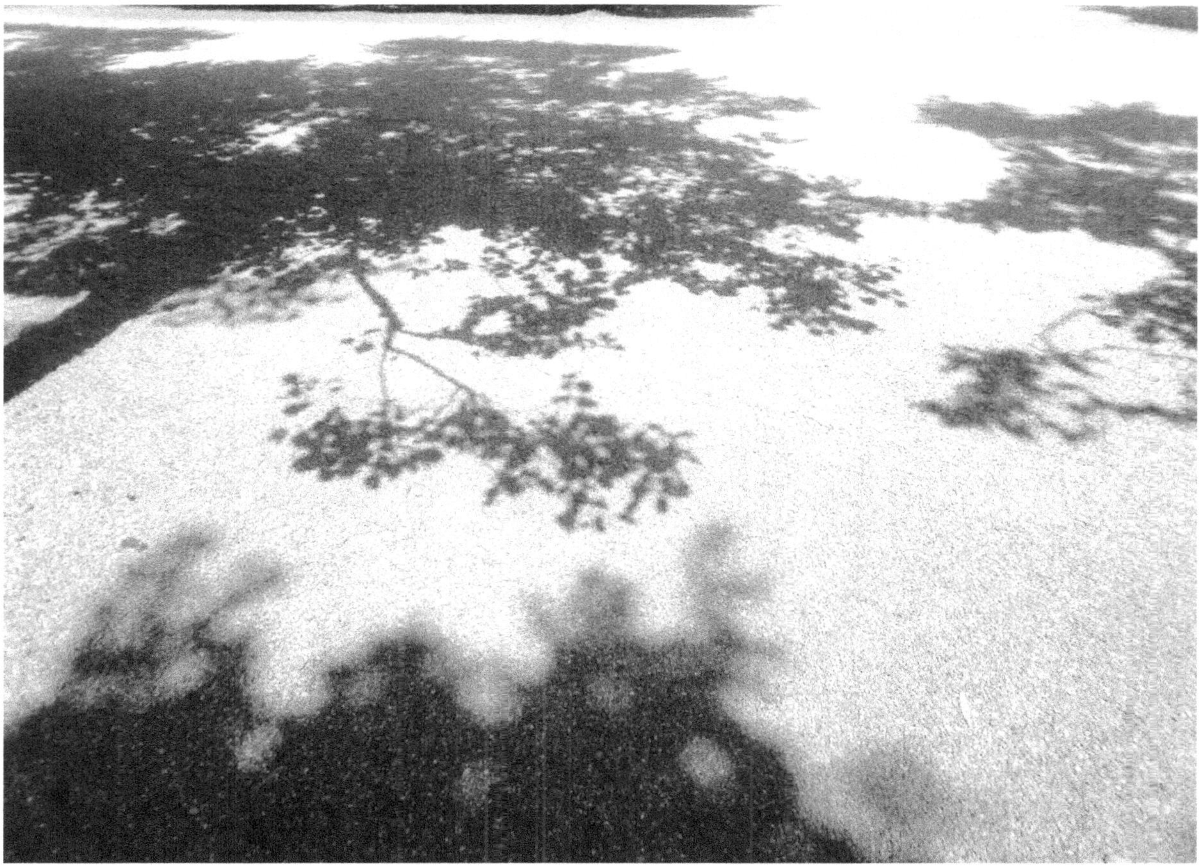

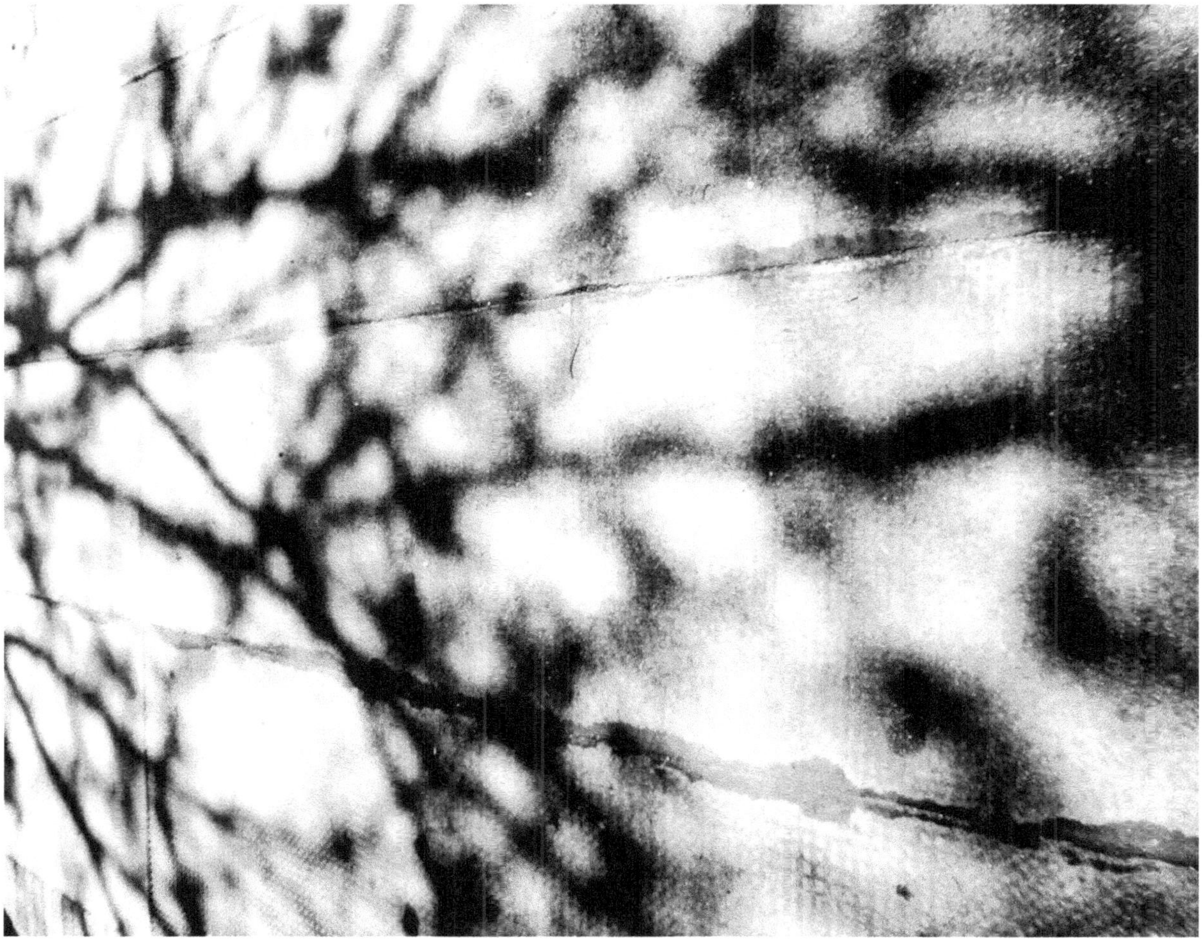

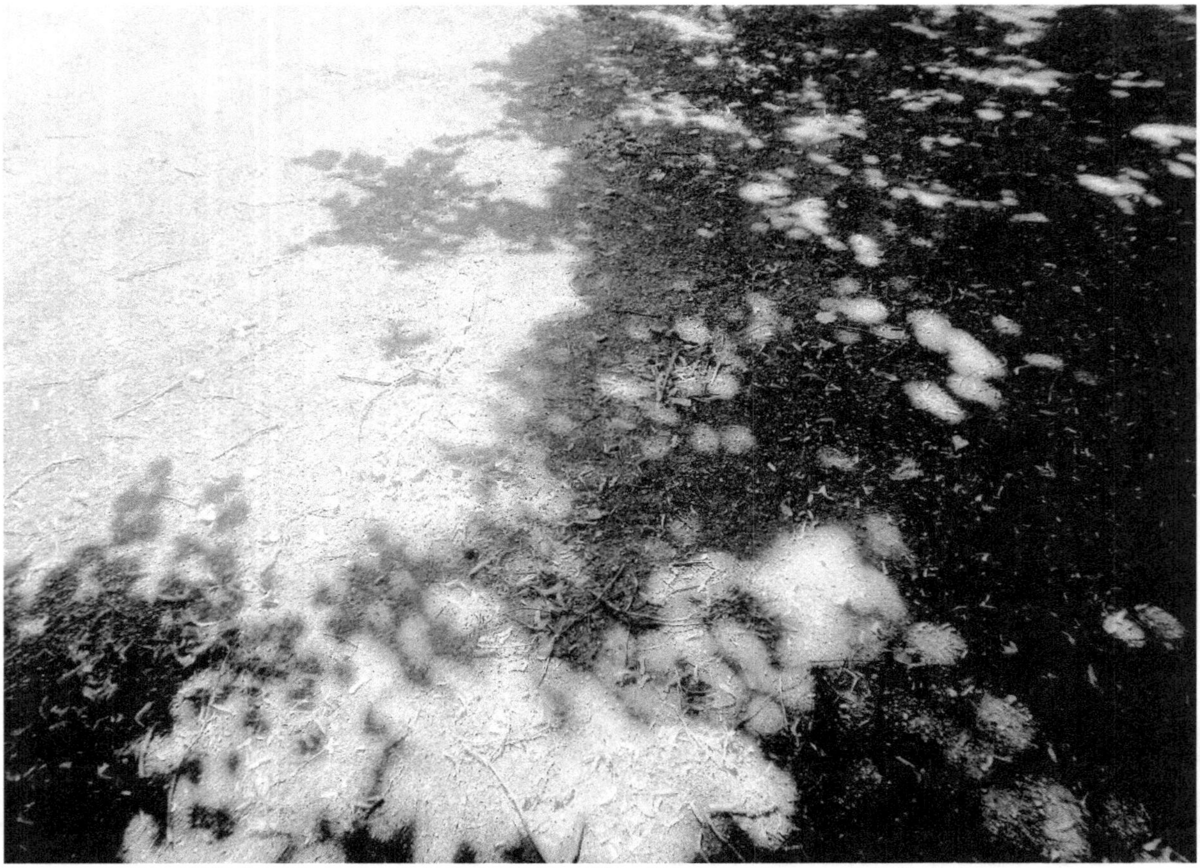

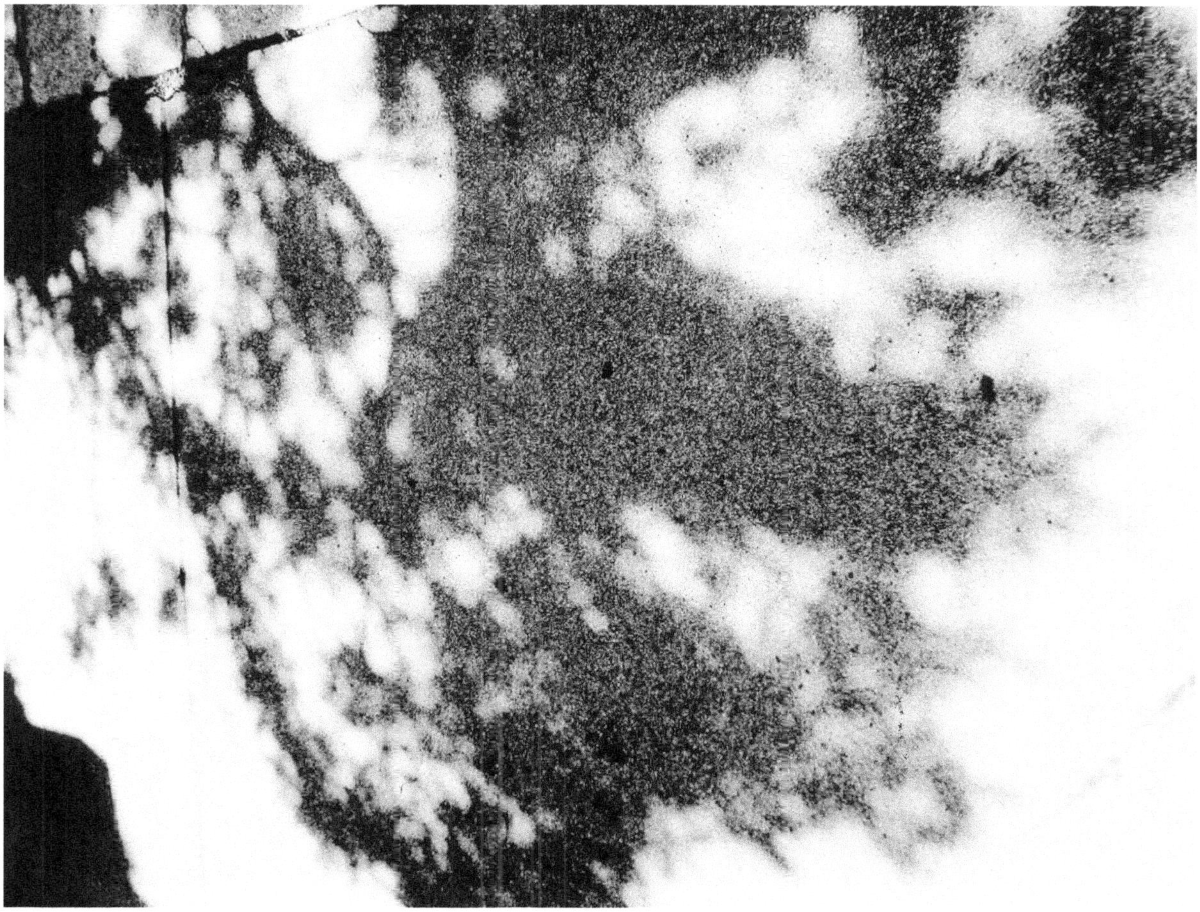

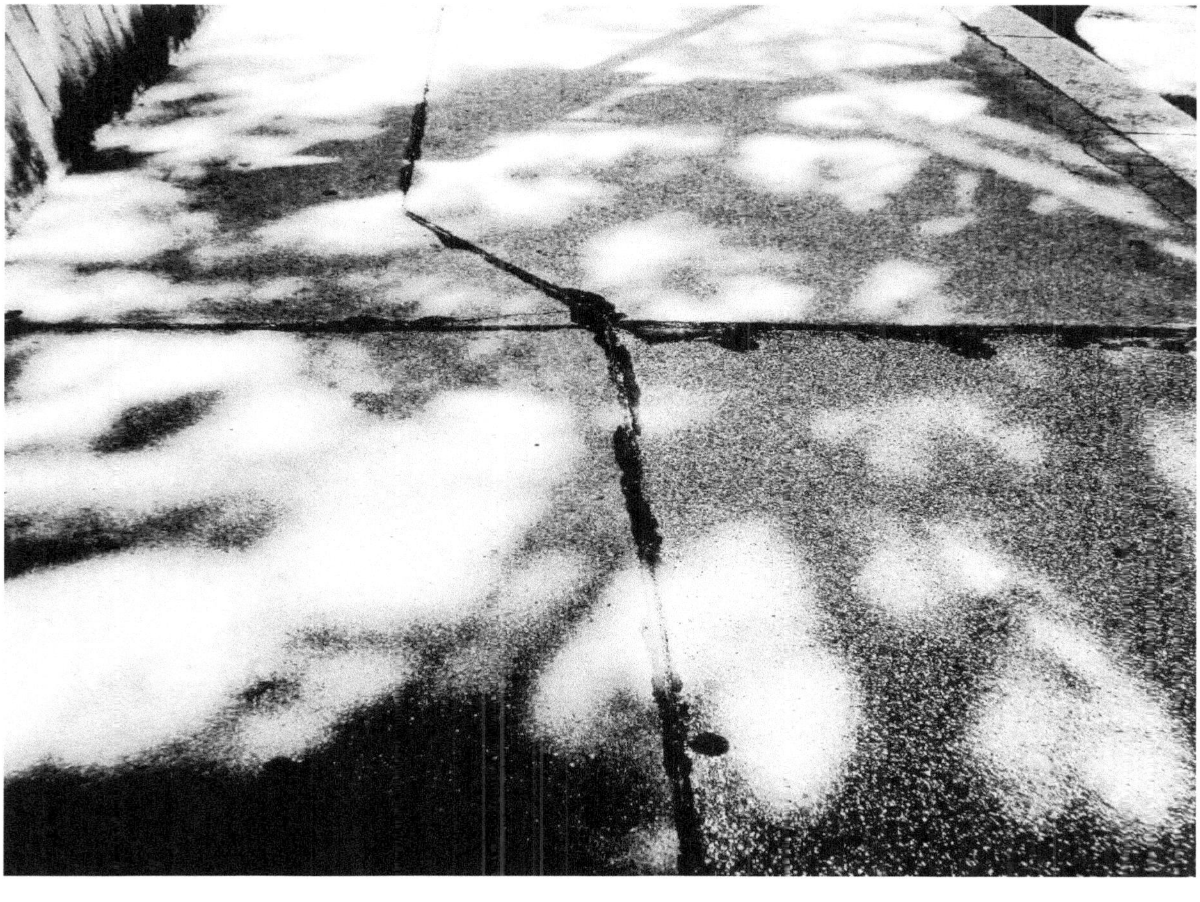

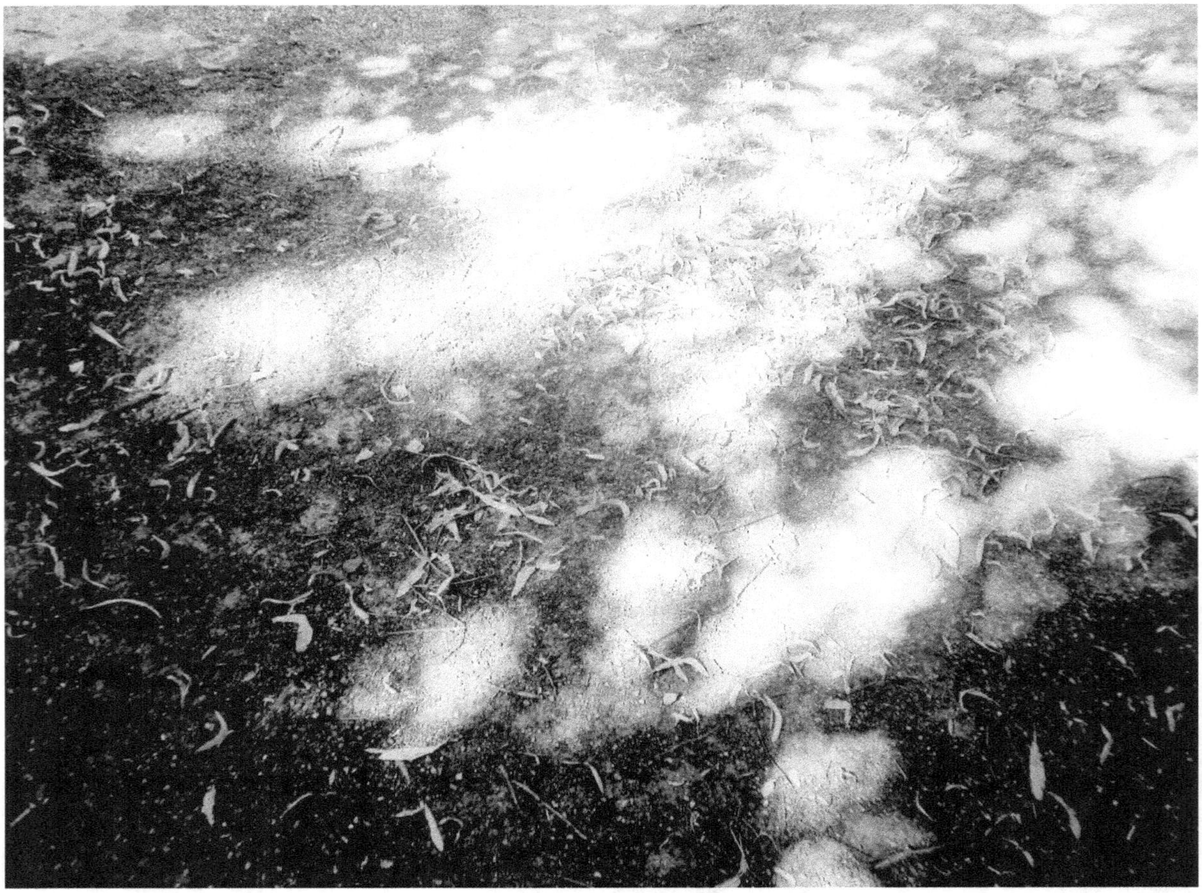

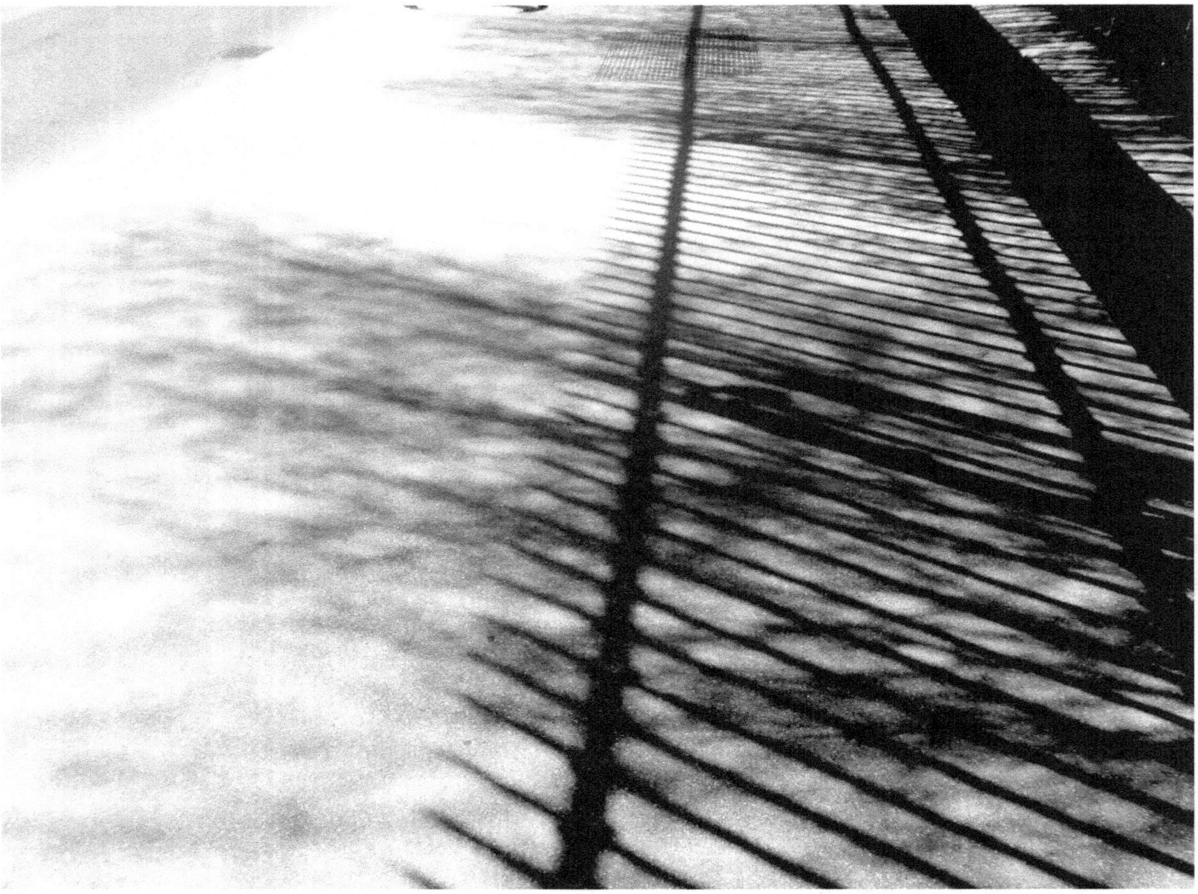

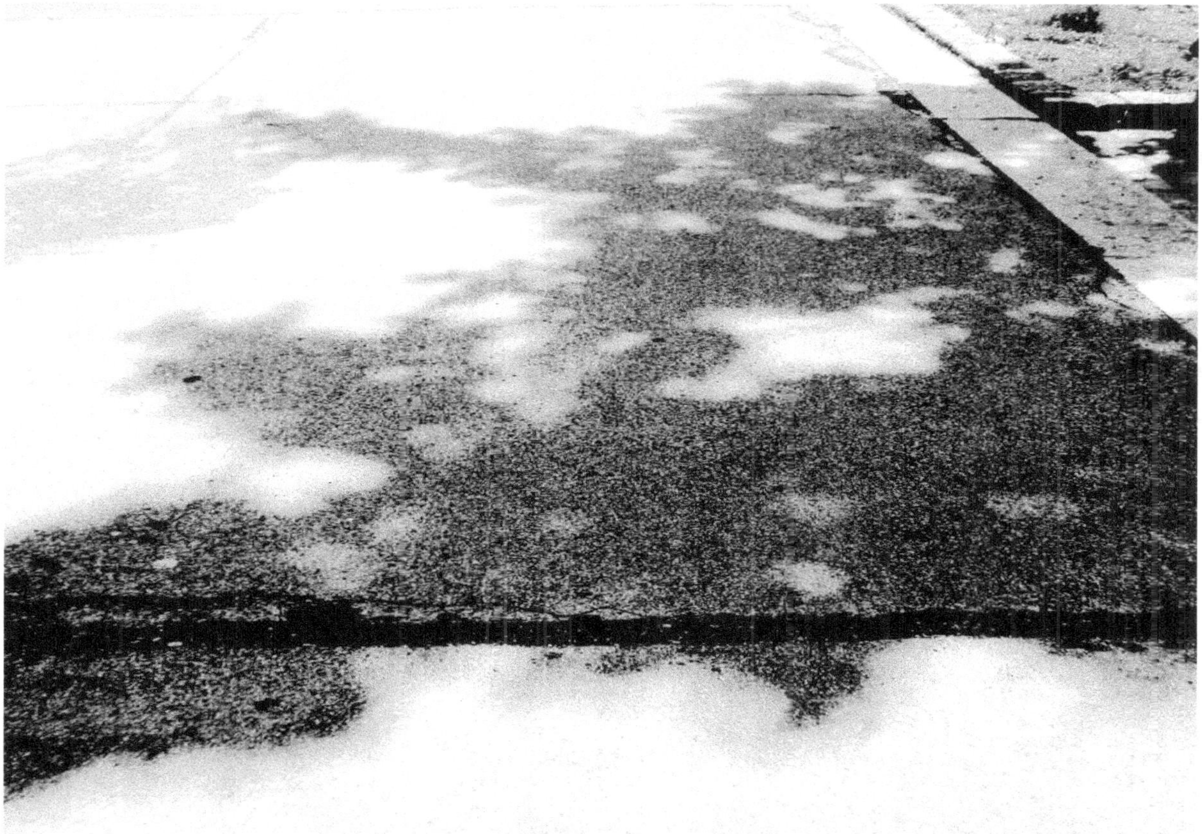

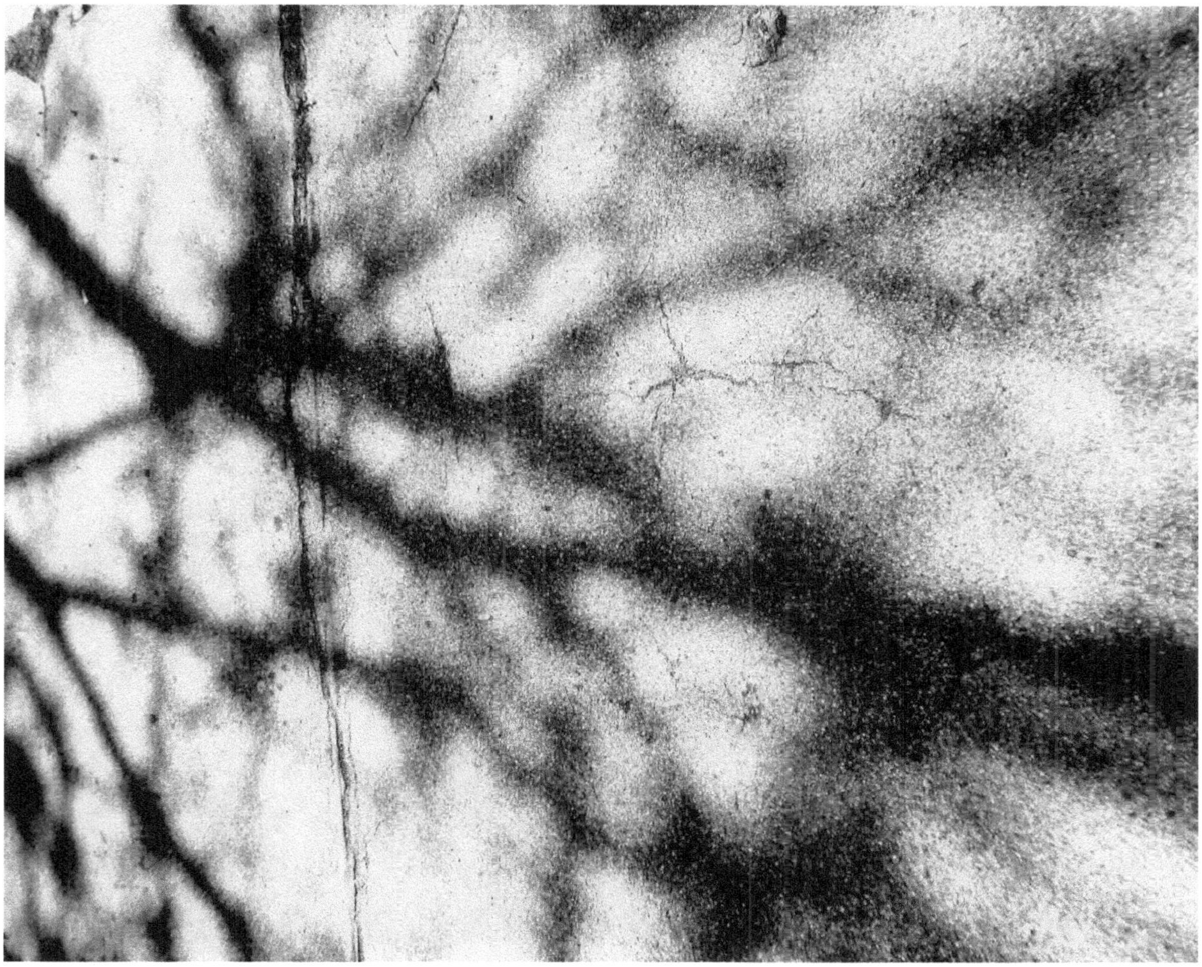

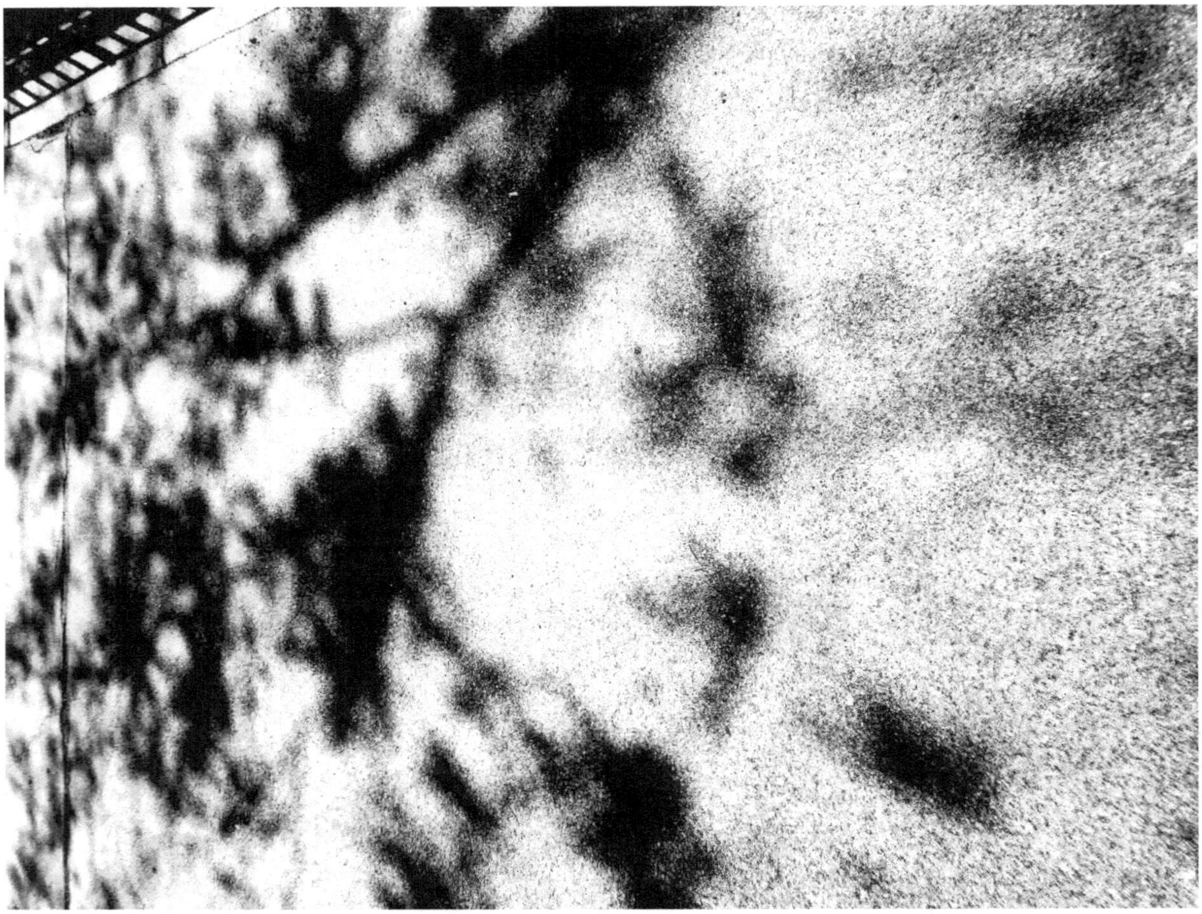

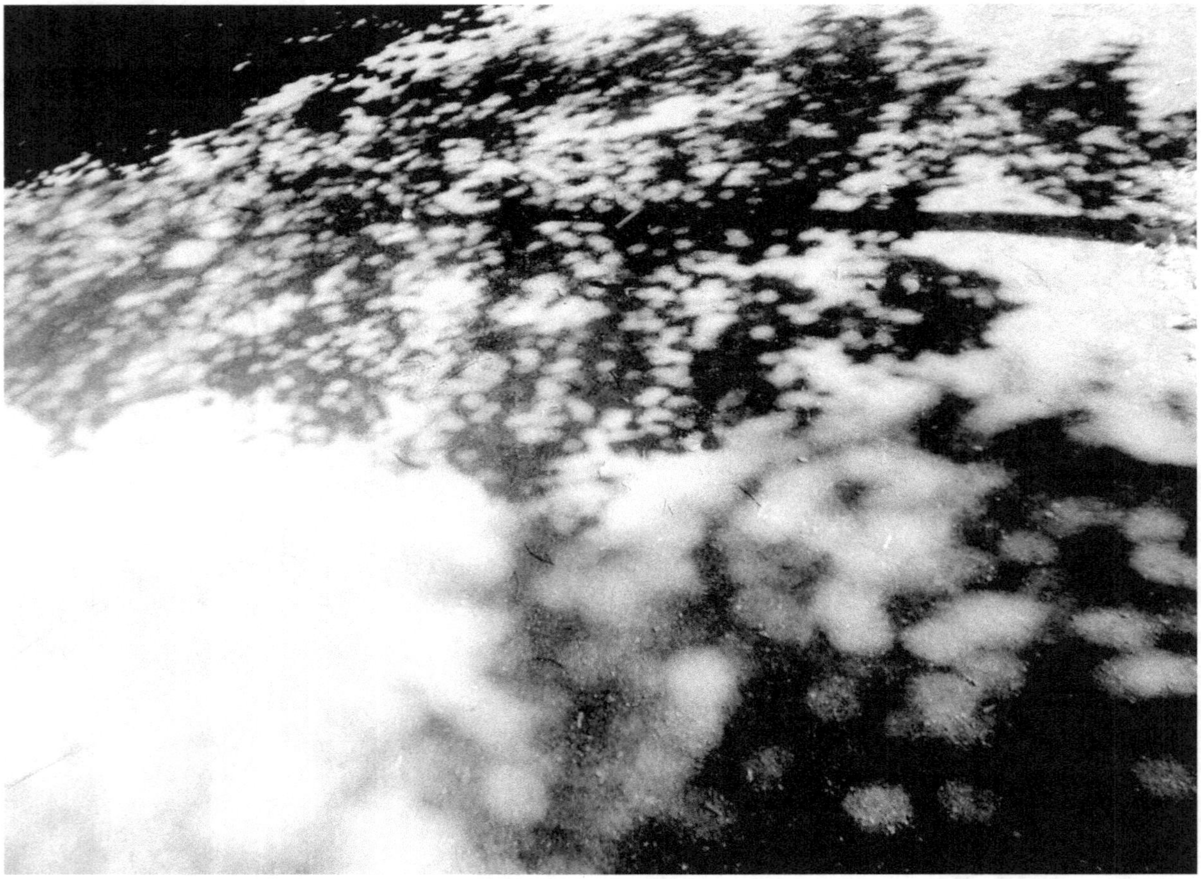

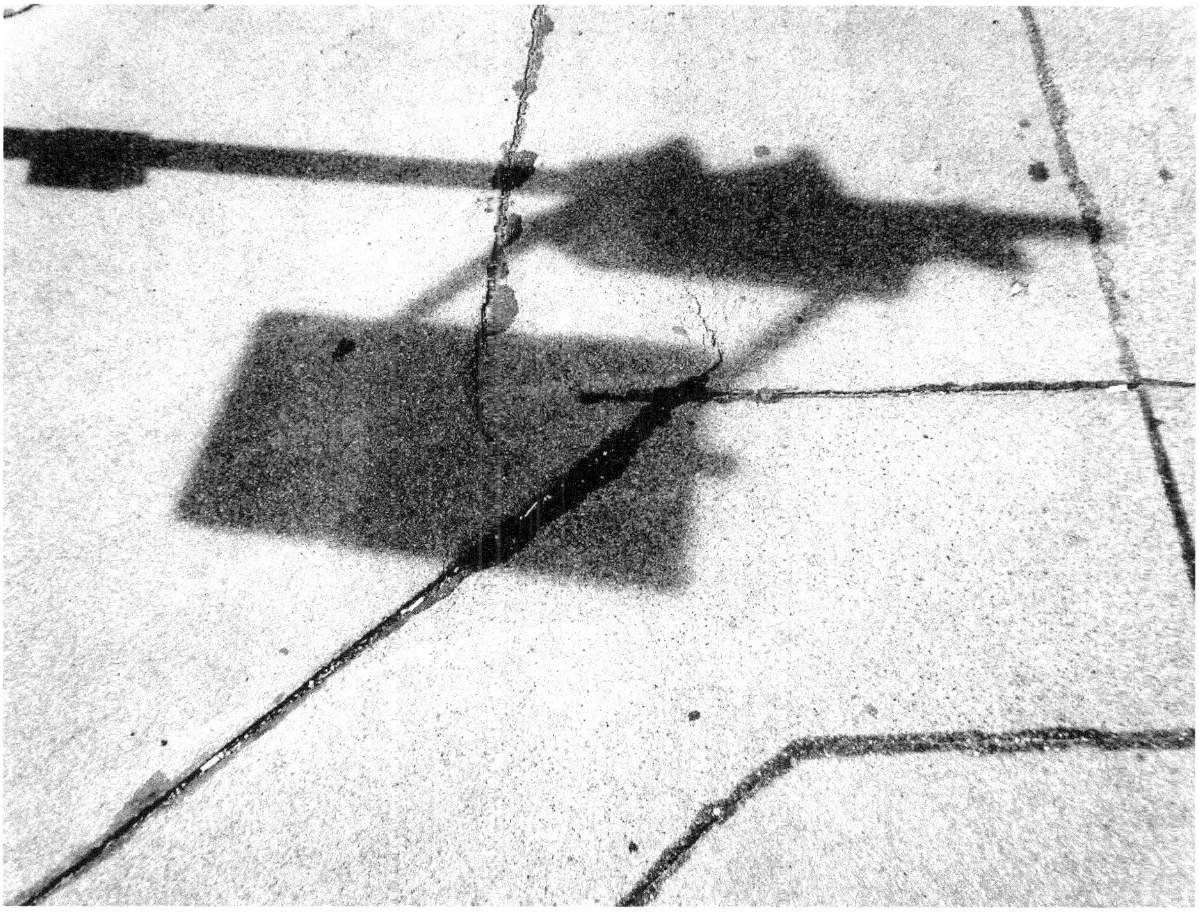

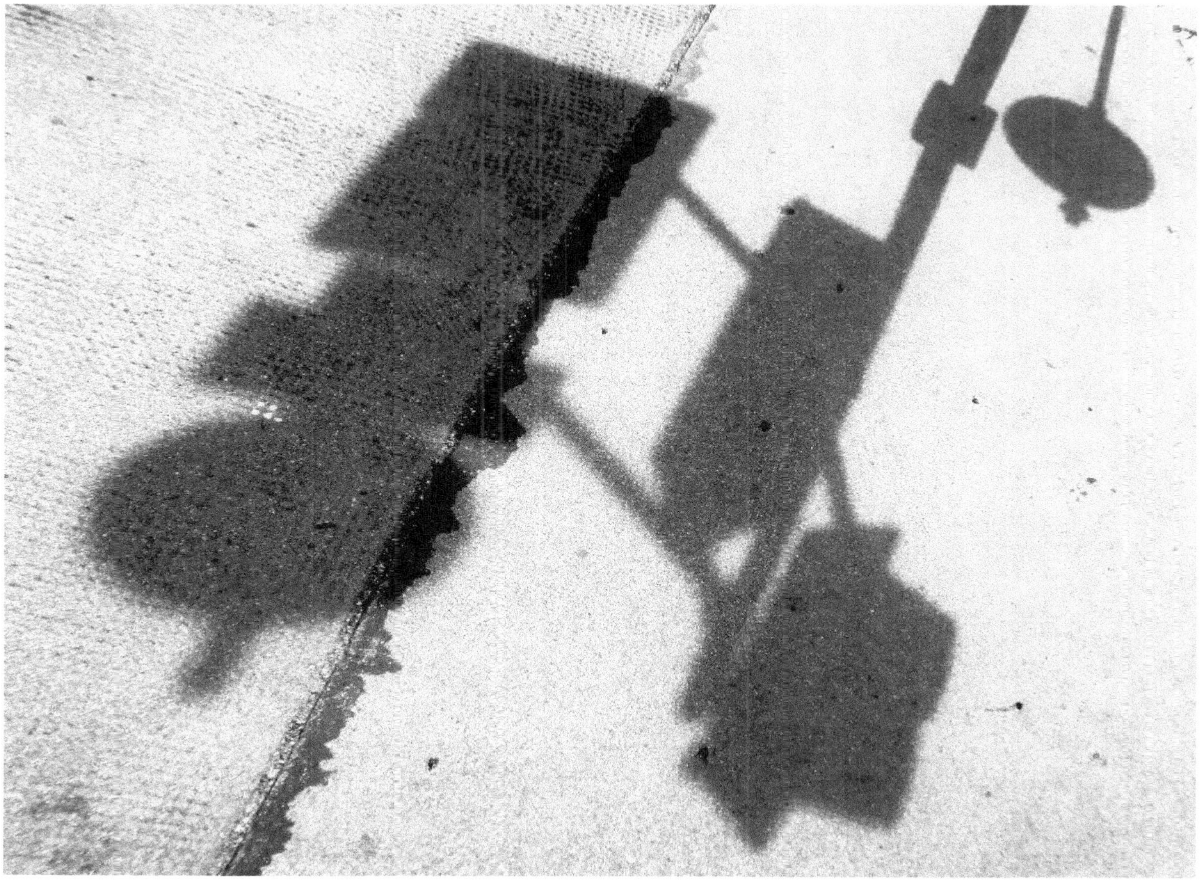

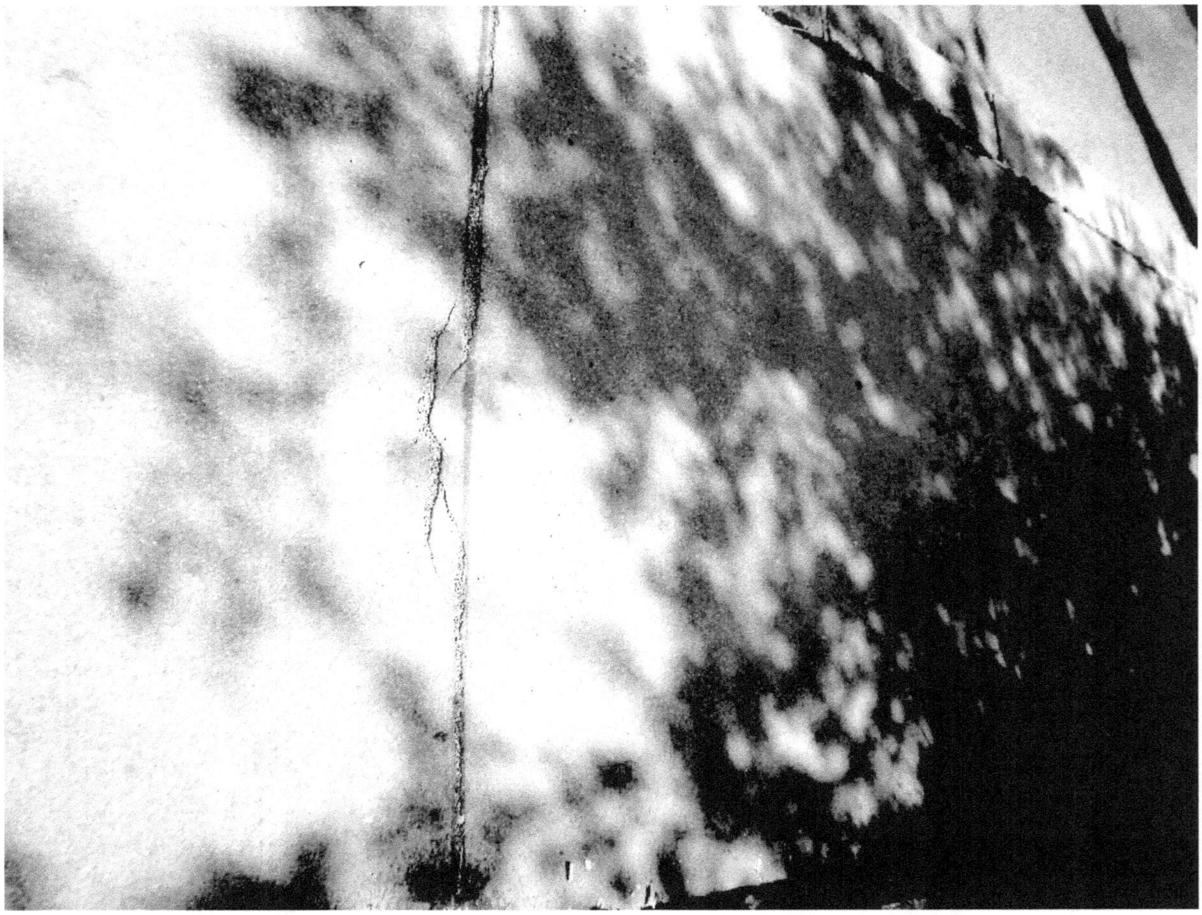

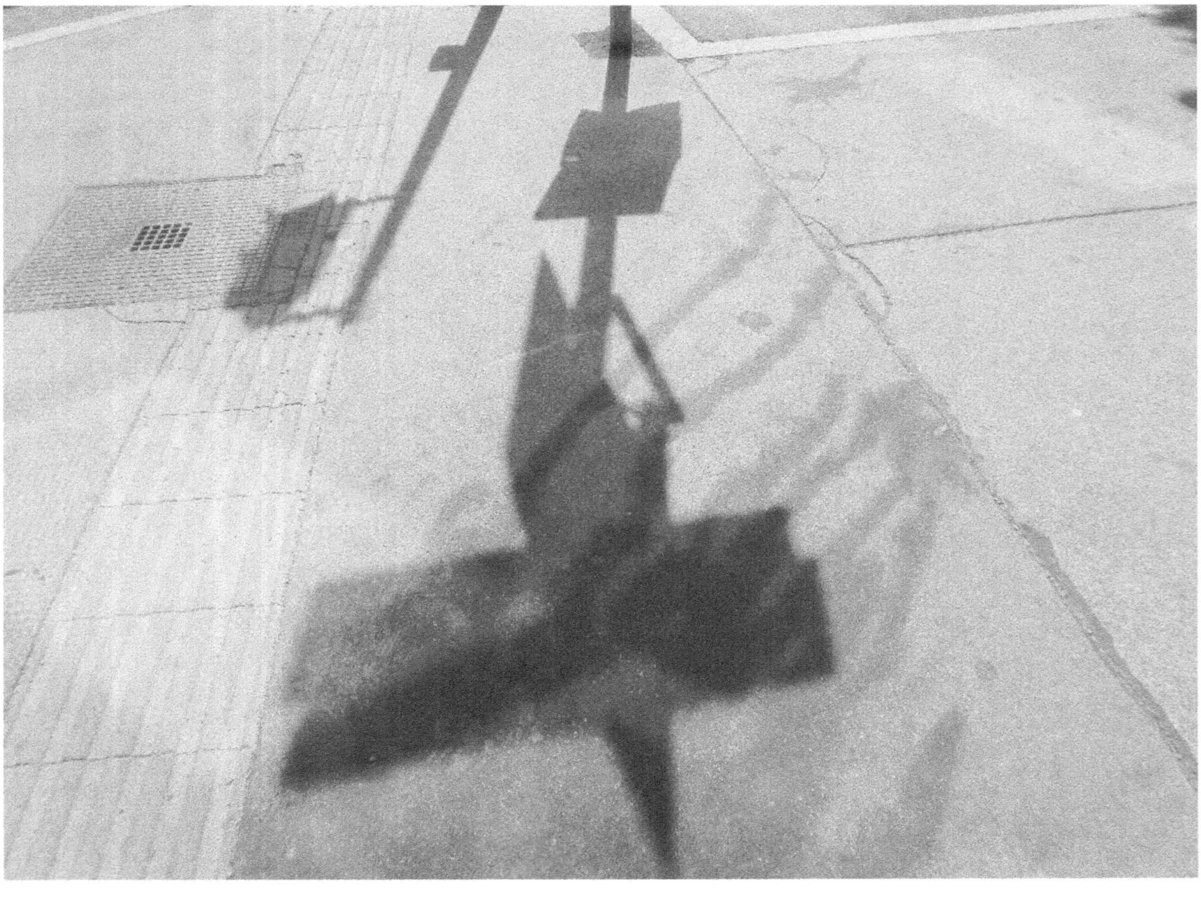

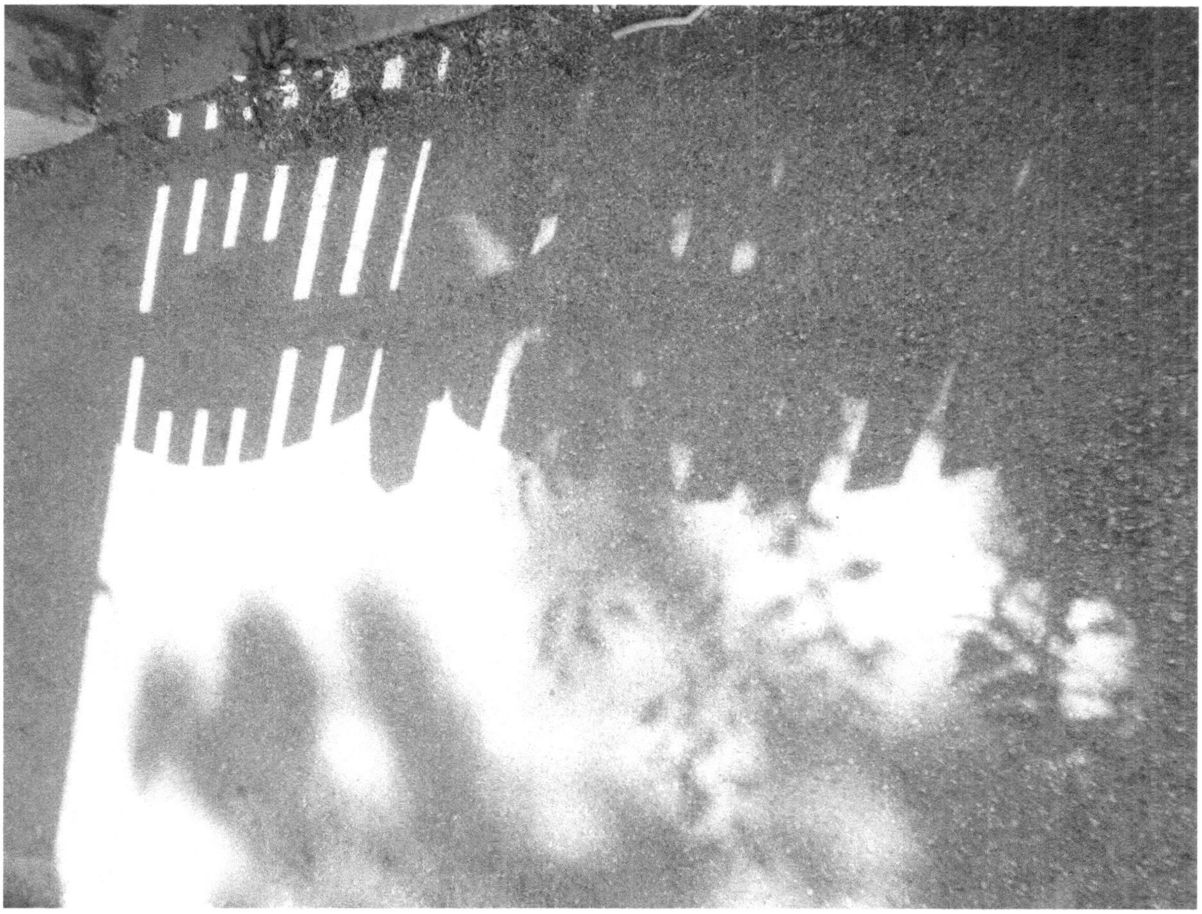

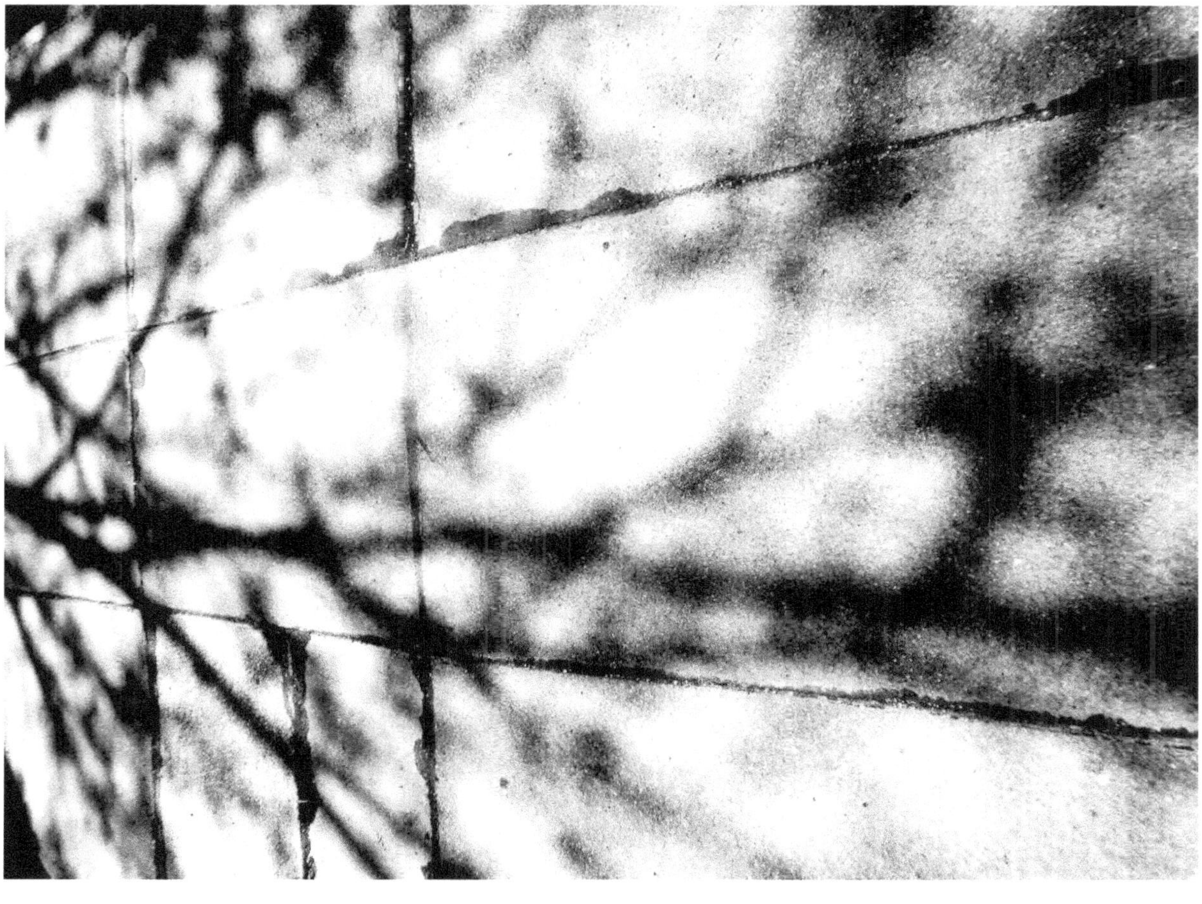

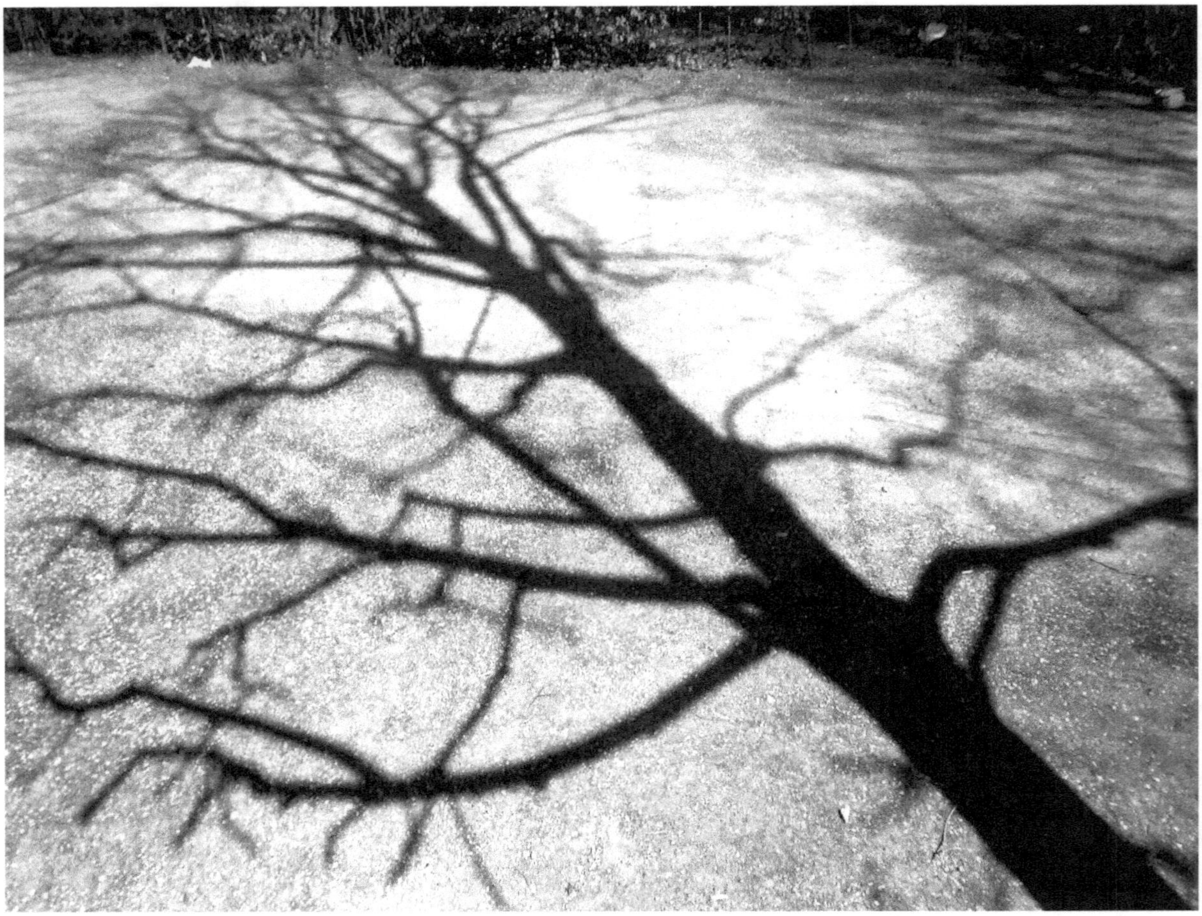

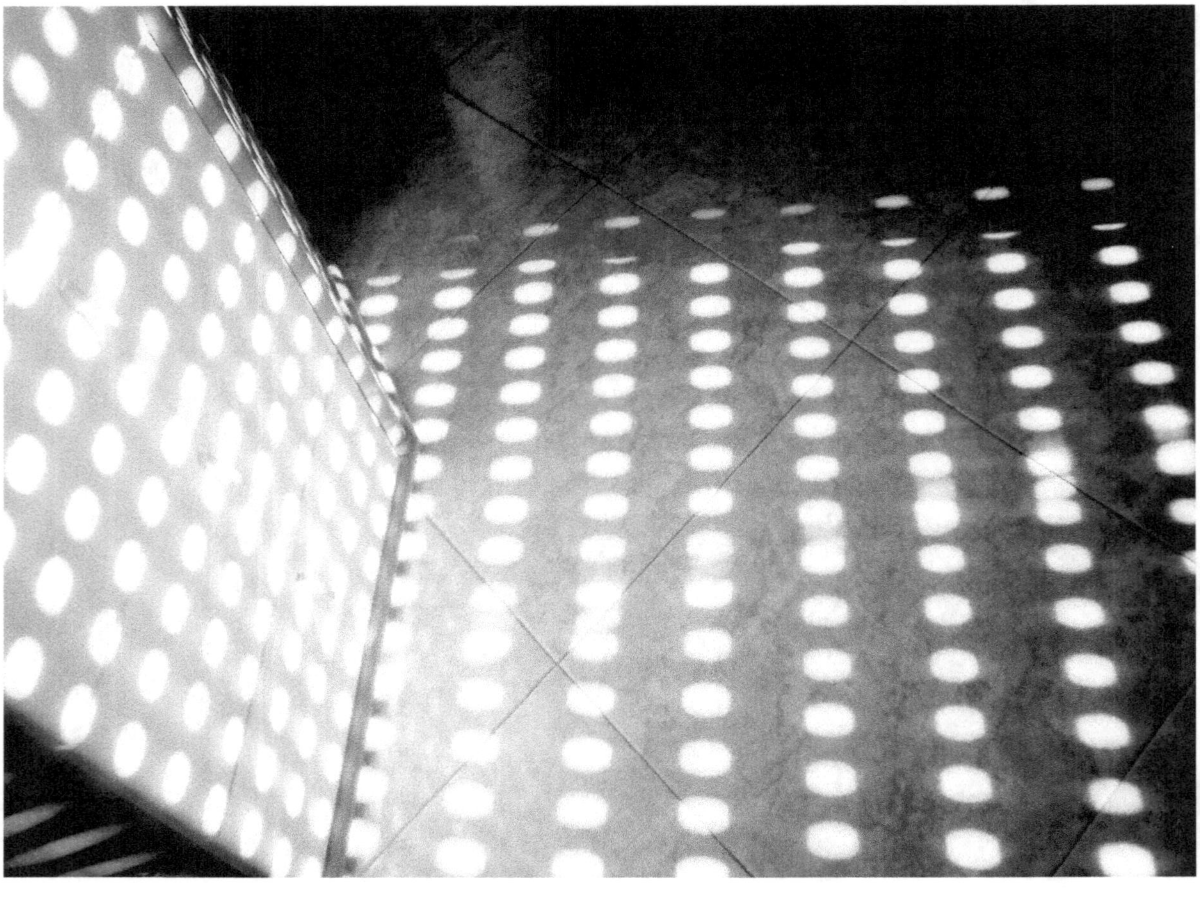

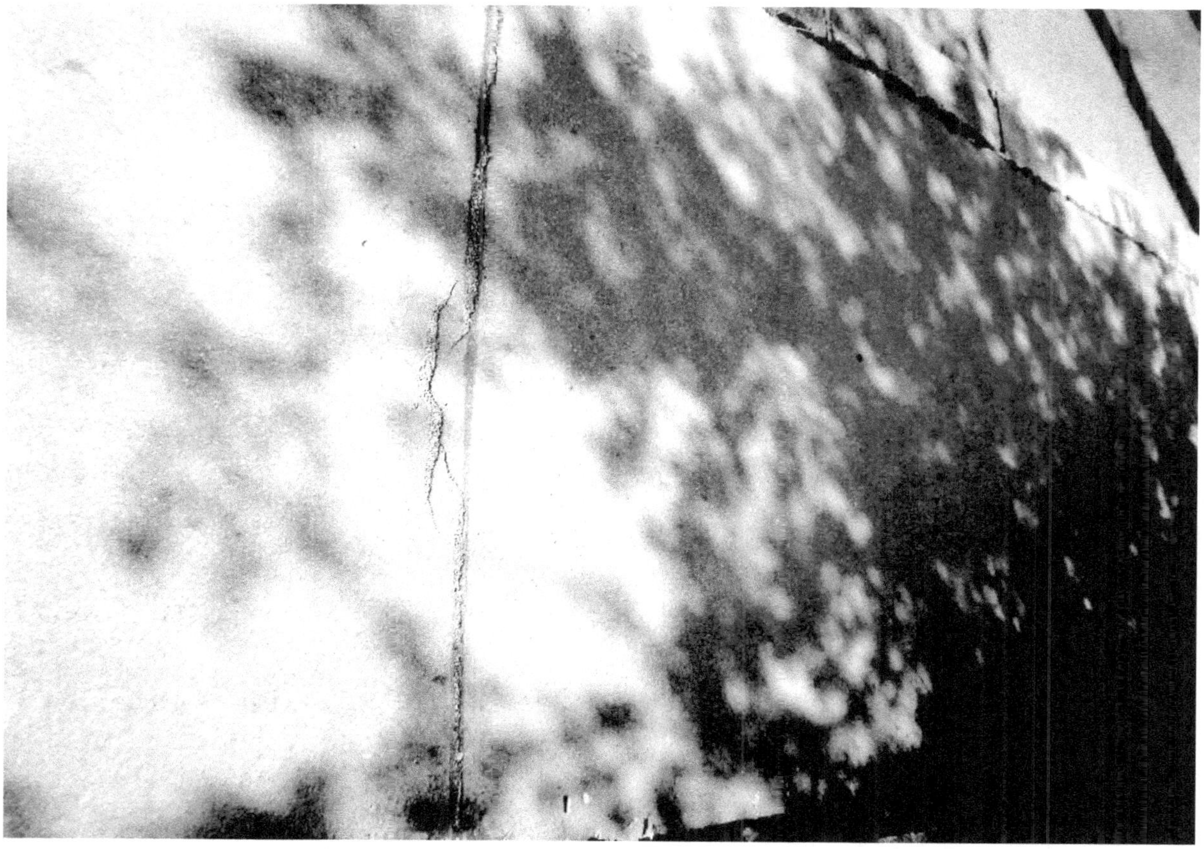

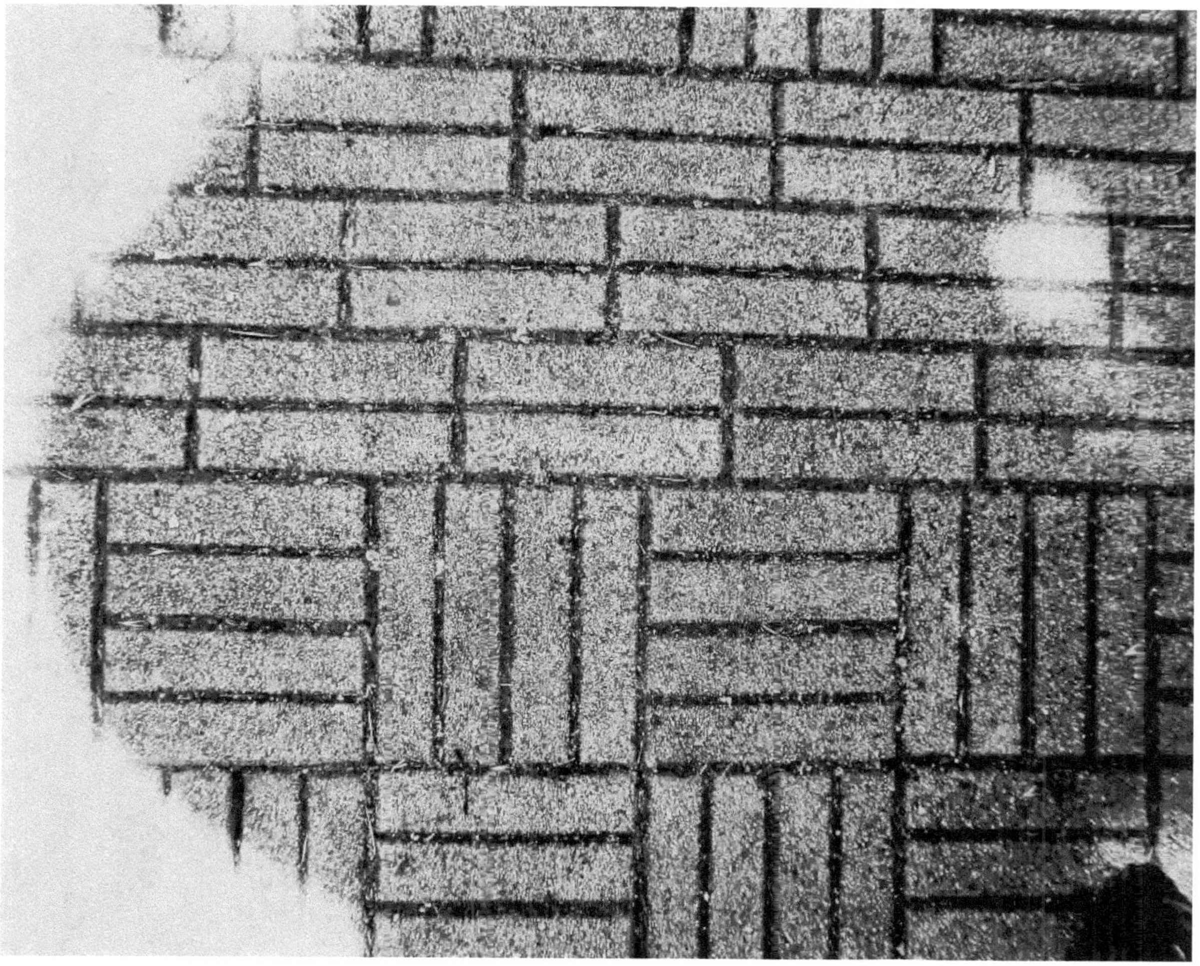

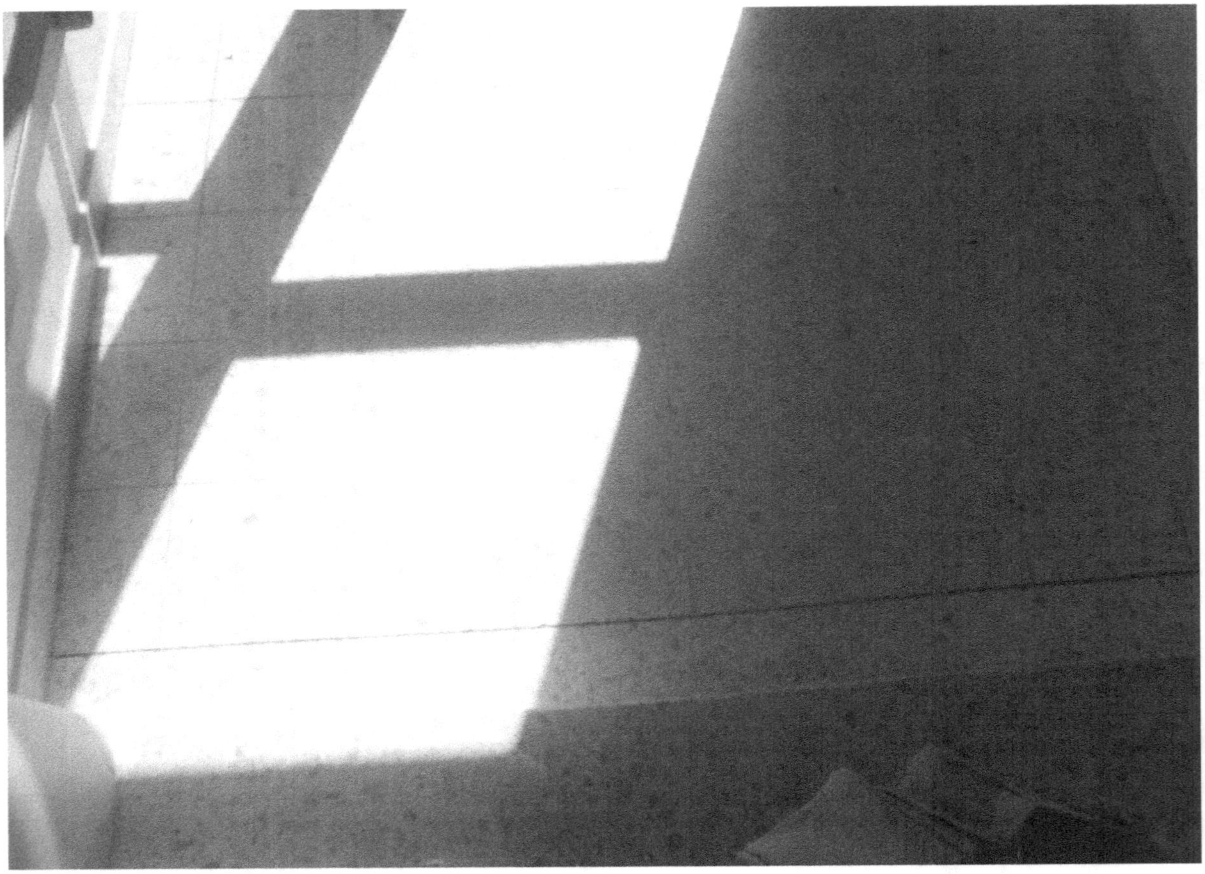
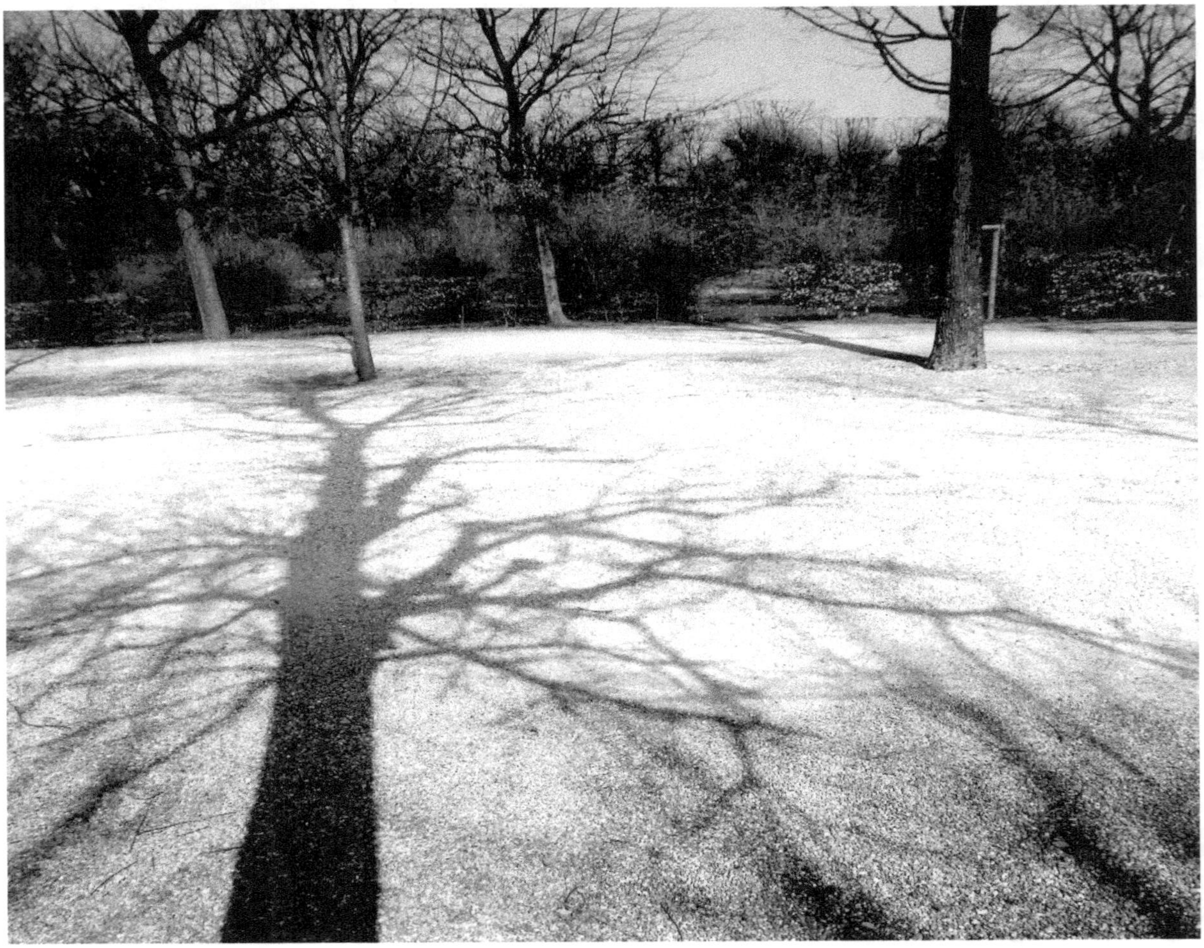

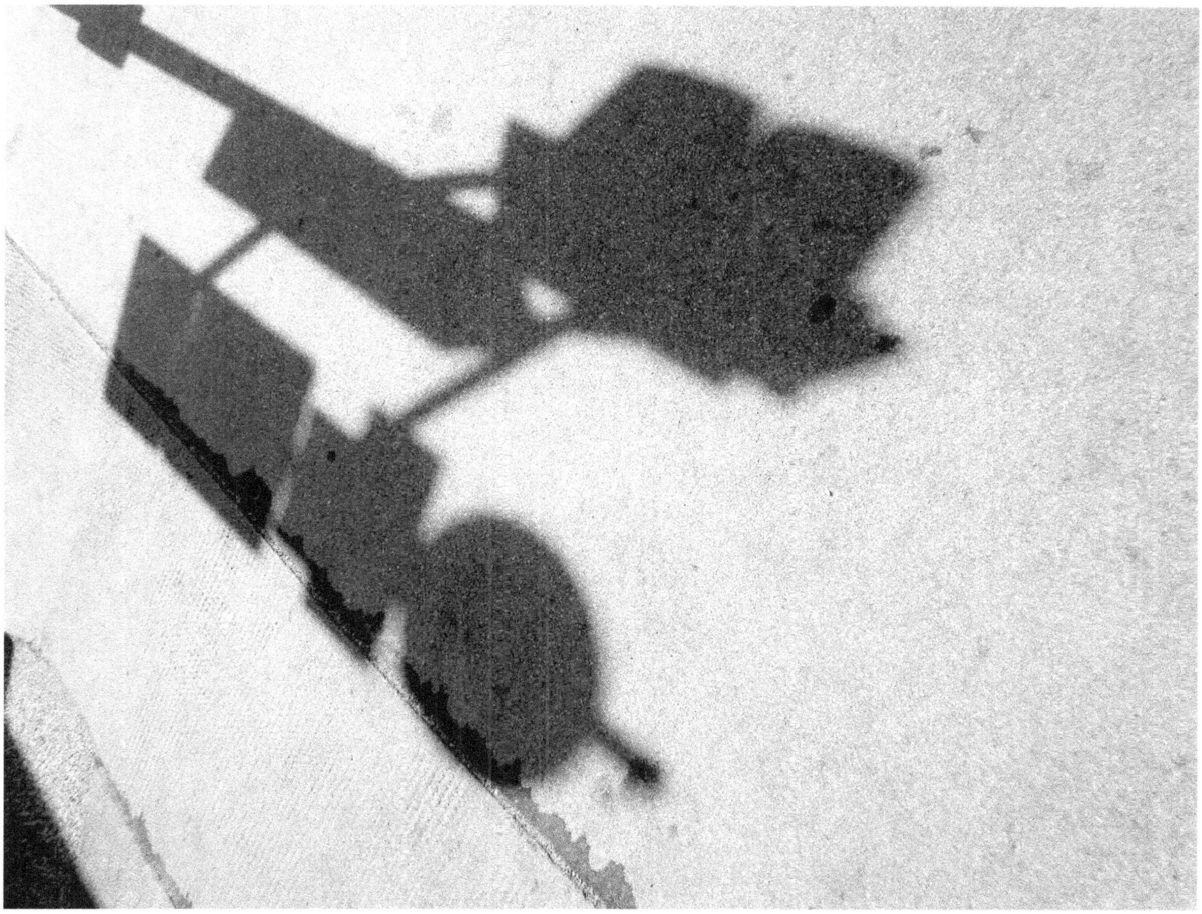

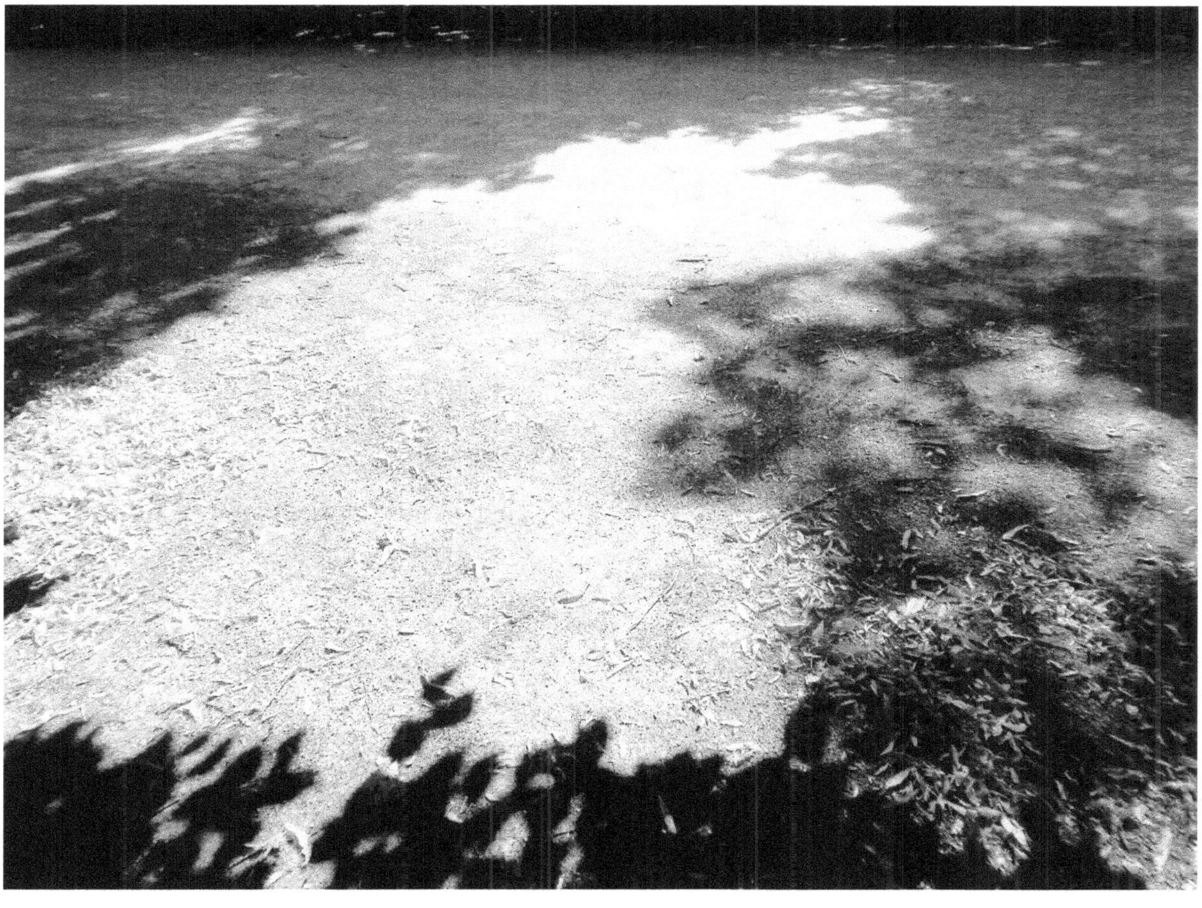

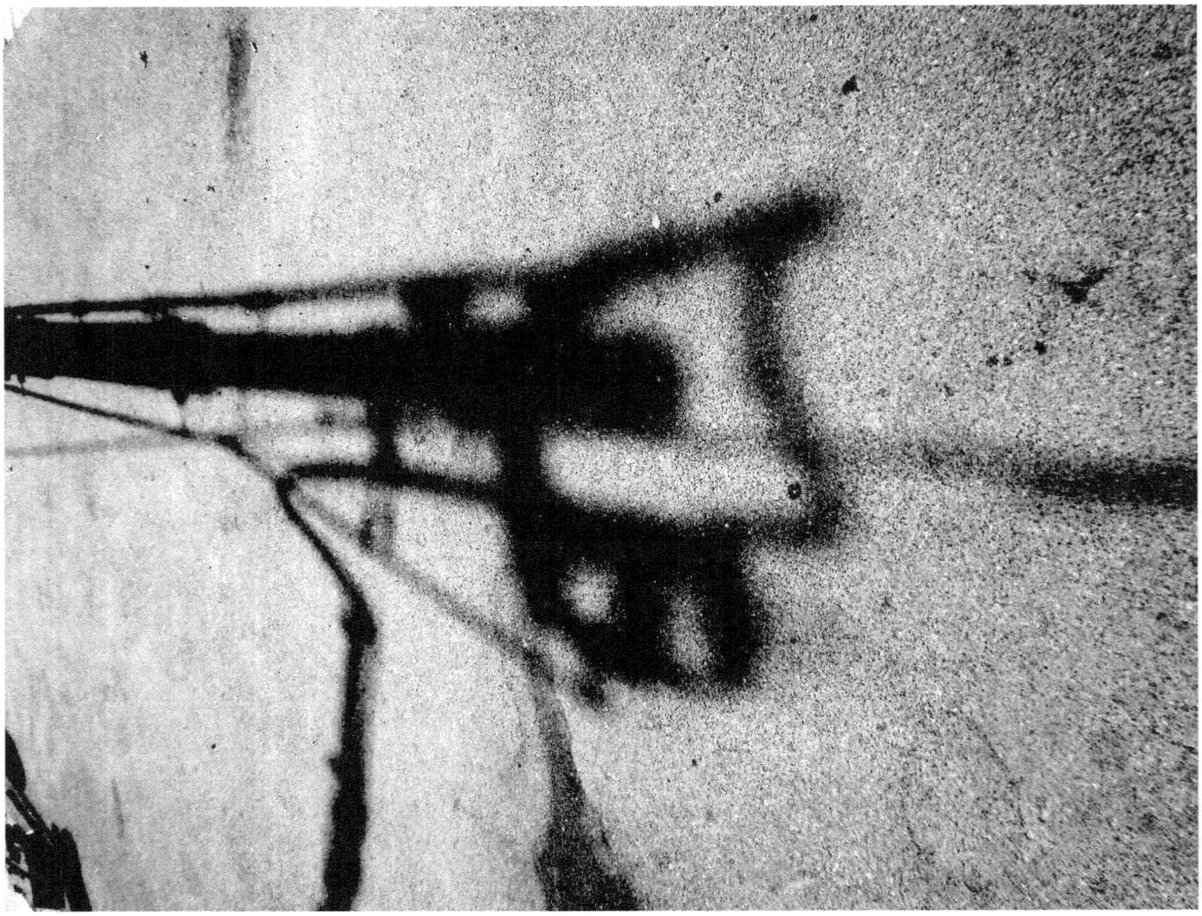

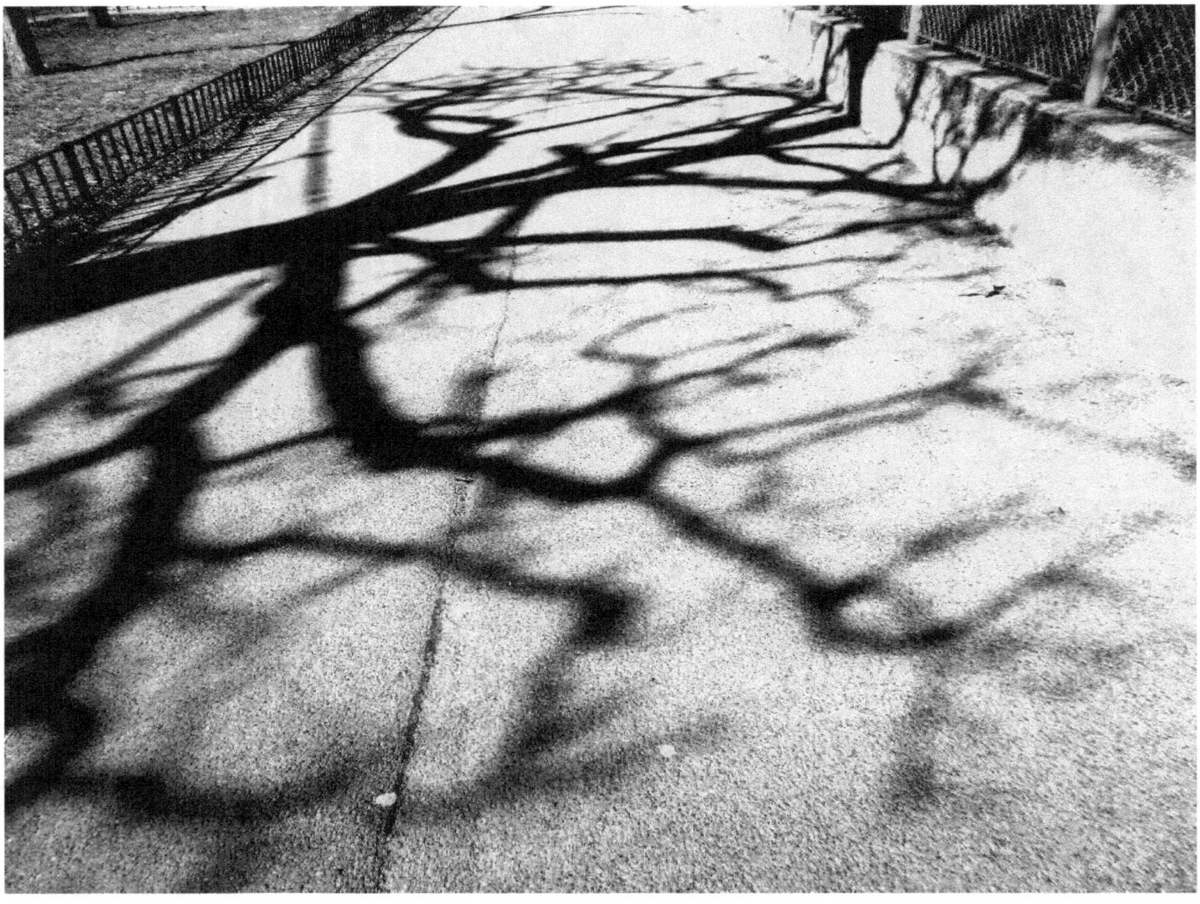

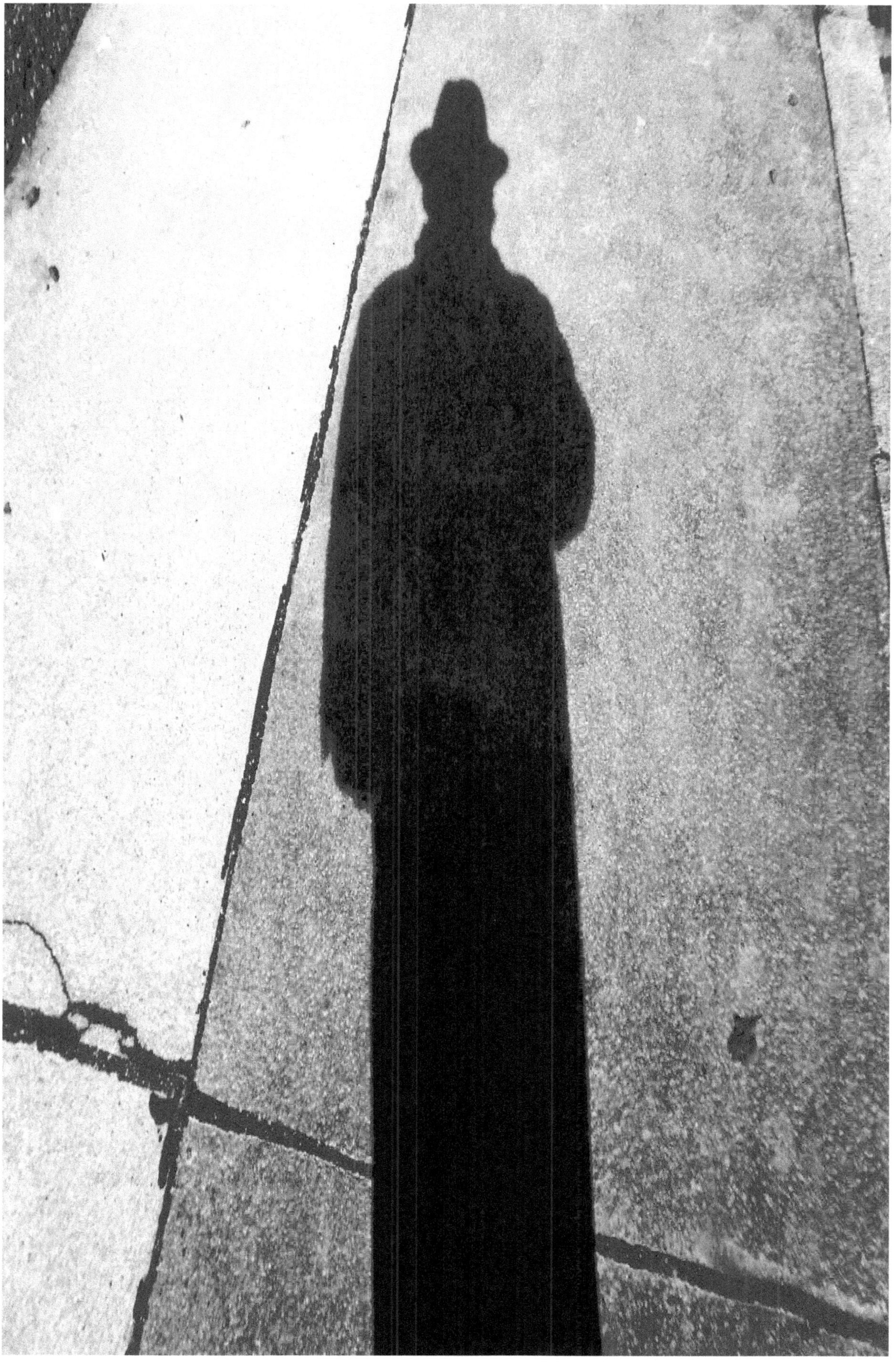

www.ingramcontent.com/pod-product-compliance
Lightning Source LLC
Chambersburg PA
CBHW080539190526
45169CB00007B/2562
9781530382378